SHADOW ON THE HILL

THE TRUE STORY OF A 1925 KANSAS MURDER

Diana Staresinic-Deane

Aventine Press

Published by Aventine Press
55 East Emerson St.
Chula Vista CA 91911
www.aventinepress.com

ISBN: 978-1-59330-815-5

In memory of Florence, John, and Roger Knoblock

A special heartfelt thanks to my husband, Jim;
early readers Rosa Lee, Yvonne, Karen, Tony, Sarah, and Jeff;
my friend and editor, Erin;
and my EPL friends who were around when I found the folder

The Family

Florence Knoblock, victim
John Knoblock, Florence's husband
Roger Knoblock, Florence and John's four-year-old son

Charles Knoblock, John Knoblock's father
Mary Knoblock, John Knoblock's mother

John Mozingo, Florence's father
Mary Mozingo, Florence's mother
John "Johnnie" Mozingo Jr., Florence's brother
Edna Mozingo, Florence's sister
Ella Kellerman, Florence's sister
John Kellerman, Ella's husband
Frances McCormick, Florence's sister
Ruth Mozingo, Florence's sister
Vesta "Vet" Mozingo, Florence's sister
Herman "Pete" Jenkins, Florence's maternal uncle
Alice Naylor, Florence's maternal aunt
Minnie "Aunt Min" Jaggers, Florence's maternal aunt

The Law

Arch C. Brown, Greenwood County deputy sheriff
Detective Maple, from the Burns Detective Agency
Frank Hunter, Coffey County sheriff
George Griffith, Coffey County deputy
Leroy Hurt, police chief in Emporia
Samuel "Sam" Crumley, Lyon County Sheriff
Steven A. Grubb, Coffey County deputy sheriff
T. H. Olinger, Coffey County deputy sheriff
William "Bill" Utesler, Coffey County deputy sheriff

The Court

A. H. Woodrow, court reporter for Judge Richardson
C. B. Griffith, Kansas attorney general
Emma Randolph, stenographer
Fred Harris, prosecuting attorney from Franklin County
Isaac T. Richardson, district court judge
J. H. Rudrauff, Justice of the Peace
Jennie Caven, court clerk
Joe Rolston, Franklin County prosecutor
John Stewart, Kansas attorney general investigator
Lon McCarty, Lyon County attorney
May Larson, stenographer
Owen S. Samuel, defense attorney
Ray Pierson, Franklin County attorney
R. C. Burnett, Kansas attorney general's assistant
W. C. Harris, defense attorney

The Undertakers/Coroner

Eugene Stone, undertaker/furniture maker
Joseph O. Stone, coroner
Roy Jones, undertaker/furniture maker

The Reporters

Reverend A. C. Babcock, correspondent for *True Story* magazine
Bill White, reporter for the *Emporia Gazette*
Glick Fockele, reporter for *The LeRoy Reporter*
John Redmond, editor and reporter for the *Daily Republican*
Lee R. Hettick, reporter for the *Gridley Light*

The Hounds

George Eaton, experienced bloodhound handler from Kansas City, Kansas
Old Bess, bloodhound from Kansas City, Kansas
Tom, bloodhound from Kansas City, Kansas

George Wilson, police officer and bloodhound handler from Lyon County (Emporia)
King Rustler, bloodhound from Lyon County (Emporia)
Queen Rosalind, bloodhound from Lyon County (Emporia)
Captain Volney G. Mullikin, owner of Rockwood Kennels in Kentucky, breeder of Emporia bloodhounds

The Doctors

Dr. A. B. McConnell
Dr. Albert N. Gray
Dr. David W. Manson
Dr. Harry T. Salisbury, conducted Florence's autopsy
Dr. Melvin Roberts

The First Jury (Franklin County)

Frank Hiles, Ottumwa Township
Oliver Kelly, Ottumwa Township, **foreman**
Jack Britton, Rock Creek Township
E. E. Baker, Rock Creek Township
George Baker, Rock Creek Township
John Clark, Rock Creek Township
W. C. Combes, Lincoln Township
E. W. Ellis, Lincoln Township
George Bruce, Aliceville

Frank Decker, Burlington
G. H. Bennett, Rock Creek Township
Charles Strickland, Burlington

The Second Jury (Lyon County)

S. C. White, Bushong
Arthur Kirkland, Bushong
A. Q. Thornbrugh, Miller
Robert Castle, Admire
Earl Stonebraker, Admire
Edward Haas, Allen, **foreman**
O. B. Rhudy, Allen
James Heironymous, Admire
H. K. Gage, Reading
W. C. Showalter, Bushong
J. R. Bennett, Miller
John Mundy, Waterloo Township

Contents

Author's Note

I'd never even heard of Florence Knoblock until her story fell at my feet.

One hot August morning in 2007, I was chasing after a group of hyper children playing hide-and-seek in the stacks at Emporia Public Library in Emporia, Kansas, where I worked as a library assistant. As I was passing through the stacks between the nonfiction collection and the genealogy area, a folder slipped off of the shelf and fell at my feet. It was thin, made with heavy green paper embossed in a faux leather pattern. Someone had scrawled "Knoblock Murder" in a shaky hand within the boundaries of the little rectangle on the cover.

The brads inside held nothing, but the right pocket contained several news clippings. "May Have Murderer," read the first *Emporia Gazette* headline. I turned the clipping sideways and saw "2 June 1925" written in the same old-style cursive as on the folder cover.

Intrigued, I carried the folder back to the reference desk to read.

I shuffled through the microfilm printouts. Twenty-two newspaper clippings from two different newspapers: the *Emporia Gazette* and the *Olpe Optimist*, which had served the small town of Olpe, nine miles south of Emporia. It was obvious that this green folder was someone's personal research folder, as each microfilm printout was dated in the same handwriting, featuring a loopy number two in the "1925." I also doubted it had been in the building very long, as it had been tucked onto the same shelf as some of our more heavily used materials. But why was this folder on the shelf at all? And why had no one found it before now?

The headlines were sensational, in bold capital letters across the width of their respective newspapers: MAY HAVE MURDERER: BURLINGTON AWAITS REPORT ON FINGERPRINTS; CALL IN DETECTIVES: KNOBLOCK MURDER PROBE WILL BE PUSHED; MYSTERY IS GROWING: NEW DEVELOPMENTS TEND TO CLEAR NEGRO; CALL OUT A POSSE: BURLINGTON THOUGHT MURDERER WAS CAPTURED, NIGHT RIDE ONLY TO FIND WEARY PEDESTRIAN.

The morning was slow enough that I was able to read a couple of paragraphs here and there between patrons needing assistance.

It was *In Cold Blood* meets the Keystone Cops. Absolute tragedy marred by klutziness and moments of humor. It was real life.

It was also gruesome. John Knoblock and his four-year-old son, Roger, returned to the farmhouse after a trip to town to discover the body of Florence Knoblock in a pool of her own blood on the kitchen floor. Florence's skull was crushed, her head having been beaten repeatedly with an iron lid from the wood-burning stove, and her throat had been slashed to the bone with a shaving razor. Twice.

Several different men were taken into custody. Florence's husband was arrested twice and then tried twice in two of the most sensational trials in Kansas.

I flipped to the last newspaper clipping in the folder. It was dated November 25, 1957. It was John Knoblock's obituary.

"There's nothing in here about how the trial turned out," I blurted out while standing at the reference desk, turning the heads of a few computer users in front of me.

Florence Knoblock's murder changed everything—for her family, for her community. I had to know how the story ended. I had to understand why a tight-knit farm community—people who worked together, worshipped together, raised their children together—would ultimately choose to believe they had identified but failed to convict a murderer rather than accept the possibility that the real murderer lived and worked among them in anonymity.

This is the story of the Knoblocks and the murder that shook Coffey County, Kansas. It's also the story of how a handful of newspaper clippings would lead to a curiosity that would take over my life for years to come. I've recreated the events that took place based on hundreds of newspaper articles, court documents, and interviews with descendants of those whose lives were touched by Florence Knoblock's murder and the subsequent investigation and trial. It is my hope that I've accurately captured the essence of this moment in Kansas's history.

Diana Staresinic-Deane

Chapter One
Across the Fence

Goodrick farm, seven miles west of Burlington, Kansas
Saturday, May 30, 1925
10:30 a.m.

Dora Goodrick stood in her pasture, a pitchfork in one hand, a sweat-covered kerchief in the other. She wiped the kerchief across her forehead. The sunshine had already burned much of the dampness out of the fields, but last night's rain had left the creeks swollen and the air heavy with humidity. Dora stabbed the pitchfork into the wet soil and, pulling her dark hair back, retied the kerchief into a square knot at the base of her neck.

"Drink."

Her husband, Charles, pressed a tin cup of cool water into her hand. Dora held the water in her mouth for a moment before swallowing. She touched the cool tin to her cheek as she joined her husband, who stood overlooking the shallow valley below them.

Leaving Oklahoma for Coffey County, Kansas, had been the right decision, Dora thought as she took in the scenery. They had made their home in the aptly named Pleasant Township nearly four years ago and hadn't looked back. The natural springs and creeks ensured that the hills were green throughout the entire growing season, and from their little perch on top of a rise, they could see for miles. Their three children, all nearly grown— Grace, their youngest, was in high school now, a fact that never failed to astonish Dora when she thought about it—loved the land and explored it on horseback every chance they got. Yet they were less than half an hour away from Burlington, a town large enough to boast several shops, a few hardware stores, an opera house, and two hotels.

Most of their neighbors were salt-of-the-earth people who had welcomed them into the Pleasant Township and the Bethel Methodist Church with open arms. The Goodricks found comfort in such a tight-knit community and had forged strong ties with many other families.

Dora's gaze drifted down the hill to the northeast. She squinted and frowned.

"There's that man again," she said and tilted her head in the direction of the creek. Dora and Charles watched him move through the thigh-high grass of the Knoblock family's pasture, past the grove of catalpa trees, until he was out of sight, likely standing on the east porch of the Knoblock house.

"Florence still having trouble with him, then?"

"He's scaring her," Dora said. "I wish he'd set his sights on someone else." Just a few days earlier, her friend, Florence Knoblock, had sought Dora's advice on how to steer the man's interests away from her.

The winds picked up from the southwest, bringing with it the sound of cattle mooing and children playing.

"Florence may look frail, but she can handle her own," Charles said. "See? It hasn't even been a quarter of an hour, and he's already hurrying back home, his tail between his legs."

Charles took Dora's tin cup and set it on top of the jug of water sitting next to the barn door. He turned back to see his son, Carl, riding his horse through the Knoblock field, until he and his horse disappeared behind the house.

"Carl to the rescue," she murmured, and Charles chuckled.

"It is a difficult lot to have, being a pretty and sweet young redhead," he said. "She has to juggle the feelings of many men, young and old alike."

"Your feelings, too?" Dora asked him, a teasing lilt in her voice.

Charles put an arm around her shoulders. "Even Florence Knoblock couldn't turn my head when I've got you. And look," he said, as their son thundered away from the Knoblock house, looking over his shoulder. "Another heart broken."

File Type: Newspaper Clipping

The most brutal murder ever committed in the
Burlington community occurred Saturday at
the farm home of Mr. and Mrs. John Knoblock
6 miles west of the McCreary corner when
Mrs. Knoblock's head was chopped and her
throat cut.

"Skull Crushed And Throat Cut: Mrs. John
Knoblock Is Found By Her Husband Saturday
Afternoon," *Daily Republican*, June 1, 1925

Chapter Two

Murder

Knoblock farm, six miles west of Burlington, Kansas
Saturday, May 30, 1925
1:40 p.m.

In his mind, Sheriff Frank Hunter knew that he was going to see a murder scene. But the newly minted sheriff, a man whose law enforcement experience began with a favorable election tally completed just months earlier, was not prepared for the blood.

He and the coroner, Joseph O. Stone, walked up the gravel path to the two-story farm house and made their way past a small gathering of people on the front porch, through the dining room, and into the kitchen. John Knoblock, the man who had called to report the murder, said nothing until both members of law enforcement were in the kitchen. He pointed toward the space near the cook stove.

"That's my Florence," he said. "My wife. She's dead."

The body of Mrs. Florence Knoblock lay on the floor in front of the stove. A black pillow covered her face, and an old blanket covered the rest of her. Her feet, spread apart, protruded from beneath the blanket. Blood, somewhat dried now, permeated the blanket in the area around her neck. The rest of the blanket wicked blood from the floor, but the blanket wasn't enough to stop the blood that had already flowed toward the southern wall of the kitchen in a path two feet wide.

So much blood.

The sheriff slid his glance to the coroner. Stone's jaw was dropped, and his color was pale, maybe a little green. Stone, who wasn't even a doctor, had as much experience being coroner as Hunter did being sheriff.

"Dr. Gray is on his way," the sheriff said to everyone and no one in particular. "I want to take a good look at the house before he gets here."

Knoblock looked from his wife to the sheriff to the coroner and nodded.

Like so many country houses, it was a mix of old and new. An old pump served as the only indoor source of water, and the rooms were still lit with lanterns. Yet a telephone sat on a table, connecting them to others through the party line.

Hunter took in the kitchen. Shards of broken dishes littered the hardwood. Bread dough, long past risen, had flowed over the lip of a crock, down the side of the stove, and onto the floor, where it began to dry out. A pan of washing water, likely pumped from the well that morning, sat on a chair.

Bloody, sooty fingerprints marked the door casings to both the closet door and the door leading out to the backyard. More prints covered the doorway to the dining room, where he found an incubator full of baby chicks on the dining table.

The rooms of the first floor flowed into each other, and Hunter crossed the threshold of the dining room, then the parlor, before entering the first-floor bedroom. Dark, sooty fingerprints were pressed into the otherwise pristine white quilt on the bed. Dresser drawers were pulled out and stained with blood and soot. Clothes littered the floor, tossed from the drawers.

A robbery? Hunter wondered.

He climbed the stairs to the second floor, where he found a second bedroom and a storage room. Both had been ransacked.

Hunter returned to the first floor. He walked out onto the porch where Knoblock and his four-year-old son, Roger, sat with an older couple he didn't know and Sam and Rose Shoup, who farmed a quarter section just a couple of miles away.

"Has anything gone missing?" the sheriff asked.

The older woman he did not know sobbed into her kerchief.

Hunter shifted his eyes from John Knoblock to the weeping older couple.

Knoblock followed the sheriff's gaze. "Mr. and Mrs. Mozingo," he said. "Florence's parents. And no, sir, nothing is missing." Unlike the woman, Knoblock's face was blank, void of all emotion.

Everyone shifted to watch a car turn off the county road onto the dirt track to the house. John Redmond, editor of the *Daily Republican*, Dr. Albert N. Gray, and county attorney Ray Pierson climbed out of the car. All three men nodded toward the group on the porch and then turned their attention to the sheriff, who led them into the kitchen.

*****

Dr. Gray studied the kitchen scene before approaching the body, noting the blood near the cabinets on the north side of the room. He squatted down by Mrs. Knoblock's head, trying not to slip on the blood.

"Let's see what she can tell us," he said and reached for the pillow.

Everyone in the room gasped as Dr. Gray uncovered her face.

"Christ," the sheriff muttered.

"Oh, hell!" Pierson said. "That's one of the redheaded Mozingo girls."

Dr. Gray studied what was left of Florence's face. She had been beaten repeatedly in the head, the worst blow crushing soot and hair and brain matter into a fracture that spread from her eyebrow to her hairline.

"Help me pull this blanket off," Dr. Gray said to the sheriff.

Dr. Gray squeezed his eyes shut for a moment, quelling a wave of nausea.

Florence Knoblock lay on her back on the hard kitchen floor. Her legs were mostly straight, but perversely parted. The perpetrator had pushed the skirt of her dress up until it was bunched around her waist, where it soaked up blood from the floor. A deep slash was visible in Florence's neck.

"Was she—" John Redmond paused, searching for a kinder word to use in the presence of the dead woman's husband. "Was she assaulted?"

"I need more light in here," Dr. Gray said.

The sheriff called out the door for more light, and a moment later, someone passed lanterns into the kitchen.

Dr. Gray had seen just about every way a body could be injured during his years of doctoring, but even he was horrified. He almost felt sorry for the inexperienced coroner, who'd likely never seen a corpse in such a condition.

Don't think about her, Dr. Gray chanted in his head. Just examine the body.

"Write this down for me, John," Dr. Gray said to Redmond. He gently prodded at the wound on Mrs. Knoblock's neck. "Florence Knoblock's throat has been cut with something sharp from ear to ear. Maybe a razor or a knife. The cut severed her windpipe and the artery. In fact, it goes all the way to the spine."

Dr. Gray braced one hand on Florence's left shoulder and the other on the back of her neck to roll her on to her side. On the floor by her head, he found an iron lid from the cookstove. A second lid lay under her left ankle.

"There are cuts and blows to both the front and back of her head. One blow in front and one in back have crushed her skull. Based on the angle of the blow to the back, I believe she was hit on the back of the head first and then hit again when she was already on the floor. The soot around the injuries tells me that she was likely hit with at least this stove lid, which appears to have blood, brain matter, and hair crusted onto it."

"I don't understand," the sheriff said. "Did she die from having her throat cut or from being beaten?"

"There isn't much blood around her neck, not like what you'd see if her throat had been cut when she was still alive," Dr. Gray said. "Whoever did that," he said, pointing to Florence's neck, "did that after."

"When do you think she died?" the sheriff asked.

Dr. Gray took in the blood that was dry and the blood that was wet. "I'm not entirely sure, but I'd say around ten o'clock, ten-thirty, thereabouts."

Dr. Gray examined Florence's thighs and womanly parts. "I don't think she was assaulted," he said, "at least, not while she was alive."

File Type: Obituary—Death Certificate

"The CAUSE OF DEATH was as follows: Murder.
Struck over head with a blunt instrument
and her throat cut from ear to ear by party
or parties unknown."

Standard Certificate of Death, State of
Kansas, for FLORENCE EMMA KNOBLOCK, filed
June 2, 1925

Chapter Three
After

Knoblock farm, six miles west of Burlington, Kansas
Saturday, May 30, 1925
2:30 p.m.

As long as he lived, John Kellerman never wanted to receive another phone call like the one he received from John Mozingo, his father-in-law.

And, as long as he lived, he never wanted to see another person he cared for sprawled on a blood-drenched floor in her own kitchen, where she should have been safe.

As he stood on the front steps of the Knoblock house, holding his sobbing wife, Ella, and her youngest sister, eleven-year-old Vesta, he realized someone needed to drive to Hartford to tell Frances McCormick, yet another of the Mozingo sisters, who was heavily pregnant and likely unable to travel to Burlington.

"You have to go," Ella sobbed. "I have to stay here for mother and Vet. Please, John."

Kellerman didn't want to leave Ella without a way to get back into Burlington, so he asked to take his brother-in-law's car. Keys in hand, he had been about to open the driver's side door when he noticed the rear tire was flat.

"Need a ride?"

Kellerman turned and found Sam Shoup standing behind him on the dirt and grass that served as a driveway to the house. He was, as usual, dressed in a good suit, with a good tie and a good hat.

"I'd be grateful. Thanks, Sam."

*****

"Mama, just look," Grace Goodrick stood at the parlor window, looking down the field at the Knoblock house. "What do you suppose is going on down there?"

Dora joined her daughter at the window and frowned. The driveway to the Knoblock house was lined with cars, and dozens of people tromped through the pasture, some with heads bent down, as if concentrating on the ground. Some were shouting and pointing. Still others walked the country roads toward the Knoblock farm.

"I don't know, Grace," Dora said.

When the phone rang, Dora answered it with dread.

*****

Ella Kellerman was too tired to cry.

Her husband and Sam Shoup returned to the Knoblock farm from Hartford just before five o'clock, Shoup looking as dignified as ever while her John looked bedraggled. Eugene Stone and Roy Jones, the undertakers, were washing Florence's hair when they arrived.

"Mrs. Kellerman?" Ella hardly recognized her own name when Roy Jones called to her. "Could you bring us some cloths?"

Ella stared at him. "Cloths?"

"Yes, ma'am," Jones said. "We need something to soak up the blood."

Ella followed her brother-in-law, John Knoblock, up the stairs to the bedroom he had shared with Florence and dug through a box of cloths in the closet. A short time later, she went back to the bedroom with John Mozingo, John Knoblock, and Eugene Stone to search for some clothing for Florence.

John Knoblock sat on the bed and sobbed.

"They want to take her to town," he said. "They said they need to take her to town, because it will be easier to get her ready for burial there."

*****

Neighbors wasted no time in reaching out to friends and family with the news. By late afternoon, a crowd of at least seventy-five people milled about the Knoblock farm, popping in and out of the house, the pasture, and the barn. But the dull roar of conversation stilled as Stone and Jones, furniture makers and undertakers, carried Florence Knoblock out of her home for the last time.

*****

The word was out that Blackie Stevens, one of the Negroes who had worked on construction projects around Coffey County two years ago, was the likely murderer. Ella wasn't sure who had started that gossip; she couldn't imagine that the man Florence had spoken kindly of after giving him strawberries just two weeks prior could have done such a thing. But then, before that Decoration Day,[1] she couldn't have imagined her sister murdered.

Rumor had reached Burlington that three Negroes had been spotted in Hartford. Ella's brother-in-law, now somewhere between catatonic and half-crazed, wanted her husband and Sam Shoup to drive out with him to see if any of them might be Blackie.

---

1 Before World War II, Memorial Day was more commonly called Decoration Day.

As the light began to fade, many of the curious went home to their families, leaving only a handful of family and close friends. John Knoblock, her husband John, and the Reverend Joseph Neden moved together from room to room, closing and locking doors so no one would be able to enter the west side or upper floor of the house. Knoblock left the exterior door in the dining room open for the use of those remaining.

"You'll be all right?" Ella's husband asked her, taking her hands in his.

Ella nodded and threw her arms around him. "Watch out for John, will you?"

Her husband squeezed her and then climbed in to Shoup's car for the second time that day.

Charles and Mary Knoblock, John's parents, sat at the dining room table with only the light of an oil lamp to keep them company. Rose Shoup, Alice Naylor, and Mr. and Mrs. Woods stood adrift in the yard.

Ella sat on the steps leading out of the dining room into the front yard, watching twilight set in. It was perverse that they were all there, guarding the house.

There was no one left to protect.

*****

Dora sat on the step of her front porch, horrified.

Florence had been murdered, and it likely happened while she and Charles were staring at her house. They were standing there, doing nothing, while Florence was beaten and her throat—. Dora ran into the field a ways and vomited.

*****

The men returned to the Knoblock farm around six o'clock Sunday morning. They had not found Blackie in Hartford, but rumor was that the Negro had been spotted in Osage City, and

Knoblock, Shoup, and Kellerman planned to head out again that morning.

Kellerman had found Ella asleep propped up against a wall in the dining room. He gently shook her awake. She'd rested some, but dark circles shadowed her eyes and her red hair frizzed out of her normally stylish bob.

"Sweetheart, let's get you home," he said.

Ella took her husband's hand and stood, groaning at the aches and pains in her back and her heart. She yawned.

"Roger's going to need something clean to wear," she said, spotting her brother-in-law. "John, could you unlock the door to his room? I'll take some clothes back for him." The little boy had spent the night with his grandparents, the Mozingos.

Knoblock fished a key out of his pocket and unlocked first the double doors to the parlor and then the door from the parlor to the downstairs bedroom.

The bloody prints on the dresser drawers and bedspread had dried to a dark brown.

Knoblock stepped into the room with Shoup, Kellerman, and Ella close behind him. Most of Roger's clothes were strewn about the floor. Knoblock reached down for a pair of Roger's overalls and a shirt and started to hand them to Ella but something caught his eye and caused him to pause.

Ella followed her brother-in-law's stare and silenced her gasp with her hand. Soon, Shoup and Kellerman were staring, too.

Lying open on the rug was an old shaving razor, the blade covered in dried blood.

File Type: E-mail
From: Mark Byard
To: Diana Staresinic-Deane
Date: April 19, 2008

   Thank you again for the email and the
work you have done to provide us with the
history around this tragic event in my wife's
past family. I was in recent communication
with two of my wife's cousins who maintain
a close tie to the Hartford/Neosho Falls/
Emporia area because their mother still
lives there. They were quite interested in
your findings (I forwarded your e-mail) and
they responded with some surprising info of
their own.
   Although they would not quote names,
they had in the years past spoken with a
resident of that area who said that her
parents actually KNEW who the murderer was
but had withheld the information probably
out of fear of reprisal. This area resident
(the parent of the person explaining this
to my wife's cousins) had actually seen a
known neighbor man ride up near the house
where the woman was killed, tie his horse,
and disappear. Later they saw the same man
removing himself from the area in great
haste! This man supposedly disappeared
from the area soon after the murder was
discovered. The witness believed that this
man thought that the home was vacated for
the day and was looking to steal items.
He was surprised/confronted by the victim

and to protect his own hide he killed the victim.

I am not at liberty to disclose any names at the request of my wife's cousins. But as they said, there was one witness . . . God Himself.

Chapter Four
Bloodhounds

Two and a half miles south of Burlington, Kansas
Sunday, May 31, 1925
6:00 a.m.

Sherman Stevens watched the sun rise over the fields in the east as he trudged along the road to Burlington. The Negro, called "Deacon" by his friends and "Blackie" by the White folk despite his skin being light brown, knew this area like the back of his hand, having sweated on the crews that built most of the culverts and bridges in Coffey County.

He'd been on his feet for hours, unable to bum a ride anywhere between Moody and Burlington. His bad right leg was giving him fits. But he was only a little over two miles from Burlington. Maybe he'd be able to find work and someplace to rest for a couple of days.

He heard a truck coming down the road and swayed off to the side a little so as not to get hit by kicked-up gravel. Instead of flying by, the truck slowed down and then came to a halt just a few feet away.

The man threw open the door and jumped out of the truck. Blackie instinctively stepped back, feeling the first prickles of fear creeping along his spine.

"Get your hands in the air!" the man from the truck shouted at him.

"Who are you?" Blackie's voice cracked.

"I said get your hands in the air!"

Not knowing what else to do, Blackie put his hands in the air.

The man walked up to Blackie and grabbed the scruff of his faded gray shirt and shoved him toward the side of the road. "Move, nigger. To that house up there."

Blackie recognized the house; it was Asa Botham's place. He couldn't think of any reason this stranger would be walking him toward it, much less with his hands in the air like some kind of criminal. But there he was, being shoved forward toward the Botham house by a very angry man.

The angry man pounded on the door.

Asa Botham answered it. "Whatcha got there, Oscar?" he asked.

"This is the nigger the sheriff wants," the man named Oscar said.

Blackie was startled. The sheriff?

"What for?" Blackie asked. "What does the sheriff want me for?" Raw panic shot through him.

"Shut your mouth," Oscar said and turned to Asa. "Where's your phone?"

Asa picked up the handset. Even at this early hour, another conversation was already taking up the party line. "I need to call the sheriff," he said, and everyone hung up. He knew they'd just wait until he was connected, then listen in. That's just how it was.

The operator came through, and he asked to be connected to Frank Hunter.

"Here," Asa said and handed Oscar the phone.

"Sheriff Hunter? This here's Oscar Morris. I've got your murderer here at the Asa Botham place."

*****

Police officer George Wilson was too tired to think. When the Lyon County sheriff got the call to bring the bloodhounds to Coffey County, George and Sheriff Crumley loaded the dogs into the car and headed for Burlington. They had arrived at the Knoblock farm at just past four o'clock on Saturday.

Poor Mrs. Knoblock had still been lying on the kitchen floor.

Wilson knew that this was the big test—it would show whether or not he and King Rustler and Queen Rosalind really knew what they were doing. They'd been practicing for weeks, ever since he took over the hounds in April. But this was the first time they'd been called to a murder case.

After sniffing the ransacked dresser in the downstairs bedroom, Rustler and Rosalind led him through the dining room door to the outside, past the dead woman's husband, and through a crowd of nearly a hundred people who were driven to the Knoblock farm out of concern and morbid curiosity. Wilson worried the dogs wouldn't be able to keep on the trail with so many distractions, but sure enough, they led him through the Knoblocks' field and into a tree-lined creek.

Here and there, Wilson caught a glimpse of tracks, some of them strangely made, like the maker had a limp. But when he and the hounds reached the water late Saturday night, the dogs lost the scent.

Now they waited for George Eaton, an experienced bloodhound man, to come down from Kansas City with his hounds.

*****

Word of the Negro's arrest spread like a prairie fire through Coffey County. So did rumors. Everyone was just sure they'd seen Blackie Stevens in the streets, on their porches, crawling around haystacks, and slinking behind barns.

George Eaton held the leads to his bloodhounds, Old Bess and Tom. The dogs were excited to have new territory to sniff. Scents were their passion, their reason for being. Nothing made his dogs happier than having a trail to follow. Tom was still a young pup, but he emulated Old Bess, and when she worked, he worked.

Eaton gave the command, and they picked up the scent.

They tracked down the field to a creek, splashing along the banks in places. They followed the scent all the way to a haystack. Tom and Bess barked, Tom bouncing in circles around the older female.

*****

"This can't possibly be where the trail ends," Sheriff Hunter said. "We've barely made it to the Shoup place. The Negro was picked up miles south from here."

"They're excited because your man spent a lot of time here. Maybe he slept here, waiting until it was dark enough to get moving again," Eaton said. He gave the leads a tug and the dogs picked up the trail. "See? Here we go."

Old Bess and Tom took George Eaton for a long walk. They followed the creek bed all the way to the Katy[2] railroad line, then they followed the tracks southeast into Burlington. They dragged Eaton east on Kennebec Street to the front porch of Cap Johnson, another Negro.

The sheriff searched Cap's house and, finding nothing, ordered Eaton and the dogs to find the trail again.

Meanwhile, onlookers were beginning to follow the dogs, Eaton, and the sheriff. Several automobiles collided, because the drivers were busy watching the dog-led parade instead of traffic.

The dogs were tiring, but they trudged on, leading the way down Sixth Street.

---

2 The Missouri–Kansas–Texas railroad line.

At the end of the pavement, they turned west to the Katy tracks near the Winwood Dairy Farm.

"Where'd you find the Negro?" Eaton asked the sheriff.

"Down that road a ways," the sheriff said.

Eaton tugged on the dogs until they were heading down the right path.

File Type: Interview

Subject: Marjorie Barrett, daughter of Velma
and Orville Haehn, friends of the Knoblocks
Date: June 9, 2009

"My dad and mother thought they knew,"
Marjorie said. "They said there was a Negro
who came to the house, and he wanted money.
And John Knoblock's brother, the one who
lived in Virginia, thought he knew who did
it, but decided not to pursue it for some
reason."

Chapter Five

Burial

Bethel Methodist Church, six miles west of Burlington, Kansas
Tuesday, June 2, 1925
2:00 p.m.

The blooms, freshly cut from country flower beds, did little to cover the smell of people packed shoulder-to-shoulder in the tiny country church. The temperature had climbed well over eighty degrees that afternoon and the previous night's rain hovered heavy and thick in the air.

Dora Goodrick stood at the back of the church, her left hand gripping Grace's and her right hand clutching her husband's. Kin of the Knoblocks and the Mozingos sat hip-to-hip on the handful of short, wooden pews, but the rest of the people from Pleasant Township lined the walls or heard what they could through the tall, open windows as they stood out in the churchyard.

"The thief cometh not but that he may steal, kill, and destroy," the Reverend Lowe said, quoting John 10:10. "I am come that they might have life and have it abundantly."

As the Reverend droned on about how society was to blame for not properly punishing its criminals, Dora wondered if he'd lost sight of the fact that they were there to grieve their lost sister and not the death of society.

Dora studied her sons. Lester shifted from foot to foot, making the floorboards beneath his feet squeak and moan each time his weight shifted. Carl stood still as a statue.

The boy hadn't said much since Saturday morning.

Dora wondered what he had seen. Or what he had done.

*****

Knoblock farm, six miles west of Burlington, Kansas
Tuesday, June 2, 1925
7 p.m.

After most folk had gone home, Dora Goodrick walked down the hill to the Knoblock farm to check on her neighbor. She followed the muddy, rocky path from the main road to the house and climbed the south porch steps to the dining room door.

"Any news, John?" Dora asked as she followed John Knoblock into the dining room.

John shook his head. "I don't know anything more than anybody else." He ran his hands over his face and his hair. He moved toward the doorway to the kitchen, and she saw it.

The bloody handprint.

She moved in a trance toward the kitchen, her hands covering the startled gasp as she stared at the floor.

"She was likely hit on the back of the head while standing in front of the cabinet there," John said quietly, "then she was dragged over there."

Her poor, sweet friend.

"Blackie is in the jail for this," John said, "but he says he didn't hurt anybody."

Unless Blackie crept up that hill like a shadow, he hadn't hurt anybody, Dora thought.

"What do you think, John?" she said, her voice gentle.

"I don't know," he whispered.

The blood had dried to the color of rust, but the air still smelled foul and metallic.

"Dora, I trust you would have said something, but I have to ask," John said. "Did you see anything? Anyone? Or maybe Grace or your boys saw someone? Or Charles? Did you see anyone come to my house Saturday morning?"

Tell him. Tell him. Tell him. The words thudded in her like the rhythm of her own heart.

The man. And her son.

"No, John," she said, not quite able to meet his eyes. "I'm sorry."

File Type: Newspaper Clipping

With the nerves of the people still on edge
following the brutal murder of Mrs. John
Knoblock on Decoration Day, it is unhealthy
for strangers to wander around much on the
country roads or even in the towns.

"Another Tourist Wandering Around Brought
To Jail," *Daily Republican,* June 11, 1925

Chapter Six
Rumors

There was right, and there was wrong, and everything about this story was wrong, John Redmond thought as he sat at his desk, wondering what he could possibly write that would neither unnecessarily frighten the citizens of Coffey County nor lull them into a false sense of security.

He adjusted his glasses and leaned back in his chair. The saddest part of this story, aside from the fact that Mrs. Knoblock was dead and her little boy would grow up without his mama, was that a reportedly kind farm woman whose greatest pleasure had been caring for her home and family was now finding her name dragged through the mud that was still fresh on her grave.

There were whispers of her infidelity in the pews of the Bethel Methodist Church before her body had even been removed from her funeral to the cemetery.

Then there was the problem of Blackie Stevens, who insisted that he had been in Independence, Kansas, at the time of the murder. When the sheriff drove Blackie down south to see if the shopkeepers could verify having seen him, they could.

Most people in town wanted to believe that Stevens did it. But Redmond suspected that many people were starting to wonder if maybe he didn't.

Redmond's wife, Maude, had reported that women around town were starting to keep loaded rifles by their doors and handguns by their stoves. No one wanted to find out the hard way that Stevens really was innocent.

"Got a minute?"

Redmond looked up to see the sheriff and the coroner darkening his doorway.

"Come on in," he said.

"We've got two things to talk with you about," the sheriff said, sitting down in a chair near Redmond's desk. Stone continued to stand.

"Oh?" Redmond leaned forward on his desk. "Any news?"

"It looks like a bunch of the Mozingos and some neighbors decided they just couldn't wait to clean the house," Hunter said. Redmond noticed Hunter's knuckles grow white as he gripped the arm rest.

Redmond was stunned. "Weren't there signs posted? 'Keep Out' or something like that?"

"There were."

"What were they thinking?"

"Depends on who you ask," Hunter replied. "Some of them are saying that the Mozingo sisters didn't think it right to leave that blood around the house and the clothes on the floor and what have you. Some people are saying that Knoblock ordered them to clean the house. And a few more are saying that the neighbors did it and Knoblock tried to stop them."

"Let me make sure I'm understanding you," Redmond said. "The murderer left behind a great deal of evidence that might indicate who he is, and the family of the victim destroyed the evidence?"

"You got it," Hunter said.

"May I report that?" Redmond asked.

"Only if you put in that story of yours how they went against my orders and now valuable evidence has been damaged."

"So what's the other thing?"

Joseph Stone, who had been fiddling with some books on the shelves along the wall, turned to Redmond. "We had an interesting rumor come our way."

"There have been many interesting rumors," Redmond said, turning to the sheriff. "Wouldn't you agree, Frank?"

"This one might be more than a rumor," Hunter said. "You know Dr. Manson?"

"Of course," Redmond said. "He's been a physician here for many years now."

"He claims that Florence came to see him recently about getting an abortion."

"Oh, my," Redmond said.

"Which makes us wonder what she might have been doing with her time when John Knoblock wasn't home," Hunter said.

"Are you telling me this because you want me to put this in the paper?" Redmond asked.

"Oh, heavens, no," Stone said. "We're telling you this because shortly after midnight, we're going to exhume Mrs. Knoblock and see if she had an abortion."

"She's only been in the ground for—" Redmond looked at the clock on his desk "—about thirty-eight hours. Doesn't it seem a little harsh?"

"The doctors tell me the evidence won't get better with age," Hunter said.

"What do you need of me?"

"You're a member of the Coroner's Jury. We need you to be there. And we need you to keep this to yourself."

*****

Sheriff Hunter paced around his office, trying to look more confident than he felt and less worried than he was. Thanks to

Florence Knoblock getting killed, his life and his job just got a whole lot more complicated. Not that her murder was the only thing he had to worry about. There were bank bandits likely to appear at any day, prison escapees in Greenwood County, and one automobile accident after another.

It was enough to make a man wish he'd stuck to farming.

His problem now was that maybe, just maybe, Blackie Stevens didn't kill Mrs. Knoblock. The shopkeepers in Independence remembered seeing him there. But then, to most people, one colored man looked just like another. Except Blackie had that limp.

Hunter knew there were just as many folk in Coffey County who swore they saw Blackie the night before the murder. But then, to them, all colored people looked the same, too.

If he let Blackie go, which is what he should do, a mob would string Blackie up.

Hunter's pacing took him to his desk. He picked up the phone and began alerting neighboring sheriffs that they needed to be on the lookout for anyone suspicious.

*****

State Highway 58, just outside of Madison, Kansas
Thursday, June 4, 1925
7:30 p.m.

John Weber hummed a little tune as he loped along the edge of the graveled highway. He was so pleased about having thought to steal several pairs of socks before leaving the asylum at Supply,[3] Oklahoma. They took his shoes away at that awful place, but with enough socks, the road was not bad. He even had extra pairs tied around his ankles for when the outer layer wore through too much to be of use.

3 In 1925, the asylum was known as Western Oklahoma Hospital. Today, it is called the Northwest Center for Behavioral Health. The city was also re-named Fort Supply in the 1940s to honor its roots as a military fort.

Horrible, horrible asylum. He was never going back. Never. It was horrible!

Weber yelped as a sharp rock pierced his heel. He stopped to examine his sock and shook his head. He pulled off the bad sock and swapped it with one of his extras.

He stood in time to see a flash of light bounce off the windshield of an automobile. As the vehicle approached, it slowed down, and Weber's heart filled with joy. At last, a ride to help him finish his journey!

The automobile pulled to the side, and a man wearing a nice clean shirt, dark trousers, and a hat got out of the car. Weber smiled at him, then caught sight of the badge pinned to his shirt. Weber stepped back as the man looked him over. No, no, no, he thought. They weren't supposed to find him.

"Good evenin'," the man said to Weber. "Is there something I can help you with?"

Encouraged that the man was keeping his distance, Weber stood up straight in his dirty nightshirt and pajama pants and introduced himself.

"I'm Deputy Brown," the man with the badge said. "I'd be happy to give you a ride if you need one. Where are you headin'?"

Weber's head bobbed up and down in a nod. "I'm on my way to the asylum in Nebraska," he told the deputy. "It's supposed to be much nicer than the one I just left in Oklahoma. Oklahoma was horrible, horrible. Horrible."

The deputy opened the passenger door for Weber, who was honored by such a kind gesture. No one ever opened a door for him in Oklahoma.

*****

Strawn farm, northwest of Burlington, Kansas
Friday, June 5, 1925
11 p.m.

The dog was barking.

Will Strawn shook himself awake and raised his head off of his pillow, listening to the dog's bark grow more furious and persistent. Alert now, he slipped out of bed and reached for his shotgun.

Strawn shifted the curtains ever so slightly to peek out the window. The nearly full moon cast just enough bluish-white light over the fields for him to see the outline of a man standing near his fence.

Strawn picked up the phone and called the sheriff.

*****

Sheriff Hunter took one look at the scene in front of him and wanted to beat his head against the steering wheel. There had to have been at least a hundred cars parked all over the street and Strawn's pasture and at least three times that many people wearing uniforms Hunter didn't recognize standing around in a field. It was nearly one o'clock in the morning, for God's sake. What was going on?

"Where's Will Strawn?" Hunter yelled over the noise.

"Over there," someone said, and Hunter walked over to a man wearing an undershirt, overalls, and shoes with no socks.

"Who are all of these people?" Hunter asked him.

Strawn shrugged. "Modern Woodsmen of America," he said. "They were having their initiation in Ottumwa. They got wind of me calling you, and they just . . . showed up."

"We got 'im!" someone shouted, and Strawn and Hunter turned to see George Hunt hauling a scrawny man up the path to the house.

"We found him in that house over there." Hunt pointed down the road.

"I didn't do anything!" the man was shouting. "I was just resting here! I didn't do anything!"

"Let's take him to the jail," Hunter said, resigned to another night without sleep.

*****

Vance Fox woke up in a jail cell adjacent to the one housing a Negro sleeping on a cot.

"Mr. Fox?" Vance turned to see the sheriff standing at the cell door with a much younger man he didn't know.

"Yessir?"

"Ray Pierson, our county attorney, would like to ask you some questions."

Fox was led to small, sparsely furnished room. Pierson told him to sit down, so he did.

"What were you doing on William Strawn's land last night?" Pierson asked him.

"I told the sheriff. I was just resting," Fox said.

"But why were you resting at Strawn's place?"

"I was tired," Fox said.

Pierson closed his eyes for a moment and tried again. "Mr. Fox, how did you get to Strawn's farm?"

"On foot."

"Where were you coming from?"

"Emporia," Fox said, shifting in his chair.

"You walked from Emporia," Pierson repeated.

"Yes, sir."

"That's a long ways," Pierson said. "When did you leave Emporia?"

"It was around three o'clock in the afternoon," Fox said.

Pierson did the math in his head. It wasn't completely impossible for a man to walk thirty-five miles in eight hours, but he'd have to keep up a pretty fast pace.

"Where were you headed?" Pierson asked.

"To my house," Fox said, "where you found me."

"But why did you go through Strawn's land?"

"I always go through Strawn's land. It saves me a few miles over taking the roads. It ain't never been a problem before."

"Mr. Strawn sure thought it was a problem last night," the sheriff said. "He almost took a few shots at you."

The sheriff stood up and walked around. He was afraid that if he stayed seated too long, he'd embarrass himself by falling asleep.

"Can I go home now?" Fox asked.

The sheriff looked at Pierson, who nodded.

"Stay off of other people's land at night, will you?" the sheriff said.

*****

John Redmond sat at his desk, shaking his head as he skimmed stories in newspapers from around the state. These sad excuses for reporting would almost be funny if they weren't so tragic, he thought. It especially annoyed him that these rogue papers were running these stories with a Burlington dateline. He was pretty sure he would have heard about a large crowd of gun-toting vigilantes showing up at the jail to lynch the Negro being held there. He could have written hundreds of column inches on how ridiculous these articles were.

But today, he wanted to bring some peace to a grieving mother who was on the edge of a mental breakdown. Mrs. Mary Mozingo called him that morning, begging him to address the rumor that Florence Knoblock had been having an affair with Charley Muscunis, a Russian immigrant who had worked for the Mozingos as a farmhand some years ago. There were two big problems with the theory that Charley Muscunis killed Florence Knoblock in a moment of passionate rage. First, he had left Coffey County in 1917,[4] when he went to the Mexican border

---

4 The *Daily Republican* reported that Muscunis joined Company C in 1917, although the official roster indicates that he joined in 1916.

with Company C of the Kansas National Guard. Second, those same Mexicans had killed Muscunis and thrown his naked body in the Rio Grande.[5]

As Redmond tapped away at his typewriter, he wondered how much longer this story would hold Coffey County's attention.

---

5 According to Ed Gerhardt, the president of the Kansas National Guard Museum board of directors, "Records at the Museum of the Kansas National Guard indicate that Company C, 1st Kansas Infantry Regiment, Kansas National Guard, Burlington, Kansas, took part in the journey to Eagle Pass, Texas, for the Mexican Border War in 1916. The roster indicates that Charley Muscunis was a private in Company C. The 1st Kansas Infantry arrived at Eagle Pass, Texas, on [July 2, 1916]. They returned to Fort Riley, KS, on [October 15, 1916]."

File Type: Interview

Subject: Deborah Kennamore, former executive
director, Coffey County Historical Society
and Museum
Date: July 2008

Deborah: You have to understand that the
people around here keep to themselves.
They're hard workers, and they're good
people. But they're not all likely to talk
to you. What you need is a gossip, someone
who knows everyone and is really interested
in the history of the place.

Chapter Seven
Burns Detective Agency

Charles Knoblock's house, Burlington, Kansas
Monday, June 15, 1925

John Knoblock stabbed the blade of the shovel into the loose soil and let go of the handle to wipe the sweat from his brow. He studied the trench and gauged that he and his father had made it about halfway from the house to the street. The downside of modern conveniences like indoor plumbing was that they required maintenance, John thought. His parents had been dealing with this leaky pipe since before Florence was murdered, but they were just now getting to it.

Before. Everything now was *before* or *after*. *Before*, he had a wife and his son had a mother. *After*, he had nothing to keep his heart company but grief and fear; he worried about Roger; he felt like a charity case, having to depend on his parents and his wife's parents. *Before*, he could trust his neighbors. *After*, those same neighbors accused him and his quiet, sweet wife of any number of horrible things. They either had John pegged as a murderer or his wife as a— he couldn't even bring himself to think it.

Well. John wasn't going to be quiet anymore.

John picked up the shovel and drove the blade into the dirt with his foot, then tossed the scoop of earth next to the pit. Step, scoop, toss. He let the process become mechanical, not thinking, just digging, easing some of the tension that had been building these past few weeks. He almost didn't hear Ray Pierson's car pull up in front of his father's house.

"Mr. Knoblock?" the county attorney called to him. Pierson, wearing his usual "lawyer" suit, walked toward the trench along with a man wearing a pale blue shirt with the sleeves rolled to the elbows, dark trousers, and a striped tie.

"Mr. Pierson?" John said.

"This man is the reporter from the *Emporia Gazette*," Pierson said. "He'd like to interview you."

"You'll forgive me for not offering to shake your hand," John said.

The reporter nodded.

"Well, I'll leave you two to it, then," Pierson said, and he headed back to his car.

John studied the reporter, who looked around for somewhere to sit and, finding none, resigned himself to standing in the sun as John and his father continued to toil in the trench.

"I've told Ray every single thing I know, and he can tell you whatever he wants to. I don't want to hide anything," John said. "But I've been advised by detectives not to talk to anyone about this except officials."

The reporter nodded. "So why did you agree to see me?"

"These rumors about my wife—" John started to say, but the anger hit him so hard, he couldn't think for a moment. Step. Scoop. Toss. "My wife never went with anybody but me," he said. "And I never have gone with anybody else. I started going with her when she was fifteen, and we've never had a bit of trouble." Step. Scoop. Toss.

Out of the corner of his eye, John saw the newspaperman scribbling furiously on a little notepad. He flipped over the notebook to a new page and crouched down by the trench.

"Mr. Knoblock," the newspaperman said, in a just-between-you-and-me whisper, "do you have any idea who murdered your wife?"

John stopped digging, and by the silence, he knew his father had, too. John raised his gray eyes to look directly at the reporter.

"I've been hoping they would get the man, but I couldn't say myself who did it," John said. "I saw something in the papers the other day, which gave me an idea. I read somewhere they had picked up a crazy man near Madison, and it's just possible that fellow might have done it."

"But what about Blackie Stevens?"

John shook his head in disgust. "He always was quiet. I don't remember of his ever having come up to this house alone, except when he was working on the bridge down near my place, when he used to come to the back door to get a drink of water. When the murder first happened, I never thought of Blackie until some of the neighbors suggested it might have been him."

The reporter stopped writing and looked from Charles to John. "You don't think the man sitting in jail for the murder of your wife did it?"

John shrugged.

"Whoever did it was a powerfully built man," John said. He closed his eyes, remembering what his wife looked like, lying on the floor. He shuddered. "My wife's wrists showed she had been gripped tightly, and the blows on her head come from that stove lid, undoubtedly. It was an awful shock when I came in and seen her lying there." His voice grew hoarse and dropped lower. "It would have been worse if I had seen her head where her skull had been broken by the blows. But it was covered with a pillow, and I didn't see that until later."

The reporter flipped the page in his notebook.

"The last time I seen her," John said, "she was standing on the porch, and my little boy had his arms around her, kissing her goodbye."

*****

Coffey County Jail, Burlington, Kansas
Tuesday, June 16, 1925
9:00 a.m.

"Listen to what he says here about cleaning the house," Ray Pierson said as he skimmed the *Emporia Gazette*. "Knoblock says, 'Yes, it certainly was a mistake; everybody should have been kept away from there.'" Pierson smacked the newspaper onto the sheriff's desk. "A *mistake*, he called it. No," Pierson said, "a mistake is when you forget to pick up flour at the bakery. When you destroy a crime scene, it's a crime!"

The sheriff leaned back in his chair and studied the county attorney. Pierson's youth was betraying him as he lost control of his anger.

"Did he say anything useful that we didn't know before?" the sheriff asked.

Pierson picked up the paper and skimmed it again. "No," he said, and dropped the paper back on the table.

*****

National Hotel, Burlington, Kansas
Wednesday, June 17, 1925
9:30 a.m.

What a bunch of rubes, Detective Maple thought for the thousandth time since arriving in this ridiculous town. The whole county was in a panic, the hicks who called themselves the law had allowed a dream-come-true crime scene to be destroyed, and now they were looking to pinch a fall guy—any guy—so that the citizens of Coffey County would stop shooting at any stranger who was spotted in town.

The problem was that most of the time, the bad guy wasn't a stranger.

Maple was a detective with the famous Burns Detective Agency, and he knew there was no such thing as a perfect crime. Billy Burns, the American Sherlock Holmes who'd made a name for himself as a masterful detective, was fond of saying that every crime leaves a track.

There were tracks all over the place, but Maple didn't believe any of them led to Blackie Stevens.

Maple buttoned the cuffs of his sleeves and was brushing lint off his jacket when he heard a knock at his door.

"Mr. Maple? These came for you," said Walter Bunge, the hotel's manager. Bunge passed a stack of folded newspapers through the partially open door and turned back into the hallway, closing the door behind him.

Maple dug through the small pile of newspapers, which were mostly from neighboring towns and counties, until he found the June 16 edition of the *Emporia Gazette*. He was curious as to whether the *Gazette* reporter had been able to get anything out of the grieving widower.

There was another knock at his door. "Mr. Maple?" Bunge called through the still-closed door. "The sheriff called. He'd like for you to meet him at the *Daily Republican*."

*****

Maple was pretty sure he was sitting across from the only intelligent man in Coffey County. John Redmond, editor and owner of the *Daily Republican*, waited to take his statement regarding the latest rumor sinking its claws into the imaginations of the local saps. The problem was that Maple wasn't so sure this rumor was entirely false. Maybe it wasn't the sheriff who was trying to frame John Knoblock, but Maple was pretty sure someone out there had an interest in Knoblock taking the fall.

"It is true that there has been an explicit understanding between Mr. Pierson, Mr. Hunter, and myself that no information is to be given to the press, except in such cases where the giving of such information may materially assist us in this investigation," Maple said. "How does that sound so far?"

"Like it's coming from law enforcement," Redmond said. "Next?"

"We had an agreement that no person should be permitted to enter the Knoblock premises without permission from Sheriff Hunter." Except for the fifty or so people who entered between the time Mrs. Knoblock was found and the house was sealed, not to mention the fact that two of Maple's key suspects had access to the crime scene the night after the murder. He shook his head in disgust and took a breath. "Mr. Pierson," the snot-nosed toddler they had passing for a county attorney, he thought, "prepared notices to that effect, and Mr. Hunter and myself posted the notices on the Knoblock place." When it was already too late to make much of a difference.

Redmond scribbled, then looked up and nodded at Maple to continue.

"I can only speak for myself, and I disclaim any knowledge of the acts or intentions of any other person. I have the key to the Knoblock house," as if any eight-year-old couldn't pick that skeleton-key lock, he thought, "and no one has been admitted to the premises by me. You can say, for me, that no one is going to be 'framed' in connection with this case while I am connected to it."

John Redmond made a final stroke with his pen and looked up at Maple. "It will run this afternoon," he said.

*****

"Listen to me," Maple said to Pierson. "You and I both know you have the wrong man in jail. You and I both also know that Knoblock likely didn't do it. You and I both know there are a couple of good suspects out there that are a better fit than Knoblock. Stop trying to force the evidence to fit the suspects. Find the suspects that fit the evidence."

Maple watched the flush creep over Pierson's face. The sheriff sat back, watching, not saying a word.

"You listen to me," Pierson growled, though Maple thought his growl was as intimidating as that of the young pooch that he was. "You might be from the big fancy Burns Detective Agency in big fancy Kansas City, but you don't know our people here. We do. I don't care what your evidence says. You don't know anything."

"Yeah?" Maple braced his hands on the table and leaned forward, right into Pierson's face. "If you know your people so well, who killed Florence Knoblock?"

"Not one of our people," Pierson said.

Maple snorted.

"You're right about the Negro," Hunter said. "We're going to have to let him go. But having him here keeps him safer than if he were out, and people won't have their guards up so high if they don't think we're questioning them to find the real killer."

"Everyone in town knows now that Blackie Stevens didn't do it," Maple said. "If they believed it was Blackie, you wouldn't get calls every single night asking you to come out and investigate whatever shadow was spotted crossing a field."

"You're right about that, too," the sheriff conceded, "but until we have a plan, I don't want to put Blackie in harm's way."

"You know what the evidence says," Maple said.

"You can't prove a thing," Pierson said.

"Are you the one trying to frame Knoblock?" Maple said.

"Let's settle it down. Now." Hunter stood up, ready to throw himself between the two men.

"I'm just glad I didn't speak for all of us when I said that no one would be framed on my watch," Maple said.

*****

Two days later, Maple was on his way back to Kansas City. He'd been given the axe.

*****

Goodrick farm, seven miles west of Burlington
Monday, June 22, 1925
2:00 p.m.

Dora looked at the first page of the *Daily Republican* with disbelief. "BURNS OPERATIVE OFF OF THE JOB—STILL NO ARREST," the lead story shouted in capital letters.

The only man trained to find killers was gone.

She thought about Decoration Day morning. She'd seen the man who bothered Florence, and she'd seen her son.

The local law was not going to do anything about the man.

But they might come after her son.

File Type: Newspaper Clipping

"It is being told," [Sheriff Hunter] said, "that we have taken for granted the guilt of a certain party and have disregarded other clews [sic], while as a matter of fact, not one clew [sic] has gone unnoticed and every rumor has been run down."

"Detective At Work: Burlington Did Not Know of Knoblock Investigator; Sheriff Hunter Resents Belief That Officers Disregarded Clews [sic] and Loafed on Job," *Emporia Gazette*, July 20, 1925

Chapter Eight
Released

Coffey County Jail, Burlington, Kansas
Wednesday, July 15, 1925

Blackie Stevens sat in his cell, wondering how much longer it would be before they let him go or, more likely, strung him up.

His leg was bothering him again, and he could feel his muscles going to fat, having been penned in this cell for almost forty-six days.

He hummed a hymn, one that had been a favorite of the wife who lit out on him nearly two years ago. *In dark days of bondage to Jesus I prayed*, he sang softly to himself, *to help me to bear it, and He gave me His aid.*

"Blackie?"

Blackie looked up and saw the sheriff standing at the bars. "Howdy, Mr. Sheriff," he said.

"Come on, Blackie. You've got somewhere to be," the sheriff said. "The judge wants to see you."

Blackie shuddered. What he had been waiting for was going to happen now. Suddenly, waiting didn't seem so bad. He fought the urge to break away from the sheriff and run, pouring his soul into the hymn he silently sung in his head:

I'm troubled, I'm troubled, I'm troubled in mind
If Jesus don't help me, I surely will die

*****

The sheriff escorted Blackie to stand in front of Justice of the Peace J. H. Rudrauff, who happened to be the same judge who married Blackie to the woman who would ultimately leave him.

"On behalf of the state of Kansas and Coffey County, I hereby dismiss, without prejudice, the charge of murder in the first degree against one Sherman Stevens, also known as Deacon Stevens, also known as Blackie Stevens."

Blackie stared at the judge in disbelief. Had he heard right?

He felt a hand on his shoulder and turned to see the sheriff steering him toward the door of the courtroom.

"You're free to go, Blackie," the sheriff said.

"I'm free?" Blackie repeated.

"You're free, but for one condition," the sheriff said. "Keep in touch and let me know where you are once a week."

"Why?"

"Just in case we need to get hold of you."

Blackie bobbed his head in a nod, but could taste the bitterness in his unspoken words. Free ain't free when you was a Negro, he thought.

*****

Sheriff's office, Burlington, Kansas
Monday, July 20, 1925

Sheriff Hunter paced around his office, across the lawn, and into the courthouse, wondering for the hundredth time why he hadn't stuck to farming. It seemed like everyone was mad at him right now. Drivers who were ticketed for running Burlington's newly installed stop signs weren't real happy with him nor were the pedestrians he had ticketed for jaywalking in the same intersection. That Mexican they had sentenced for carrying a gun last month escaped the road gang he was assigned to, and now Hunter and his officers were arresting people for spitting tobacco on the sidewalks and walls of buildings. And all of that was just a drop in the bucket compared to the still-unsolved Knoblock murder.

Having reached the end of the hallway, the sheriff pivoted on his heels and paced back across the yard to his office.

He had wanted to think the reward money would be enough to entice information from even the most secretive type. But nearly a month had passed since the county had announced a $500 reward, and nearly three weeks had gone by since the state had added another $200 on top of the county's cash.

The sheriff pivoted in front of his desk and headed back across the yard.

Maybe they waited too long to offer the reward, he thought. Maybe the eleven days between the murder and the announcement was enough time for the murderer to put some fear into any potential witnesses. Or offer them more cash than the government could.

Or maybe the only person who knew for sure who the killer was lay buried in Graceland Cemetery.

Still, the things people were saying about him and his officers stung. He couldn't come right out and say that many of Coffey County's citizens were wasting his time with rumors and lies, because he didn't want to discourage someone from passing along a rumor that might be true. But those people had no idea how many man-hours he and his men were putting into this case. He may have been new to solving murders, but George Griffith and William Utesler, his deputies, were experienced lawmen. While most of Coffey County was sleeping, they were working night and day, crouching in ditches watching potential suspects, hoping to find the clue they needed to break the case.

The sheriff made one more trip around the courthouse before heading back outside for some air.

*****

Mozingo farm, seven miles west of Burlington, Kansas
Tuesday, July 21, 1925

Florence being dead didn't make John Knoblock any less his son-in-law, John Mozingo thought as he took his chair at the supper table. His wife, Mary, and his daughter, Vesta (whom everyone called Vet), brought greens, boiled potatoes, and chicken to the table. Knoblock and little Roger settled into their chairs as Mary spooned potatoes onto plates.

Mozingo said grace and the family ate, mostly in silence, though Roger and Vet chattered on between themselves. When the plates were empty, Mozingo asked Mary to take the children outside to play.

Mozingo studied his son-in-law. The past two months have been hard on all of them, Mozingo thought, but hardest on Knoblock. His hair was grayer, his face had grown hollow, and the crinkles around his eyes were deeper. His slightly nervous mannerisms grew more noticeable each day. And he knew that what he was about to tell Knoblock wasn't going to help.

"John," Mozingo said, "I've been in touch with Harris & Samuel in Emporia. They're the very best attorneys in the area. They've agreed to take us as clients."

Knoblock looked up at him. "We've come to that, then," he said.

Mozingo nodded.

"It's going to get a whole lot worse before it gets better, John," Mozingo said. "But I'll do my best for you. And I wouldn't do that if I didn't believe, absolutely, that you would never hurt Florence."

"Will it be enough?"

"We've got to hope so."

*****

Six days later, John Knoblock was called to the state attorney general's office in Topeka for questioning for the first time.

File Type: Newspaper Clipping

Public sentiment over the county has changed
radically in the last month, possibly
due to the many rumors which have been
in circulation in an endless stream, but
public sentiment is very uncertain under
any conditions, and is not worth much in
a trial in court, and officers can not make
arrests without substantial evidence.

"No Developments But Many Rumors In Knoblock
Case," *Daily Republican*, July 17, 1925

Chapter Nine
Arrested

Kansas Attorney General's Office, Topeka, Kansas
Thursday, August 6, 1925
11:30 a.m.

Attorney General C. B. Griffith's office was silent except for the ticking of a clock, which chimed every fifteen minutes from its perch on top of a bookcase to the right of Griffith's desk. Griffith; his investigator, John Stewart; Ray Pierson; Franklin County prosecutor, Joe Rolston Sr.; and Sheriff Frank Hunter had heard the clock chime eleven times since John Knoblock was supposed to arrive for his second round of questioning.

Hunter studied Griffith, who sat behind his desk wearing an expression that waffled between exasperation and anger. Despite the August heat, there wasn't a hint of sweat around the man's dark, wavy hair. He was ageless, really, a man who could be anywhere from thirty-five to fifty, until you looked at his eyes—eyes tired from taking on the Ku Klux Klan and other injustices against people of color. Hunter wondered why Griffith deemed the Knoblock case worth his valuable time.

Griffith turned his attention to Stewart. "Tell me again what John Knoblock said when you told him to be here today?"

"I told him that he needed to come to Topeka this morning to go over all of the evidence," Stewart said. "Knoblock said that he would start out early in the morning if the roads weren't too muddy, and if he couldn't make it, he would call your office."

The clock chimed a quarter until noon.

"Get Mr. Knoblock on the phone for me," Griffith said. Stewart picked up the upright on Griffith's desk and made a long-distance call to Charles Knoblock's house in Burlington. Once Knoblock was on the line, Stewart passed the phone back to Griffith.

Hunter couldn't hear what Knoblock was saying, but he could tell from Griffith's reaction it wasn't good.

"Mr. Knoblock says he won't be making the trip to Topeka," Griffith said after he ended the call.

Hunter sighed. "I didn't think the roads were that wet out by the Mozingos," Hunter said.

"Oh, he didn't say he wasn't coming today because of the roads," Griffith said. "He said he wasn't coming. At all."

Hunter closed his eyes a moment and shook his head. He couldn't believe Knoblock would be so stupid. Or maybe it was that Knoblock was smart enough to know he was in a heap of trouble. Either way, Knoblock now had an enemy in the attorney general.

*****

Charles Knoblock's house, Burlington, Kansas
Friday, August 7, 1925
8:30 a.m.

John Knoblock dressed in his work clothes and tied his shoes. He'd promised both his father and father-in-law that he'd help them with chores during the next few days. He was still angry after yesterday's call from C. B. Griffith. What more could he tell them? Didn't they understand that he had work to do? They were paid to investigate. He was not paid if he didn't work, and he had a boy to feed and clothe. What little he had owned had been auctioned off to pay bills. And already he was tired of feeling like he was living off of his family's charity.

As he fished out his work gloves, he heard a knock at the front door. He opened it to find the sheriff standing on his parents' porch.

"Sheriff," Knoblock said.

"Mr. Knoblock," the sheriff said.

Knoblock held up his gloves for Hunter to see. "I need to get to work."

"The attorney general is requesting your presence in Topeka today," the sheriff said.

Knoblock stared at the sheriff for a moment. There was something different—a cold, hard edge—to Hunter this morning. Knoblock didn't like it.

"I told Mr. Griffith that I was not going," Knoblock said. "I told him everything I know. I don't have time to go to Topeka today. Or any day. He's wasting my time."

"Mr. Knoblock," the sheriff said. "Charles Griffith wants to see you in Topeka. Today."

Knoblock looked over at the sheriff's car. Pierson and another man sat inside, watching the exchange on the front porch.

"I have work to do," Knoblock said as he tried to push past the sheriff.

The sheriff grabbed Knoblock's arms and turned him around. "John Knoblock, you're under arrest for the murder of Florence Knoblock."

"What?!" Knoblock shouted as the sheriff muscled Knoblock into the back of his car. "You don't believe that!"

"What I believe doesn't matter," the sheriff said and pointed the car toward Topeka.

*****

John Mozingo and Charles Knoblock stormed into the sheriff's office, only to find Hunter out and his deputy sheriff, T. H. Olinger, in charge.

"Where's my son?" Charles shouted.

"Like I told you over the phone, I don't know," Olinger said. "I myself didn't know he'd been arrested until you called me. I don't know where he is. Whatever is going on, the sheriff and the attorney haven't told me a thing."

"Where's the sheriff?" Mozingo demanded.

"I don't know that, either," Olinger said.

"What *do* you know?" Charles yelled.

"I meant what I said. I. Don't. Know. The sheriff hasn't checked in yet today," Olinger said. "I. Don't. Know."

Mozingo steered Charles out of the office. "Come on," Mozingo said. "We need to go to Emporia."

Knoblock's father and father-in-law made the trip to the law offices of Harris & Samuel in record time, only to find the attorneys out of town. They drove back to Burlington and placed several long-distance calls to Topeka. But no one would tell them what had become of John Knoblock.

*****

John Knoblock fought tears as the sheriff and Pierson drove him back to Burlington. The grilling had begun the moment the sheriff opened the door to Griffith's office. Knoblock's words were thrown back into his face over and over again. Did he not realize that his stories varied some? Did he not know they knew he was lying? Had he been stepping out on his wife? Wasn't Florence sickly? Was she standing in his way? The attorney general asked questions over and over again, confusing Knoblock to the point that even he didn't know what was true anymore. By the time the day was over, Knoblock was so tired he didn't even care what anyone was telling him. He just wanted to go home.

The car stopped just outside the little brick jail on the

courthouse lawn in Burlington. Knoblock's eyes widened in horror as Hunter opened the door and yanked Knoblock out by the bib of his overalls.

"Your new home," the sheriff said and locked him in the same cell the Negro had recently vacated.

*****

When Knoblock's attorneys told him that his bail had been set at forty thousand dollars, he told them he didn't want the money raised. He couldn't do that to his family. He wouldn't take any more charity. Ten days, Owen Samuel had said. He would try to get the preliminary hearing set within ten days.

"I'll stay here for ten days," Knoblock had told them. "Maybe it will satisfy some of those who have been hounding me if we get the hearing done with."

Now, as he awoke from his seventh night in the little brick Coffey County jail, he wasn't sure he'd make it ten days. He was a man who liked to work. He had rough hands that did well in the fields and even better with woodwork. But here, in this jail, his tanned skin was beginning to peel. He felt grimy and, worse, useless.

Knoblock was shaken out of his self-pity by the clanking of metal.

"Mr. Knoblock?" Deputy Sheriff Olinger unlocked the cell door and pushed it open. "You made bail. Come on back to the courthouse with me."

On shaky feet, Knoblock followed Olinger out into the sunlight.

*****

Owen S. Samuel was, in general, a likeable man. He gardened and fished. He'd spent some time working for the Santa Fe Railroad and had coached football at both the College of Emporia and the Kansas State Normal.[6] He was also a top-notch attorney who had more than twenty years of experience under his belt. If Knoblock had a chance, Samuel and his partner, the former judge, W. C. Harris, would get it for him.

Samuel looked around the room, amazed by the outpouring of support. This, he thought, was Knoblock's greatest defense: twelve friends and family members who were willing to risk it all because they believed this husband could not have killed his wife. The dead woman's father had put up one of the largest portions of the bond. What kind of father would do that if he wasn't absolutely sure his son-in-law was innocent?

Samuel stood when a bedraggled man wearing bib overalls and a dirty collared shirt was led into the room. Everyone else cheered. Mrs. Mary Knoblock threw her arms around her son despite the filth, as any loving mother would. John Mozingo gave him a hearty pat on the shoulder and led him to the empty chair next to Samuel.

"This sure was a surprise for me," Knoblock told him.

"No more than it was for me," Samuel said. And he meant it. This room full of farmers and retirees managed to qualify for forty-six thousand dollars in bond money.

"But why?" Knoblock asked.

"Mr. Pierson called this morning and asked if we could postpone your hearing. I said absolutely not, unless the bond was lowered. Judge Rudrauff agreed to lower the bond to twenty-five thousand, and here we are."

Raw disappointment swept across Knoblock's face. "So there'll still be a hearing?"

Samuel nodded.

*****

Sheriff's office, Burlington, Kansas
 Friday, August 21, 1925

6 Kansas State Normal was renamed the Kansas State Teachers College in 1923. Today, it is known as Emporia State University.

Sheriff Frank Hunter wondered for the thousandth time why he had gone into law enforcement. The state livestock commissioner was in town investigating two reported epidemics of rabies among pets and livestock, which meant that every third Coffey County citizen who saw a stray dog in the streets was calling to report a possible rabid dog on the loose. George Luther Knoblock, a roundabout cousin of the now-out-on-bond John Knoblock, had escaped from the prison farm in Lansing and was thought to be on his way to Burlington. And a group of thieves were busy in Agricola and Waverly, breaking into four different businesses the previous night.

He could always go back to farming, Hunter thought. Then the only people he'd have to worry about were his own kin, and the only land he'd have to worry about was his own property.

Deep in thought, the sheriff didn't notice Ray Pierson's head poking in through the partially open door until Pierson cleared his throat.

"Sheriff? A moment of your time?"

Hunter sighed and waved the county attorney into a chair.

"I've been going over all of the evidence in the Knoblock case," Pierson said. "And I can't help but wonder if I'm missing something."

Hunter wanted to roll his eyes at the man. "You think so?"

"I'm sure it's just that there is something you haven't handed over," Pierson said. "I can come up with enough to prove that Knoblock had the time to commit the murder, but I can't figure out why."

"Maybe he didn't do it," the sheriff said.

"Of course he did," Pierson said.

The sheriff shrugged.

"He did it," Pierson said, more firmly.

"All right," the sheriff said. "But why?"

"Florence was sickly," Pierson said.

"Lots of folk out there are," Hunter said.

"He was a healthy man. Men have needs," Pierson said.

"That they do," Hunter said. "But you've got nothing that says Knoblock's 'needs' were so important he had to get rid of his wife."

"But I will," Pierson said. "Because he did it."

The sheriff shrugged again. "You don't have to convince me. I can't convict him."

Pierson scooped up his papers and stood. "I will prove he killed her."

"Yeah? Well, then, I hope it's true."

*****

Coffey County Courthouse, Burlington, Kansas
Wednesday, September 9, 1925

John Redmond took his seat next to the staff correspondent for the *Emporia Gazette*. By his estimation, nearly one hundred and fifty people were packed into the benches, and even more lined the walls. Men and women jostled in the hallways, hoping to squeeze in. Still others were blocking the light coming in through the windows as they pressed their faces and ears against the glass, hoping to catch some of what was going on inside.

The woman from the *Gazette* leaned toward Redmond. "Who's who?' she asked, and Redmond obliged by pointing out the key people.

"The younger man is Ray Pierson, our county attorney. It looks like Joe Rolston, a prosecutor, is assisting him. I'm not sure what became of R. C. Burnett. He was supposed to be assisting on behalf of the attorney general, but I heard he was pulled off the case."

Redmond paused to give her a moment to finish spelling out the names among the scribbles in shorthand.

"Coming in now are Owen S. Samuel and the former judge, W. C. Harris, both of whom I'm sure you know, as they're from Emporia. And that is John Knoblock."

Redmond watched as the *Gazette* reporter scribbled Gregg lines to describe the defendant. He caught "graying hair" and "nervous" and something that looked like "twitching."

The bailiff shouted for everyone to quiet down and stand as Judge Rudrauff entered the courtroom.

"The State wishes to make a motion," Ray Pierson said.

"Go ahead," Rudrauff said from his seat.

Pierson held a piece of paper in front him with a shaky hand. "Before J. H. Rudrauff, a justice of the peace of the city of Burlington, Kansas, the *State v. John Knoblock* comes now the plaintiff by Ray S. Pierson, county attorney of Coffey County, Kansas, and moves the court to dismiss the hearing to this case."

The spectators roared in surprise.

"Objection!" W. C. Harris stood from behind his table.

"How could you possibly object to having the hearing dismissed?" Pierson said.

"You aren't dismissing the charges, you're dismissing the hearing," Harris shouted.

"On what grounds are you requesting the hearing be dismissed?" Rudrauff said.

"Your honor, the state has not had enough time to prepare—"

"That's ridiculous," Samuel said. "You've had three months to investigate this case—"

"I asked our defense," Pierson shouted so Rudrauff could hear, "For a continuance, and they refused to cooperate—"

"We already gave you a continuance, and if you can't prove your case by now, you never will."

"Order!" Rudrauff pounded the gavel until everyone inside the courtroom settled. "Defense, what is your objection to the motion?"

"Your honor, the motion's wording renders it meaningless. The defendant is entitled to one of two things. Either dismiss the charges and release Mr. Knoblock from the bond under which he is being held or proceed with the hearing."

The crowd broke out in applause.

"Order!" Rudrauff shouted.

"When Knoblock was let out of jail, I submitted a list of twenty-one witnesses to be subpoenaed," Samuel said. "I came down here several days ago to get ready for this and I scratched a few names from the list and added a few more. Now none of them have been subpoenaed. The state has had almost a hundred days to get ready, and now we are no nearer the end than we were before. We are entitled to a subpoena hearing. We have tried and can't get it. I want the *case* dismissed. Not just the hearing."

The crowd broke out in applause again.

"Order!" Rudrauff shouted. "This isn't a theatrical performance! Stop applauding or you'll all be removed from the courtroom."

"This is ridiculous," Pierson said. "The state is entitled to adequate time to build a case."

"There are only two courses," W. C. Harris said. "Go to trial or wipe out the charges. We demand a hearing and your honor has no right to refuse."

Rolston, Pierson, Samuel, Harris, and Judge Rudrauff were all shouting at the same time. Redmond glanced over at the *Gazette* reporter. Her hand and pencil rested on her notepad as she watched the spectacle with her eyes wide and her jaw dropped. Redmond couldn't blame her. It looked like the five men were on the verge of breaking into a brawl.

"Dismissing the hearing and dismissing the charges mean the same thing," Pierson whined.

"Absolutely not," Samuel said, turning to Rudrauff. "If you believe this, then I take it your honor is not a lawyer and is not schooled on these terms. It is a play on words. We want to feel when we leave here that Knoblock is as free as if the charges had never been made."

The courtroom went silent at Samuel's attack on the judge, who bristled. Rudrauff closed his eyes and pursed his lips as he considered.

"Prosecution, what is your true intent with this motion?"

Pierson glanced at two angry attorneys and a bewildered defendant to his left.

"To dismiss the charges," he said slowly.

"Then reword the motion and read it again."

Pierson and Rolston scribbled notes on their paper and Pierson reread the motion to dismiss the charges and release Knoblock from his bond.

"Does that satisfy the defense?" Rudrauff asked Samuel and Harris.

"Yes, your honor."

"Very well, then. The charges against John Knoblock are dismissed and he is released from his bond."

Redmond and the *Gazette* reporter studied John Knoblock, who remained seated long after the mob of spectators filed out of the courtroom. Today he wore black trousers, a light blue shirt, and a black tie, a far cry from the farm attire he wore in the photo shot by the *Gazette* only a few weeks ago.

"He's an attractive man," the *Gazette* reporter said. "Pity about his wife."

Redmond stood to listen as Knoblock talked with family and friends. Knoblock's mother, eyes red with tears, approached her son thirty minutes after his case had been dismissed.

"Are you going to sit there all day?" she asked him.

"I'm going to stay here until I know just where I am," Knoblock said, rubbing his face with his hands. "I want to get this thing settled one way or the other."

File Type: Newspaper Clipping

To the citizens of Coffey County:

I am a writer and am researching the murder
of Florence Knoblock, who was killed in
her home on a farm just a few miles west
of downtown Burlington in 1925. While
I have accumulated numerous newspaper
articles and some other paper work, I am now
very interested in finding family stories
pertaining to Mrs. Knoblock's death and its
effect on the community.

Do you remember first-hand when this happened?
Did your grandparents tell you about
testifying at the first trial or serving on
the jury? Have you picked up some legends
regarding this tragic event? Then I'd like
to hear from you.

Please send your stories to: Diana Staresinic-
Deane, P.O. Box 515, Emporia, KS, 66801, or
1925.knoblock.murder@gmail.com. Be sure to
include how you heard the story (i.e., first-
hand or from a neighbor), and, if possible,
your contact information in case I have
questions.

Thank you in advance for your assistance.

Diana Staresinic-Deane

Coffey County Republican, editorial page,
August 8, 2008

Chapter Ten
Rearrested

Mozingo farm, seven miles west of Burlington, Kansas
Monday, November 2, 1925
11:30 a.m.

Sheriff Frank Hunter turned his car onto the dirt drive to the Mozingo home, taking in the tidy house and the large barn that said the man had done well for himself. Hunter sat, unmoving, before tossing open the door and marching up to the Mozingo's front porch.

Mrs. Mozingo opened the door before the sheriff could knock. She greeted him because her proper good nature wouldn't allow her to be rude, even if she wanted to chuck him headfirst into the yard.

"I'm here to see John Knoblock," the sheriff told her. As if she didn't know. As if everyone in the county didn't know, he thought. Coffey County had been holding its breath to see when Pierson would make his move after being embarrassed at the hearing in September.

Mrs. Mozingo nodded. "He's out shucking corn. May I bring you anything?"

The sheriff shook his head. "No, ma'am. Thank you."

The sheriff stood in the parlor, studying the black-and-white photos of the Mozingo children and some of the grandchildren. Photos from happier times, Hunter thought. A picture of Florence, holding a little boy of about two, was tucked behind the frames of other pictures.

"You here for me?" Knoblock said, pulling Hunter's mind back into the room.

Hunter turned. Knoblock stood in the doorway, shielding his mother-in-law. He wore dirty overalls and held a pair of stained work gloves in his right hand.

"I'm here to arrest you," Hunter said.

Knoblock nodded.

"You mind if I change my clothes first?"

Hunter nodded. "I can wait."

*****

Goodrick farm, seven miles west of Burlington, Kansas
Monday, November 2, 1925
4:00 p.m.

"How could they arrest him again? They have nothing," Dora said. "Half of Coffey County saw John Knoblock in town that morning, running his errands." Dora set the *Daily Republican* down on the dining table and looked up at her husband. "We've got to say something. We've got to tell what we saw."

Charles, who had been pacing the length of the dining room, sat down in the chair across from Dora. He reached for her hand. "Listen to me," he said. "We can't prove anything. All we can do is tell them we saw two people approach the house. As soon as we do that, the focus will be on our boy. All of our friends will think we're trying to hide the truth. You just said yourself they have nothing on John. That will come out at the preliminary hearing. Then they'll let him go. The law will do what's right."

Dora wiped tears from her eyes. "The law hasn't done what's right yet," she said. "That Burns detective would still be here, arresting that man we saw, if the law was doing what's right."

"Dora, we don't know he did anything, either. We saw him go to the house, then we saw him leave." He held up a hand before she could speak. "Just like we saw Carl go to the house, then leave."

"Ma?" Dora turned to see Carl standing in the doorway. "You all right?"

"Carl, come. Sit," she said, and patted the chair next to her.

Carl pulled the chair out and folded his gangly limbs under the table.

"I'm going to ask you a question, Carl, and I want you to tell me the truth, now," Dora said. "We saw you ride up to John and Florence's house the morning that Florence was killed. Did you see Florence? Alive or dead?"

Carl sat, still as a statue. Dora couldn't even swear he was breathing.

"Carl," Charles said, "answer your mother."

Carl turned his face towards Dora. "No, Ma, I didn't see anything," he said in a harsh whisper.

Dora looked into the eyes of the man who was once her little boy.

She was wanted to believe him.

*****

Ray Pierson's house, Burlington, Kansas
Tuesday, November 3, 1925

Ray Pierson sat in his favorite chair, still floating on the high of having Knoblock rearrested. Sure, Knoblock hardly had time to warm the cot in his cell before he was out on bond again, but he was arrested, the public knew it, and Pierson would make sure Knoblock had his day in court.

Pierson was pleased to see Knoblock still merited front-page coverage in the *Daily Republican*.

"The arrest of John Knoblock yesterday was expected by all who had kept in touch with the case," Redmond had written, and Pierson couldn't help but smile. That's right, he thought, everyone knew he was going to be arrested, because everyone suspected him.

"There has been so much discussion of the mysterious murder and so many rumors of all kinds that many people felt that Mr. Knoblock was entitled to have the matter settled and the case brought to trial," Redmond's article continued.

Pierson frowned. Redmond made it sound like the general public thought Knoblock deserved the trial so he could be vindicated.

"The county officials have impressed their firm belief in Mr. Knoblock's guilt and in their ability to prove it and say that considerable corroborative evidence has been discovered since the former case against him was dismissed," the article said. "Mr. Knoblock still adheres to his story of the happenings of that day and insists that he is innocent."

Pierson set the unfinished newspaper on the small table next to his chair. If he didn't know better, he'd think Redmond didn't believe he could pull off this conviction.

*****

Carl Goodrick stood on the wooden platform, watching the Katy line train slow to a stop. His neighbor, John Dornes, stood nearby, a small bag at his feet.

"Are you sure you don't want me to stay?" Carl asked his father as the conductor called for passengers to board.

"We'll be fine," Charles said. "The wages you earn will help this winter."

Carl didn't look back as he boarded the train.

*****

Daily Republican office, Burlington, Kansas
Saturday, November 7, 1925

John Redmond proofed the latest Knoblock story one more time before sending it to press. "Are Preparing For Hard Fight At Preliminary" certainly wasn't the longest piece he'd done on the murder, but the list of names subpoenaed to appear was substantial and reviewing each name was tedious.

Neighbors, friends, family, and strangers were about to be thrown into the arena, fighting it out with their testimony in hopes that the truth would ultimately be victorious.

*****

Sheriff Hunter's automobile was stuck. Again.

Hunter looked at the last of the pile of subpoenas he needed to deliver and wondered if he'd have an easier time walking than trying to move his Ford through the muddy country roads. He flipped through the pile and planned out the fastest route in his head. No, he thought. If he wanted to finish before nightfall, he was going to have to use the car.

He cranked the steering wheel right, then left, and rocked the car until he broke free from the mud.

*****

"Mama, the sheriff's here." Grace found her mother in the kitchen, preparing supper. Dora wiped her hands in her apron and walked out to the front room, where a weary sheriff stood holding three folded pieces of paper in his hand.

"Mrs. Goodrick, I'm here to serve you, your daughter, and Carl with subpoenas for the Knoblock hearing on Monday," Hunter said. He handed her an official piece of paper that was folded once and then again. He gave Grace a similar piece of paper.

"Where's your son, Mrs. Goodrick?" Hunter said.

Dora looked up from her subpoena. "He's picking corn in Iowa with John Dornes," she said. "He won't be back until December."

The sheriff studied her for a moment, then pulled an ink pen from his pocket to mark the subpoena "Not Found."

*****

Coffey County Courthouse, Burlington, Kansas
Monday, November 9, 1925
9:00 a.m.

County Attorney Ray Pierson was ready. His notes were in order. His suit was immaculate. He'd had a good breakfast. And he'd had a realization that would make this preliminary hearing a whole lot easier: He didn't have to prove that Knoblock was guilty or even that Knoblock had a motive. All he had to do was prove that there was enough evidence to suggest Knoblock *could* have killed his wife, and Pierson only needed to prove it strongly enough that the judge would agree that Knoblock should be bound over for trial.

Pierson stood tall, took a deep breath, and opened the door to find the county prosecutor, Joe Rolston, poised with his knuckles ready to knock.

"There's been a delay," Rolston said. "Fred Harris' train is running late from Ottawa."

That's not good, Pierson thought. Harris, a highly skilled attorney from Franklin County, was being brought in to help with Knoblock's prosecution.

"And W. C. Harris and Owen Samuel are stuck on a muddy road somewhere between here and Emporia."

Pierson poured himself another cup of coffee and sat back down in his chair.

*****

Justice of the Peace J. H. Rudrauff stepped out of his chambers and into pandemonium.

The hallway leading to the courtroom was packed with people standing shoulder-to-shoulder, with small children squeezed between legs or clinging to necks.

"Excuse me," Rudrauff said. "Please, step back." The sea of people parted just enough for Rudrauff to muscle his way through to the doors. What he saw made him shake his head. Every seat—nearly two hundred—was occupied, sometimes by more than one person. Every inch of wall space was lined with bodies. Men sat on the radiators and on the window sills, women sat on the floor. Bodies filled the space inside the railing and on the platform by the judge's bench. Most disconcerting was the number of faces pressed against the glass from the outside of the courtroom, hoping to see what was happening inside.

He was relieved, at least, not to find anyone sitting on his bench.

The attorneys and the defendant were already in place, and the crowd became astonishingly quiet as he called the hearing to order.

*****

John Redmond sat next to the correspondent for the *Emporia Gazette*, scribbling his impressions of the courtroom before the hearing was fully underway. By his estimation, at least six hundred people had gathered for the trial. Redmond glanced over at his colleague's notes and suppressed a smile when he saw she estimated at least one thousand people were in attendance.

Redmond wondered if Pierson would manage to secure a trial.

*****

Sheriff Hunter stood when he was called to the stand. This wasn't the first time he'd been called to testify. Hell, it seemed like he'd spent more time on the stand than any of the criminals he'd arrested. The hardest part was feeling like he was on trial when he was actually just a witness. Even during those cases when he knew he'd done everything by the book and there was no question that he was in the right, he could feel the bottom drop out of his stomach and his guts churning right up until he was called to the stand.

Today, his stomach was churning extra hard.

*****

John Knoblock sat with his attorneys, trying very hard not to look worried. "Remember, it is not your job to prove you're innocent today," Owen Samuel had told him during their last meeting before the hearing. "It's the state's job to prove they can scrape together enough evidence to merit a trial. It's your job to stay calm. The state is going to say hurtful things about you and about Florence. Try not to listen too much. It will only upset you."

Then the sheriff was called to the stand.

"Sheriff, describe to us how you first learned about the murder."

Hunter cleared his throat. "I was called to the Knoblock farm by John Knoblock. He told me over the phone that his wife was dead and to bring the coroner along."

"And what did you see when you arrived, sheriff?"

Images flashed in Knoblock's mind as the sheriff described the kitchen. Try not to listen too much, he chanted inside his head. He caught himself gripping the fabric of his trousers and fought to relax his hands.

"And what did Mr. Knoblock tell you with regards to his whereabouts that day?"

The sheriff blinked and took a breath. "He described his trip into town and how he arrived home between noon and one o'clock and stopped on the porch—that's the east porch—and took an armful of packages into the kitchen. He said he went back for another armful when he saw his wife lying dead on the floor, cold and stiff. He said he called Florence's father, John Mozingo, to come right away and then called me and asked me to bring the coroner."

"What did he tell you he did then?" Harris asked.

"He said that he wanted to cover Mrs. Knoblock with a blanket. That he took the quilt off the bed, but he didn't want to ruin it, so he took an old blanket instead."

The bailiff brought out the wool blanket. "Is this the blanket?" Harris said.

Knoblock looked down as the blanket was unfolded. He couldn't bear to look, but knew by the murmurs and movement that everyone in the courtroom was trying to catch a glimpse of the dark red stain, the blood absorbed from the deep slash in Florence's neck.

When the bailiff brought out the pillow that had covered Florence's face, Knoblock closed his eyes.

*****

Dora Goodrick closed her eyes a moment after her name was called before she stood to approach the stand. What if they asked her what she saw that day? None of the lawyers—not Pierson or Rolston or John's fancy lawyers from Emporia—had asked her any such questions when they paid her and Grace a visit over the weekend.

But what if they asked now?

"Mrs. Goodrick, please tell us what John Knoblock told you when you visited his farmhouse after the murder," Fred Harris said for the state.

"He said it looked as though the murderer might have come in the door and struck Florence on the head as she was raising up from picking up the dishpan or soap or something. Oh, and that his razor had been used to cut her throat but that it was missing."

"Did he show any grief?" Fred Harris asked.

The poor man had been too numb to show grief, Dora thought. She shook her head. "No."

"What else did he say?"

"He also said that he was going to cover her with the quilt, but he was afraid it wouldn't wash and got the blanket out instead."

"Thank you, Mrs. Goodrick," he said.

She sat still on the stand, waiting.

"You may step down now," Rudrauff said.

As she took the seat by her husband's side, she thought about how much telling the truth had felt like telling a lie.

*****

John Redmond was called to the stand.

Redmond relayed his interview with Knoblock. He told of the prints on the white bedspread in the bedroom and recalled what Knoblock had told him about errands in town that morning. During his testimony, Redmond watched Knoblock. The man was trying so hard to sit still, Redmond thought. Knoblock was a jittery, nervous man by nature, and by sitting still, he only drew more attention to himself.

"Did you ask who he thought did it?"

"He said he had no definite suspicions, but two weeks before, his wife had been frightened by a man in the yard and she believed it was a colored man," Redmond said.

*****

Knoblock hung his head and fought the urge to cry as Eugene Stone, the undertaker, described Florence and the things he saw in the house that day.

"Can you tell the court how long Mrs. Knoblock had been there?"

"When I saw her?" Stone asked. "I have no way of knowing."

"Did you hear Mr. Knoblock say anything about his wife?"

The undertaker hesitated. "I heard him say that he would buy his wife a nice tombstone," he said. "And that he could 'cash in' on her death 'for five thousand or six thousand dollars.'"

*****

Redmond listened to the undertaker describe the sooty prints on the drawer pulled out of the dresser. When the defense asked for the drawer to be presented so that Stone could identify it, the county attorney said he didn't have it.

"Your honor, we'd like to call Ray Pierson to the stand, please," Owen Samuel said, annoyed.

Ray Pierson glowered at Owen Samuel and placed himself on the witness stand.

"Mr. Pierson, do you have the drawer?"

"No, I do not."

"Do you know where the drawer is at this time?"

Pierson shifted in his seat. "No, I do not."

"Do you have the contents of the drawer?" Samuel said.

"No, I do not."

"Are you aware of where the contents might be?"

"No."

Samuel shook his head. "No further questions."

*****

John Knoblock forced himself to sit still as his late wife's aunt, Minnie Jaggers, was called to the stand. Aunt Min, he thought, was nothing but trouble. He just knew she was going to say something awful. He didn't dare turn around, but he figured if he did, he'd see his in-laws readying for the worst, too.

A sixty-two-year-old widow who worked as a seamstress from her home, Aunt Min was formidable, difficult, and one of types who could do more damage by being well-intentioned than someone who was bent on injury. Because she was dependent upon family to drive her into town as she herself could not drive, she was also hard to evade.

"Mrs. Jaggers, tell us about your conversation with John Knoblock," Fred Harris asked for the state.

"I asked John if anything had gone missing, and John said nothing was missing except maybe some valuable papers, but no money, because he took everything they had in the house with him when he went to town," she said. "He even took the money that was in the baby's bank."

Knoblock heard some murmurs in the crowd before the judge ordered silence.

"I asked John why he didn't offer a reward, and he said he didn't want to help the law, because he didn't want them to blame it on him and say they'd get a convict to swear he did it like they did in the Governor Davis[7] trial," she said.

"And then what did you say?" Harris asked.

"I said he should at least offer to get his fingerprints taken, but he refused. He said he wasn't going to help them."

*****

"Tell us about Mr. Knoblock's relationship with Florence Knoblock's sisters," Fred Harris said.

"John acted familiar with the girls, but that was his way," Jaggers said, frowning in disapproval. "But I don't like that, because things like that lead to trouble."

"What do you mean, Mrs. Jaggers?"

"Well, when we were all in the dining room the Sunday after Florence died, I saw John walk up behind Edna Mozingo and try to put his arm around her."

7 In 1925, near the end of his term, Kansas Governor Jonathan M. Davis and his son, Russell Davis, were arrested for accepting bribes. The accuser was a banker convicted of forgery, Fred W. Pollman (*Time*, January 19, 1925). Davis was tried twice and ultimately acquitted (National Governors Association, http://www.nga.org).

The crowd murmured.

"What did Edna do?"

"She scowled at him and walked away."

"Mrs. Jaggers, were you aware that the Knoblocks' house was going to be cleaned?"

Jaggers lifted her chin and the wrinkles in her face crinkled further. "I was present when Ruth Mozingo asked John for the key to the house. I told them they shouldn't touch anything until they'd phoned the sheriff."

"What did Mr. Knoblock say after that?" Harris asked.

"John said that it was all right because he was a friend of the sheriff."

*****

Unlike many of the Knoblocks' and Mozingos' closest friends, Sam Shoup was not inclined to help with John Knoblock's bond. It wasn't that he wanted to see the man hang or that he even believed Knoblock was guilty. It was just that Shoup, a businessman and a community leader, believed his energy was better spent supporting his longtime neighbors as a friend than publicly taking sides in a matter as important as a murder case. Shoup did not need to involve himself further into John Knoblock's problems. The day of Florence Knoblock's murder was still fresh on his mind: Florence's blood, his friends' pain, the excited folk buzzing around the house.

Shoup gave his friend John Mozingo a single, supportive nod as he made his way to the front of the courtroom.

"No, Knoblock wasn't excited when Rose and I arrived that afternoon," Shoup said. "But he was grieving."

"Mr. Shoup, did the sheriff post any signs forbidding anyone disturb the property?"

"I helped John and John Kellerman post signs on the doors and the gate that said, 'Keep Out—by order of the sheriff.'"

"And when did you do that?"

"The evening of the murder."

"Yet the next day, you were back on the property."

"We didn't imagine that warning was for family and close friends."

"Tell us about the sack."

Shoup shot Mozingo an apologetic glance. That Sunday morning following Florence's murder, he and his wife, Rose, had stopped by the Knoblock farm to lend a hand. Mary Knoblock had handed him a sack to destroy. When he had smelled the blood burning, he knew he was touching the crime, touching horror and fear, touching the remains of Florence Knoblock's life.

But on the witness stand, he just said, "When I arrived at the Knoblock farm Sunday morning, Mrs. Knoblock, John's mother, gave me a sack to burn. It was a bundle of rags or something wrapped in a gunnysack. I didn't look inside, but it smelled bad. I wanted to make sure it burned, and so I asked John if he had some coal oil. When it burned, it smelled like blood."

*****

Shortly after her husband finished his testimony, Rose Shoup was called to the stand.

"Mrs. Shoup, tell us what Mr. Knoblock said about the razor," Fred Harris said.

"I heard John say that he was glad it wasn't his new razor that was used in cutting his wife's throat," she said.

*****

Redmond scribbled notes as the sheriff and the county attorney testified to the condition of the house Sunday morning. "When I was at the Knoblock house on Sunday, it had not been cleaned up and the fingerprints and such were still there. But when I was out there next, it had been cleaned," Sheriff Hunter said.

"And did you give permission for the house to be cleaned?" Fred Harris asked.

"No, sir, I did not."

Ray Pierson was called to the stand a second time. "Mr. Pierson," Fred Harris said, "Describe your efforts to preserve the evidence in this case."

"On the day Mrs. Knoblock was buried, I placed some signs throughout the house."

"That would be Tuesday, June second?"

"Yes."

"Three days after the murder."

"Yes."

"What did you do with these signs?"

"I placed them on the bedspread, the dresser and its contents, the bedstead, and other places, warning people not to touch them. The Burns detective didn't have his camera with him when he first came here and couldn't immediately photograph the fingerprints, hence the signs."

"Did you give permission for the house to be cleaned?"

"Absolutely not. But the house was cleaned anyway, and the fingerprints were mostly wiped out."

Owen Samuel approached Ray Pierson. "Tell me, Mr. Pierson, had something prevented you from taking the doors and bedstead with you? To preserve the valuable evidence?"

Pierson shifted in his seat.

"It wasn't necessary," Pierson said. "That's what the signs were for."

"And what happened that day when John Knoblock was in your office?"

"Mr. Knoblock said that his family was cleaning the house."

"And what did you do?"

"I told him nothing must be touched."

"And what did Mr. Knoblock do?"

"He phoned the farm and told them to quit."

*****

The state rested its case at four thirty-five that afternoon. Redmond and several others lucky enough to have seats stood and stretched. He knew many of the onlookers today had been at the courthouse since six o'clock that morning, waiting to get inside. He groaned as the defense moved to begin its questioning.

*****

Sheriff Hunter walked to the witness stand for the third time that day.

"Did you accompany the bloodhounds after the murder?" Samuel asked the sheriff.

"Yes, sir," the sheriff said. "I walked with the bloodhounds as they followed the footprints. Some of the tracks were plainly marked, some places showed heels on shoes, and other places showed no heels. The dogs went across a wheat field where there were no visible tracks."

"How did the dogs behave?"

"The man holding them often pulled them," Hunter said. "Sometimes he pulled them in a direction different from the one they apparently wanted to go."

*****

Owen Samuel looked at the time and smiled. The mud that had delayed him and W. C. Harris might have been a nuisance, but slowing the hearing down meant that the judge and the general public would leave the courtroom on the words of the defense's two most important witnesses.

Samuel stood as Margaret "Grandma" Winchester, age seventy-six, approached the stand.

"Mrs. Winchester, please tell the court where you live."

"On the George King farm. Route four, seven miles southwest."

"Tell us what you heard, Mrs. Winchester," Samuel said.

Mrs. Winchester sat stiffly upright, her chin raised a fraction. "The Knoblocks are on the same party line as we are. The morning of the murder, I overheard Mrs. Knoblock calling the bakery on the party line to ask Ray if their lard had come. Then I heard someone on the other end ask her if she wanted the hundred-pound can. Then Mrs. Knoblock said, 'John is here, I'll let him talk.'"

"At what time did this happen, Mrs. Winchester?" Samuel asked.

"It was after breakfast," she said. "About eight o'clock."

*****

Rosa Knapp was just sure she was going to be sick. The girl, just a few days shy of her sixteenth birthday, walked to the witness stand on shaky legs. She hated crowds, and here she was, testifying in a room so stuffed full of people that she had to step over legs and between knees to reach the chair next to the judge's bench.

"Miss Knapp, please tell us about what you saw that morning," Samuel said in a gentle voice.

"I was in the car with my father and brother that morning," Knapp began, trying to control the tremor in her voice. "We were on our way home after going to town. About three miles east of the Knoblock farm, we passed a car being driven by Mr. Knoblock. His little boy was in the car. As we drove past the Knoblock farm, I saw a man standing on the east porch. He wasn't moving, except to turn his head toward our car."

"Could you describe the man?" Samuel said.

Rosa closed her eyes, trying to remember. "I couldn't see his face. I don't know if he was white or colored. I remember he was wearing something dark, like overalls. After I heard about the murder, I remember telling my family about seeing him."

"Could you have been mistaken? Perhaps you saw a tree or a bush?"

Rosa heaved a frustrated sigh. "That's what Mr. Pierson and the man from the office in Topeka said, too. But I went to the house and looked around and there wasn't anything there I could have confused for a man."

*****

Despite the numerous witnesses called during the second day of the hearing, not much was added to the story, thought Redmond, as he proofed the Wednesday article about the case. Ex-sheriff William Utesler and former undersheriff George Griffith both stated that John Knoblock wasn't very cooperative but that he answered questions when asked. And there was a long and tedious discussion about some bloody cloth. Yet there was nothing concrete that said John Knoblock was responsible.

After the defense rested at two-forty that Tuesday afternoon, Ray Pierson asked the state to have John Knoblock bound over "for the reason that the state had proven that a crime had been committed and that it shown that Knoblock was the last person known to be with the murdered woman."

"There was no evidence of robbery or that any other person had been at the place," Pierson said. "Knoblock did not cooperate with the officers in their efforts to find the murderer, and he declined to offer a reward for the arrest of the murderer. And, his general demeanor is that he was guilty and therefore should go to trial."

And Judge Rudrauff had agreed with him, thought Redmond, as he titled his story, "Knoblock Bound Over On Charge Of Murder—Gives Bond For $25,000."

File Type: Newspaper Clipping

Among the witnesses on the list for the defense is Blackie or Deacon Stevens . . . Deacon was released with the agreement that he was to report once a week to Sheriff Hunter, but no word has been received from him for a month or so. He reported regularly for some time, and at the last report was at Garnett, but, according to reports from that place, he is not there now.

"Crowd Jams Court Room For The Knoblock Murder Preliminary—Deacon Stevens Can't Be Found," *Daily Republican*, November 9, 1925

Chapter Eleven
Fair Trial

Offices of Harris & Samuel
Emporia, Kansas
Tuesday, December 8, 1925

John Knoblock sat in the big, leather-clad chair, his hands in his lap under the table where his father-in-law and lawyers wouldn't see his fidgeting. His attorneys, W. C. Harris and Owen S. Samuel, sat in similar chairs across from him. Everyone—his attorneys, his wife's family, and his friends—were telling him a trial would be a good thing.

"You'll be cleared in people's minds if you're cleared in a trial," Samuel had said to him after the preliminary hearing. "Otherwise, there will be that little hint of doubt that will make people wonder if you did it and got away with it."

After watching the crowd watching him at the preliminary hearing, John wasn't so sure it would be that easy.

He caught himself clutching at the creases in his trousers and tried to relax his hands.

"A fair trial will find you innocent, Mr. Knoblock," Samuel was saying as John's mind wandered back to the conversation. "But the key is that we have to get you a fair trial."

"What do you want to do next?" Mozingo asked.

"Our goal is to get you a change of venue," Harris said. "Have your trial heard by people who haven't had a chance to read all about it in the newspapers and hear about it from their neighbors. That way, they can make up their minds based on the facts, not the gossip heard at the barbershop or the hardware store."

John knew that people were speculating about his upcoming trial. The day after his preliminary hearing ended, the *Daily Republican* had tossed around the question of whether or not he could get a fair trial. Redmond had written that he thought maybe John could, but John wasn't so sure.

"What do we have to do? To move the trial, I mean?" John asked.

"We're going to draft a petition to change the venue," Harris explained. "You'll take it back with you this afternoon. Just give it to the county attorney, and the judge will take it from there."

*****

After getting wind of the petition, John Redmond headed to the county attorney's office for an interview.

"I'm going to run a copy of the petition in tomorrow's paper," Redmond said to Ray Pierson, who sat behind his desk, stacks of paper spread out in front of him.

"I expect you will," Pierson said amiably.

"There probably isn't a man in the county who hasn't heard and read about this murder," Redmond said. "Do you really believe that Knoblock can get a fair trial?"

Pierson set down the pen he had been holding and looked up at Redmond.

"Take careful notes, Mr. Redmond," Pierson said. He leaned back in his chair, his elbows on the armrests, his fingers interlocked in front of him. "I am confident there will be no difficulty in securing a qualified jury in this county. In fact, I think it would be as easy here as in any neighboring county. You saw those outside papers. They printed more sensational stories of the murder than the home papers, and the people in the other counties seem to have more thoroughly formed opinions in the mystery than have the people of this community, who have kept in close touch with the actual developments from time to time."

"Doesn't having any knowledge about the rumors and gossip prejudice a jury?"

"The rumors and gossip are mostly here, in Burlington," Pierson said. "Coffey County is a big county. There are a lot of folks in the county who rarely get into Burlington. Besides, even those people who attended the preliminary ended up with less of an idea as to Mr. Knoblock's guilt than they had coming in."

That didn't sound very promising for the prosecution's case, Redmond thought, but he kept that to himself.

"Besides, even Knoblock said he was happy with the way the paper has been covering the murder investigation. What better endorsement do you need than that?"

*****

Coffey County Courthouse, Burlington, Kansas
Monday, December 21, 1925
10:15 a.m.

District Court Judge Isaac T. Richardson climbed out of Woodrow's new Ford and marched up the steps to the courthouse. Upon entering his chambers, he checked the time and frowned at A. H. Woodrow, his court reporter.

"We were due to start the hearing at ten o'clock, Mr. Woodrow," he boomed.

"I apologize, your honor," Woodrow said. "But you know how it is with a new car. You have to take it slow."

As the little judge with the big presence donned his robes, he gave Woodrow a glare that made the court reporter squirm. As he marched into the courtroom, he shook his head at the number of people packed into the room. Didn't these people have anything better to do four days before Christmas?

Judge Richardson set in motion the hearing for the change of venue.

*****

In hindsight, thought defense attorney Owen S. Samuel, it would have been better not to have called witnesses. There was irony in that Fred M. Harris, one of the prosecutors, initially objected to the oral testimony, stating that the statutes provided only for affidavits and counter-affidavits. But Judge Richardson had decided in favor of using witnesses, and Harris and Samuel had thought it their victory at the time.

After presenting the formal petition for a change of venue, the defense called George Crotty to the stand.

"I hear the murder being discussed by people in both Burlington and in the country all the time," he said. "But they don't seem to be as prejudiced against Mr. Knoblock as bad as before."

"People talk about it constantly in Gridley," said Lee R. Hettick, a reporter for the *Gridley Light*.

"Do people express opinions regarding Mr. Knoblock's guilt or innocence?" Samuel asked.

"Sure," Hettick said. "But since the preliminary hearing, a lot of folks who were convinced of his guilt are doubtful now. I'd say most people are open-minded enough now for a trial."

As witness after witness undermined the defense's argument for a change of venue, Samuel wanted to pull his hair out. Instead, he called the next newspaper man to the stand.

"Mr. Redmond, what, in your opinion, was the attitude of the crowd at the preliminary hearing?"

"The *Daily Republican* has published the evidence given as fully as possible. Yet while people are interested, I have not witnessed manifestations of prejudice against the accused."

Samuel closed his eyes for a moment and called the county attorney to the stand.

"Is it true that you told John Knoblock and John Mozingo that ninety percent of the people of Coffey County believed he murdered his own wife?" Samuel asked.

"I believe I did say something to that effect," Ray Pierson said easily. "I was trying to persuade Mr. Knoblock to offer a reward by pointing out that people would assume he was guilty if he didn't. That doesn't mean I was telling the truth."

*****

It was all John Knoblock could do to not rub at the twitching muscle under his eye. Despite Owen Samuel presenting more than two hundred signatures supporting John's request to have the trial moved, Fred Harris, the Franklin County attorney lending a hand to the prosecution, stood up and offered one hundred and forty-five signatures saying the trial should stay put.

Perplexed by the volume of contradictory opinions, Judge Richardson asked both the prosecution and the defense to each produce three witnesses from around Coffey County to report on the various citizens who signed the affidavits on behalf of the defense.

Al Rickman was called to speak for Waverly, a town northeast of Burlington. O. B. Richardson was called to represent Gridley, a town southwest of Burlington. From Burlington itself, the lawyers chose W. W. Sanders Jr., F. W. Haight, M. A. Limbocker, and John Redmond.

Didn't seem like a real even distribution of opinions, John Knoblock thought as he rotated first his left foot, then his right.

The men were sworn in. Hoping to reveal any underlying motives of those who signed the affidavits, the judge read each name on the defense's list of affidavits and asked the ad hoc jury to describe what they knew about them, particularly their relationship to the Knoblocks and the Mozingos.

Most of the people who signed the petition in favor of a change of venue were friends or family of John Knoblock.

Most of those opposed to the change of venue were not.

After closing words from the lawyers, Judge Richardson rendered his decision. The defense had not proven that John couldn't get a fair trial in Coffey County, and the judge overruled the motion for a change of venue.

File Type: Interview
Subject: Dorene Smith
Date: July 15, 2008

Dorene: My family lived on the farm just to the west of the Knoblocks. Florence and my grandmother were friends.

Diana: Did your grandmother or mother ever talk about what happened to Florence?

Dorene: My grandmother said there was a man who was bothering her. Someone was scaring her for weeks before she was murdered. Neither my mother nor my grandmother believed for one second that John Knoblock killed his wife. They didn't believe it was that bridge worker [Blackie Stevens], either. Innocent.

Chapter Twelve
Dockets

Daily Republican **office, Burlington, Kansas**
Saturday, January 2, 1926
7:45 a.m.

John Redmond reviewed the bar dockets for the January term of the Coffey County district court. Forty-four cases would normally mean a light month. Forty were on the civil docket: six divorce cases, four cases involving real estate, eleven mortgage foreclosure cases, seven cases on notes, seven cases for the recovery of money, two cases to partition real estate, two receiver's final reports in the matter of closed state banks, and one case to condemn a site for a school house. In addition, there were only four cases on the criminal docket: one for assault and battery, one burglary, one grand larceny case that was expected to be dismissed, and one murder case.

Redmond knew that as far as most of the citizens of Coffey County were concerned, there was only one case that mattered— the *State of Kansas v. John Knoblock*. Judge Richardson, in his infinite wisdom, had set the court docket so that the murder case would be heard first.

A venire of thirty-six regular jurors was ready, and the names of an additional seventy-five men had already been drawn for the special venire.

John Redmond double-checked the spelling of the one hundred and eleven potential jurors and ran the story.

*****

Judge Richardson was sitting behind his desk when the court reporter knocked on his door.

"I've got John Redmond on the telephone for you, sir," Woodrow said, and Richardson picked up the phone.

Richardson got right to the point. "I would like the *Daily Republican* to run a story about the conduct that will be expected at the upcoming Knoblock trial," Richardson said.

The phone crackled just a little as Redmond said, "After the spectacle at the preliminary, I don't blame you."

"That's exactly my point," Richardson said. "This isn't a spectacle. A man's life is at stake here. That mustn't be taken lightly. John Knoblock is entitled to a fair trial, and that won't happen if half the county is there treating it like a theater production."

Richardson skimmed the notes he made earlier that morning.

"First, remind your readers that the courtroom is small. The seats will be reserved for the people who need to be there. When the seats are filled, the doors will be closed. There will be no 'standing room.' No sitting on the radiators. No sitting on the floor. And no pressing faces up against the glass.

"Admission cards will be given to the people who need to be there—witnesses, jurors, and the like. They will be seated first. No exceptions.

"Once the jurors are selected, they will be placed in the custody of a bailiff until the close of the trial. Their board and room will be provided by the county until the trial is over.

"We will clear the courtroom two or three times during the day to allow the room to air out. And another thing," Richardson cleared his throat. "Find some nice way to say that it would be helpful if those attending the trial cleaned themselves up. You weren't far off when you wrote that the place smelled like feet at the preliminary."

"No foul-smelling feet," Redmond said.

"No one, and I mean *no one*, will remain in the courtroom during the lunch recess. And no one will be allowed to bring food into the courtroom. The courtroom isn't a lunch room, after all."

"Of course not," Redmond said. "Anything else?"

"It would be helpful if the community could stop discussing this case until a jury is named," Richardson said.

Richardson could almost see Redmond's raised eyebrows through the phone line.

"I know, I know," Richardson said, tapping his fingers on his desk. "But perhaps you can remind them that the longer it takes to select a jury, the more expensive this trial will be."

*****

Pueblo, Colorado
Monday, January 4, 1926

More than five hundred miles of grassland separated Carl Goodrick from Coffey County, but when John Stewart turned up at the boarding house Carl temporarily called home, he knew he hadn't gone far enough. Stewart, who introduced himself as the Kansas attorney general's investigator, cornered Carl in the shabby dining room.

"John Knoblock is about to be tried for murder," Stewart said.

Carl stepped around the dining table, trying to reclaim his control over the room. "Mr. Knoblock isn't a killer."

Stewart studied him for a moment. "And you know this how?"

Carl looked the older man in the eye. He knew he couldn't show fear. He had to stand firm, be a man, or Stewart would walk all over him.

"What," Carl said, trying to make his voice sound firm, "do you want?"

Stewart pulled out a sheet of paper and waved it in front of Carl's face. "Do you know what this is, Carl? Do you?" Stewart snatched it away as Carl reached for it. "This is a warrant for your arrest, signed by the sheriff of Coffey County himself. I am supposed to haul you in across the state line if you don't sign this. It's a statement the county attorney wrote up just for you."

Stewart pulled out another sheet of legal paper and thrust it at Carl to read. Carl studied the paper and frowned.

"I, Carl Goodrick, hereby swear that on the morning of the thirtieth day of May, 1925, I visited the home of John and Florence Knoblock and saw Florence Knoblock murdered on the kitchen floor of her home," the statement read.

Carl's heart hammered in his throat. He wondered if Stewart could see it. He took a deep breath, hoping the investigator thought he was shaking with rage instead of fear.

Had Rosa Knapp decided the man on the porch was Carl?

Stewart couldn't control his mouth, which slid into a sly smile.

They didn't know anything. Stewart was fishing.

"I won't sign this," Carl said, his voice quivering. "I'm not a liar."

"Then I guess you'll be coming with me," Stewart said.

"I won't be doing that, either," Carl said.

"I have a warrant for your arrest," Stewart waved the first paper around again, just out of Carl's reach.

"Let me see that," Carl said.

Stewart tucked the paper back into his coat pocket. "You're not worth the bother," he said, and turned for the door.

*****

Daily Republican office, Burlington, Kansas
Friday, January 8, 1926

"My goodness," Maude Redmond said as she looked over the list from the county attorney. "He's really going to subpoena all of these people?"

John Redmond took off his glasses and rubbed the sides of his nose with his thumb and forefinger. "Apparently so," he said. "I still haven't received anything from Harris and Samuel. The rumors are that they'll either call very few people and hope the cross-examination will prove Knoblock is innocent, or they'll call one hundred and fifty people."

"My goodness," she repeated.

"The defense is desperately looking for Blackie Stevens," Redmond said. "They've sent subpoenas to three different counties in hopes of finding him. If their defense will be to try to pin it on the Negro, then I wouldn't blame Blackie one bit if he remained out of sight."

*****

The next morning, Maude reviewed the list of individuals subpoenaed by the state. In addition to the nearly fifty called by the prosecution, fifty-four would be called by the defense.

*****

Goodrick farm, seven miles west of Burlington, Kansas
Monday, January 11, 1926
6:00 a.m.

Dora Goodrick closed the barn door and walked back to the house. Spikes of grass poked through the thin layer of snow and sleet that had settled over the Pleasant Township in the early hours of the morning.

The sound of her feet crunching through the ice resonated into the little valley below her.

Dora turned to study the empty house below her field. This time last year, she would have seen Roger playing in the snow. Lantern light warming the windows. John tending to the livestock. Smoke curling from the chimney, flattened by the cold air.

The house was abandoned now. A ghost. A shadow, gray and dark, halfway up the hill.

A lone headstone in a graveyard.

How quickly it all changed.

As she stared down at the remnants of the Knoblock family's home, she wondered, as she wondered every day, about Rosa Knapp's testimony. *I saw a man standing on the east porch*, she had said. *He wasn't moving, except to turn his head toward our car.*

Dora wondered. Had Rosa seen the neighbor? Or had she seen her son? Or someone else altogether?

Would she ever know? Would she ever remember? Would she tell?

The unmistakable sound of an automobile crunching along the rough country road turned her head, and Dora frowned when she saw the sheriff turning onto her farm.

Sheriff Hunter caught sight of Dora, standing out in her field. He carried those dreaded papers in his hand.

"Subpoenas for the trial?" she said, in lieu of a proper greeting.

"For you, Grace, Charles, and your boys," Hunter said. She watched him as he turned to look down at the Knoblock house.

"It's hard not to look, isn't it?" he said. "It's hard not to wonder."

Dora said nothing for a moment. "My sons aren't here," she said. "Lester's on his way to the Philippines. He took a job with the postal service. And Carl's joined the service. He's in Colorado. But then, you know that, don't you?"

Hunter turned to look at her, to really look at her.

"Carl's in Colorado?" he asked, confused.

"Don't pretend you didn't know," Dora glowered at him. "Did you think I wouldn't hear about you trying to arrest him in Pueblo? Did you think my boy wouldn't tell me?"

"Mrs. Goodrick, I don't know anything about your boy in Colorado, and even if I wanted to, I couldn't arrest him across the state line," Hunter said.

Dora's breath made white clouds in the cold winter air. "Sheriff, some investigator showed up in Colorado and told my son he was under arrest if he didn't swear that he saw Florence Knoblock lying murdered on her kitchen floor."

"Ma'am, I don't know anything about that," Hunter said.

"Of course you do!" Dora snapped. "The man waved a warrant you signed in Carl's face!"

Tears were streaming down her cheeks now, and she wiped at them.

"Mrs. Goodrick." He was silent for a moment, and she realized he was waiting for her to turn to him, look at him. She saw the concern on his face.

"Mrs. Goodrick, I promise you, I didn't sign any arrest warrant for your son."

His eyes were honest, she thought, at least about this.

She nodded once, then turned back toward the valley below and the sky above.

The storm was moving in, and Pleasant Township was in its path.

File Type: Newspaper Clipping

Judge Richardson said that contrary to the
common idea, a man is not rendered ineligible
to jury duty by reading newspaper accounts
of a crime, even if he has formed an opinion,
if the opinion would readily yield to the
testimony on the stand.

"Preparing for Battle in Knoblock Murder
Trial—Hundreds Sign Affidavits," *Daily
Republican*, December 23, 1925

Chapter Thirteen

Jurors

Coffey County Courthouse,
Burlington, Kansas
Tuesday, January 12, 1926

As soon as he was sure Judge Richardson's attention was elsewhere, court reporter A. H. Woodrow gave in to the yawn he had been fighting for most of the past two days.

Fearing snow, he and the judge had made their way to Burlington by train Sunday evening and were staying at a hotel in town. The accommodations were adequate if sparse, but far better than how the jurors would be spending the next week or two. The county commissioners, none of whom would likely have to take advantage of their self-proclaimed generous accommodations, had arranged for six double beds and a cot for the bailiff to be placed in the detention room at the southwest corner of the courthouse basement. The jurors would cross the hall to take their meals. They would be escorted up the stairs to the courtroom for the trial and back down the stairs to wait out the night.

The funny thing, Woodrow thought, was that the jurors were practically in prison, while the defendant, John Knoblock, would sleep in his own bed every night during the trial.

Woodrow looked across the room and saw John Redmond smiling at him. Woodrow rolled his eyes heavenward and prayed Redmond wouldn't record his yawning in tomorrow's paper.

Had he not had to record every question and answer presented, Woodrow would have slept through most of the proceedings the past two days. Disappointed townspeople milled outside the courtyard and chattered in the nearby businesses, speculating on who would be selected and how that would affect the outcome of the trial. Little did they know, Woodrow thought, how very monotonous the jury selection process could be. Most of Monday was taken up by the judge and the attorneys arguing over procedure. Today Woodrow felt his eyes cross with each new potential juror. Name? Are you related to the defendant? Have you an opinion on John Knoblock's guilt or innocence?

Woodrow watched them stir in their seats, restless, not wanting to be there. Everyone wanted to watch Knoblock hang, Woodrow thought, but no one wanted the responsibility of tying the noose around his neck.

Woodrow smirked and picked up his pen.

*****

Charles Strickland had seen just about everything there was to see in Coffey County, seeing as how he and his parents had arrived to the area in a covered wagon when he was just ten years old. But even he was surprised by the gruesomeness of that poor Knoblock woman's murder. Maybe that was why he felt such a weight on his mind as he took the eleventh seat in the jury box. He knew in his heart that this trial mattered, and he had sworn to God almighty that he would get it right.

Strickland studied the evident reluctance on the faces of the ten other men destined to spend the next few days in the courthouse. Most were from the northern or eastern parts of the county, unlike himself, who was spending his older years in the heart of Burlington. Frank Hiles and Oliver Kelly were from the

Ottumwa Township. Jack Britton, E. E. Baker, George Baker, and John Clark were from the Rock Creek Township, in the far northeastern part of the county. W. C. Combes and E. W. Ellis hailed from the Lincoln Township, near the city of Lebo. George Bruce, a former county clerk, hung his hat in Aliceville, and Frank Decker farmed land southeast of Burlington.

He figured if any of them felt the way he did, they didn't want to be responsible for that Knoblock fellow's fate, either.

Strickland watched as G. H. Bennett, another man from Rock Creek Township, took the twelfth and only remaining juror's seat. The trial could begin.

File Type: Newspaper Clipping

While there are people who firmly believe
that the defendant is guilty, and others who
believe just as firmly that he is innocent,
the general public seems to take the position
that someone certainly killed Mrs. Knoblock
in a most brutal manner, and whoever killed
her should be punished.

"Trial Of John Knoblock Begins In Coffey
County District Court—First Thing Is To
Secure A Jury," *Daily Republican*, January
11, 1926

Chapter Fourteen
Blankets and Razors

Menard farm, five and a half miles west of Burlington, Kansas
Wednesday, January 13, 1926

Stella Menard rose early to give herself extra time to primp before she and Joe headed for town. She leaned toward the glass, inspecting each black curl in her fashionable bob of hair. If she was called to the stand today—and in all likelihood, she would be—she would have a large audience in the courtroom and even more who would hear about her testimony afterwards.

It just wouldn't do to have a hair out of place.

She admired her dark eyes, surrounded by her dark coiffure. Her dress flattered her figure. She was pleased, as pleased as any woman over thirty could be with her appearance. She scooped up her dainty mesh bag and called for her husband. She was ready.

*****

Coffey County Courthouse, Burlington, Kansas
Wednesday, January 13, 1926

Judge Richardson stuck to his own rules, and the decorum inside the courtroom far surpassed the behavior demonstrated at the preliminary hearing. What's more, Sheriff Hunter didn't trip over a single leg or skirt on his way to the witness stand.

Hunter sat on the hard chair, trying to look comfortable with his broad shoulders wedged into his best Sunday suit. Exhaustion etched his face. Of all the nights to get a call about a stolen Hudson coach, he thought. Especially after spending part of the day delivering more subpoenas. Didn't those Emporians know he had a trial today?

Hunter fought to keep up with Joe Rolston, the prosecutor, who walked him through every waking moment of the day Florence Knoblock was murdered. No, he'd never met John Knoblock before Knoblock called to request that he and the coroner come out to his house. He'd left town around one o'clock and arrived at the Knoblock farm between half-past one and a quarter-to-two. He'd entered the house through the dining room, where Knoblock stood just inside the door.

"I asked him, 'What is the matter?' He didn't answer, just walked through the doorway to the kitchen, then said that it was his wife on the floor, dead," Hunter said.

Hunter closed his eyes a moment, picturing the gruesome scene the day poor Florence Knoblock got herself killed. He wished he could say he didn't remember, but he knew if he lived to be a hundred, he would still see that blood-soaked kitchen in his dreams. He told them about the blood on the floor and broken dishes, about the pan of water on the chair and the bread starter running over the side of the crock on the stove. He talked about the black pillow on Mrs. Knoblock's face and the blanket soaked with dried blood covering her body. The dark memory of the sickening metallic smell rose in his mind as he told the courtroom full of Mrs. Knoblock's kin how someone had defiled the farmwoman's house with her own blood.

"What did Mr. Knoblock say after you entered the kitchen?" Rolston said.

"I talked with Mr. Knoblock, who told me his wife was stooping over getting something from the cabinet when she was hit from behind. He pointed out the spot of blood there and said that she was dragged over near the stove. Then he said her throat was cut with his old razor."

"Was the murder weapon there?" Rolston said.

"I asked him where the razor was. And he said, 'that's for you fellows to find out,'" Hunter said.

"What did you say?" Rolston said.

"I asked him where he had been. He said he had been to Burlington, leaving home between eight and eight-thirty. He said he went to his folks' house, then to the produce house and several other places. He told me all about who he met up with where around town," Hunter said. "Then Mr. Knoblock said he came home and brought in a load of groceries. He said he saw his wife on the floor, and after bringing in more groceries, he covered his wife up, loaded a shotgun and called me. He said he also called the Mozingos about the same time. He said his wife's clothes were pulled up to the waist and he went to get a quilt to cover her but decided it would be hard to wash, so he got a blanket instead."

"How did Mr. Knoblock seem to you that afternoon?" Rolston asked. "Was he excited?"

"No."

"Grief-stricken?"

"No," the sheriff said. "He didn't seem sorry and there were no tears."

*****

Dora Goodrick sat with her husband, Charles, and her daughter, Grace, in the drafty hallway outside the courtroom doors. The waiting gave her time to think about what questions she might be asked and about what answers she might give. Her sons were safe, outside the reach of the local law, but she couldn't stop wondering, worrying, about how the attorney general's office had found her son and why they would try to scare him with a fake arrest warrant.

She looked down the hallway at the other witnesses subpoenaed.

The man was one of them.

Her stomach lurched.

She squeezed Charles' hand. He squeezed back.

The door to the courtroom opened and one of the bailiffs came out.

"Dora Goodrick?" he called.

Dora stood, straightened her dress, and followed him into the courtroom.

*****

"I saw John Knoblock around four o'clock that afternoon," Dora Goodrick said. "John came out of the dining room and sat down on the porch. He told me about finding Florence's body on the floor and that he first thought of covering her with a quilt, then thought how hard it would be to wash and got the blanket and said it looked like she had stooped to pick up a dish pan and soap and was hit on the head, and her throat was cut with his razor."

"Did he say where the razor was?" Rolston said.

Dora shook her head. "No, he said he didn't know where the razor was but that the box was on the floor. He said he supposed it was Blackie who killed her."

"Did you talk with Mr. Knoblock about his wife's murder at any other time?" Rolston said.

Dora's gaze flitted briefly to Knoblock before turning back to the prosecutor. "The Tuesday evening after the funeral, I went into their house. John invited me. He showed me where his wife fell and showed where she was dragged. There was still a bloody place where he said she fell in front of the cabinet, a little east of the center of the kitchen."

*****

Grace Goodrick was missing a day of high school to testify at Mr. Knoblock's trial. She sat ramrod straight, her hands neatly folded in her lap, hoping she looked more mature than her sixteen years yet wishing her mother had been allowed to stay in the courtroom with her as she testified.

"I had been at the Knoblock farm the evening before Decoration Day," Grace said. "I helped Mrs. Knoblock pick strawberries for about an hour, just before the sun set. Mr. Knoblock was around the front yard and the barn."

"When were you next at the Knoblock farm?" the prosecutor, Joe Rolston, said.

"With my mother, after the murder," Grace said. "Mr. Knoblock said he supposed whoever killed her came in and hit her on the head with a stove lid when she was stooping over to pick up soap or something. He said that her throat had been cut with his razor and that the box was on the floor, but he didn't know where the razor was."

*****

Stella Menard gave her curls one final pat as she followed the bailiff to the witness stand.

"Why, I've been a good friend of Florence Knoblock for at least a decade, and I've been neighbors with them both for a while now," she said. "That afternoon, I got to the Knoblock place about three o'clock.

"John didn't show any grief at all," Stella continued, tilting her head in what she believed to be a flattering way. "But he was awfully excited. He talked all the time until dusk. He told me all about how she must have been killed. He said she must have come into the house after feeding the chickens and that she stooped over to pick up a dish pan or something when the man struck her."

"Tell us about what you saw in the house." Ray Pierson, the county attorney, took over the questioning.

"In the bedroom, the dresser drawers were all pulled out. There was blood on some ironed clothes. A small boy's trousers were on the floor in front of the dresser. I saw a lady pick them up and open them."

"And who was that lady?"[8]

Stella shook her head, her curls swaying ever so slightly. "I didn't know her," she said. "After she looked at the trousers, she set them back down. Coroner Stone walked in just then and spoke with us. The lady said, 'It must be a very small boy to go through life without a mother.'"

"Did you see anything on the floor beneath the trousers?" Pierson said.

"Not a thing," she said.

"Did Mr. Knoblock say anything else to you that day?"

"Not to me," Stella said, "but I overheard him saying that he hoped they'd get Blackie right away and hang him and have it over with."

*****

Coffey County Courthouse, Burlington, Kansas
Thursday, January 14, 1926

"Mrs. Menard," Owen Samuel, one of the defense attorneys, began, "you said you were a close personal friend of Mrs. Knoblock."

---

8 In an April 7, 1926 article in the *Daily Republican*, the lady mentioned by Stella Menard was a showgirl listed as Mrs. Lavelle, who performed with the Brunk's Comedians tent show.

"That's right," she said.

"How often did you visit Mrs. Knoblock?"

"I've never actually been to her home," Stella said, "other than the day of the murder."

"Why were you in the house that day?" Samuel said.

"I wanted to see and know as much as possible," Stella said. "And I wasn't the only one. There were several other women doing the same thing. Oh, we didn't touch anything. We were just looking around. The coroner invited me in."

"The coroner, Mr. J. O. Stone, invited you in?"

"Yes. He said I would be a good detective, but I told him I wasn't a detective nor would I act like one."

"You saw the dresser?"

"Yes," Stella said.

"And what did you see on the dresser?" Samuel said.

"There was money on the dresser."

"You made a statement yesterday about a woman picking up clothing on the floor."

"Yes."

"And you said you didn't know that woman."

"That's right," Stella said.

"And you said you spoke with her for several minutes."

"Yes."

"And that she picked up an article of clothing off of the floor."

"That's right."

"Mrs. Menard, at the preliminary hearing, you said you didn't pick up the article of clothing in front of the dresser," Samuel said.

"That's correct. I did not."

"But yesterday, you said that if there was anything else on the floor, you didn't see it," Mr. Samuel said.

"That's right."

"But why didn't you mention at the preliminary hearing that you saw this other woman pick up the trousers?"

"Because, Mr. Samuel," Stella said indignantly, "I told you about it the afternoon you visited my home, but you assured me it wasn't important."

*****

Joe Menard took the seat vacated by his wife. He didn't know what she had said or what she was asked, as he had been sitting in the hallway on a hard folding chair until the bailiff came out with Stella and escorted Joe into the courtroom.

"Yes, sir, I've known John Knoblock for at least seven or eight years, maybe a little longer," Menard told Rolston. "We were just speaking acquaintances, you understand. But we threshed at the same place."

"And when did you arrive at the Knoblock farm, Mr. Menard?" Rolston asked.

"It was about three-thirty or so. We stood outside along with a good fifty or a hundred people, arguing over how to catch the killer," Joe said. "I was there when a man asked about a track. John and I went out to the yard and looked at it, and John said it wasn't his track. John showed us the footprints he made going to and from the shower and then there were these other tracks."

*****

"Her throat was cut from under one ear to the other," said Dr. Albert N. Gray. "I thought at first there was just one slash, but after Mr. Stone, the undertaker, dressed the body, I realized there were two cuts."

"And were you able to discern what was used to make those cuts?" Rolston said.

The fifty-four-year-old doctor nodded. "A very sharp instrument, probably a razor. The cuts had severed the artery and the windpipe."

"What other injuries did she have, Dr. Gray?" Rolston said.

"I found several cuts on the back of her head and others on the front. Two of the blows had crushed her skull. The one in front was the worst. It extended from the eyebrow to the hairline. The instrument used penetrated the brain and pushed soot and hair into the injury."

"Dr. Gray, how do you believe these injuries were committed?"

"The blows indicate that Mrs. Knoblock had first been struck on the back of the head while standing. It would not have been possible to make those blows once the penetrating injury in the front had been made, unless her body had been turned over. Her throat was cut while she was on the floor. Otherwise, blood would have spurted out over the waist of her dress."

"What, in your expert opinion, was the exact cause of death?"

"The blows to the head," Dr. Gray said. "Her throat was cut after she was already dead."

From the corner of his eye, Dr. Gray saw Mr. Mozingo shudder and his wife stifle a sob with her handkerchief.

*****

Eugene A. Stone, furniture maker and undertaker, sat in the witness stand, his paralyzed right arm clutched to his side.

"There were no wounds below the breast on her body," he said. "There was a scratch on her arm, like a severe fingernail scratch. The wounds to her head contained soot, likely from the stove lids. And the stove lids had hair stuck to them the same color as Mrs. Knoblock's hair. The worst cut was an open one that went from the eyebrow to the forehead. I found a piece of skull about three-fourths of an inch wide and an inch and a half long loose, and there was soot and hair in the cut. There was also a cut on the side of her face."

"Did you notice any other injuries?" Rolston said.

"The fingers on her left hand were skinned back toward the hand where she had been struck, and there was soot on these wounds. There were finger marks under her chin and hand marks on her throat. And even though her eyes were closed, there was soot in them."

"What do you believe killed her?"

"I can't rightly say," Eugene said. "But I believe the blows to the front of her head were made after she was already on the floor, and her throat was cut after she was already dead. Otherwise, the blood would have squirted out more."

"Mr. Stone, what did you see in the bedroom that afternoon?" Rolston said.

"I went in there once with the coroner and once with John Knoblock," Eugene said. "The dresser drawers were open, and the contents were ruffled up. One of the drawers had a pistol and two old razors. There was also a pair of boy's trousers on the floor, which Coroner Stone picked up."

"Was there anything beneath them?" Rolston said.

"No, sir."

"You didn't see a razor on the floor beneath the trousers?" Rolston said.

"No, I did not."

File Type: Newspaper Clipping

Most people who haven't had experience in court think every witness is supposed to tell 'the truth, the whole truth, and nothing but the truth,' but that isn't the case. The witnesses are supposed to answer the questions put to them—but very few of them do.

"Notes on the Trial," *Daily Republican*, Thursday, January 21, 1926

Chapter Fifteen
Crime Scene

Coffey County Courthouse
Burlington, Kansas
Thursday, January 14, 1926

As the trial continued, Sheriff Frank Hunter replayed the scene in his head over and over again: sitting on the witness stand, staring back at the disapproving faces of his constituents.

"There were a hundred or more people there that afternoon," Hunter remembered saying. "They were going in and out of the house, the barn, the chicken house, and every other building on that farm that afternoon. I told people to stay out of the kitchen, but some went in there anyway."

Heads shook in disgust. Hunter wanted to shake his head right back at them, since chances were good some of these people were the ones who had trampled the grass around the Knoblock house that day.

*****

"We've been close neighbors for five years," Erky Woods said. "The day of the murder, I saw him about twenty-five

minutes before one o'clock, near the lumberyard across from
the courthouse. After I heard about the murder, I headed for the
Knoblock farm."

"Did you speak to Mr. Knoblock?" Rolston said.

"He said, 'I am glad you saw me in town today when you
did. Some people will accuse me of this murder.' I said, 'My
God, you don't mean that anyone could accuse you of that?' and
he said, 'Yes, there will be some.' Later, he said, 'This place will
be for rent. I wouldn't stay here.'"

*****

Bill White would have much preferred to be in Paris or
London or New York or even Boston, but instead, he, the son of
the great William Allen White, owner and editor of the *Emporia
Gazette*, was covering a trial in a town where the newspaper
had to remind its county residents to bathe before entering the
courtroom. Bill White, wearing a tailored Brooks Brothers suit,
scanned the room, shuddering inwardly at the Sears catalog
dresses and bib overalls.

John Redmond, Burlington's own herald and a man who
had served under Bill's father long before Bill White was born,
looked around the courtroom and took in the hodgepodge
of people watching the proceedings. Several members of
the Mozingo clan were present, publically supporting John
Knoblock, perhaps regardless of how they felt privately. There
were several community members who'd managed to snag seats
before the courtroom filled. And there was a strange gentleman
with long, flowing gray hair sitting back a few rows, a desk over
his lap, reading a movie magazine.

"Do you know that man there, sitting in the back?" White
asked Redmond.

"That would be the Reverend A. C. Babcock," Redmond
said. "He's a minister with the Christian church in LeRoy. He
claims he's a correspondent for *True Story* magazine."

"I see," White said. He wasn't sure which was less likely: that Babcock was a preacher or that Babcock was a writer.

"He says he's covering the trial for the magazine," Redmond said and flipped a page in his notes. "He's also working on a book, which he will title *The Fighting Minister: Or, Forty-Three Years on the Firing Line.*"

White could almost taste the Chesterfield cigarettes tucked into a monogrammed case in his breast pocket. It was a shame the judge didn't allow smoking in the courtroom.

*****

Coffey County Courthouse
Burlington, Kansas
Friday, January 15, 1926

"You saw spots of blood on a pair of blue trousers when you went upstairs, is that correct?" Owen Samuel asked during the cross-examination.

"Yes," Eugene Stone said. "Mr. Knoblock picked them up, and we looked at them. There seemed to be blood on them."

"When you were questioned about the trousers early in the investigation, you didn't mention picking them up. Why?"

Eugene Stone fidgeted in his seat. "I wasn't under oath at the time, was I?"

*****

Through all of this, John Knoblock sat quietly at the table with Owen Samuel and W. C. Harris, who spit tobacco into a cuspidor on the desk with the regularity of a heartbeat. Yesterday, Samuel had given him a notepad and some pencils. "Take notes, write letters, sketch people in the courtroom. It doesn't matter. Just keep your hands busy so you don't look so nervous," Samuel had said.

He had managed to listen to the sheriff and the undertaker say what they had to say about him. They didn't really know him or his family. But when the parade of neighbors and friends—or, at least, people who used to be friends—began to testify, he could hardly stand it. These were people who knew him, who knew his family. How could they say such terrible things?

He looked down at Roger, who sat on the floor by the legs of his chair, playing with some toys his mother-in-law had thought to bring. The little boy would turn five years old in just fifteen days. Would John be around to share the day with him? Or would he be writing his son a birthday letter from the penitentiary in Lansing?

When Elam Underwood took the stand, John picked up a pencil and began to write.

*****

"How long have you known Mr. Knoblock?" Rolston asked.

"Eighteen, maybe twenty years now," Elam Underwood said. "I farm land near a mile and a half from the Knoblocks."

"And what did Mr. Knoblock say to you that day?"

"He told me he found his wife dead on the floor when he returned from town," Underwood said. "He said her clothes were up and her knees were upright. He was going to adjust her clothing but then thought better of it and left it for people to see. I asked him if there was anything I could do, and John said, 'If it was your wife, I'd go out and try to find the person that did it.'"

*****

William V. Pennington had lived in Coffey County since its earliest days, having moved into the area just nine years after the county lines were drawn. He had known John and Florence Knoblock for many years.

"It must have been about two-fifteen when I arrived at the farm that day," Pennington said. "John was standing on the south porch, talking about fixing the pasture fence. He said he didn't have the money to buy the wire."

"He was talking about fixing a fence an hour after finding his wife murdered?"

"Yes, sir."

"And with whom was he talking?"

"I didn't know the man. I assume someone who had an interest in the fence," Pennington said. "I heard John tell the man that he had seen the nigger two weeks earlier, while he was milking the cows. He said he told Blackie to stay away, because the cows wouldn't stay still when he was nearby."

*****

Warren Ellis was an oil man from Gridley who had the bad luck to be in Coffey County with newspaper man Lee Hettick and hotelier Charley Dewey, both also from Gridley, when the hoopla over the murder started. He barely even knew John Knoblock, and he'd never even set eyes on him before the day of the murder.

"I heard him say he was glad he wasn't around when it happened," Ellis told the court. "I heard Mr. Knoblock say that her throat was cut with his old razor. He said he took in some groceries, saw his wife on the floor, and then went back to the car for the rest. Then he went to his wife."

"Did you see any cows at the Knoblock farm?" Rolston said.

"I saw some milk cows, and in particular, a red cow with a white face. Her udder was full and the milk was dripping out of the back teats. I noticed the milk buckets were clean."

"Did you see the victim?" Rolston said.

"She was laying on the floor. I saw her after coming in off the east door. I noticed before I came in the house there was a broken window, part of it being out."

"Did you see Mrs. Mozingo that day?"

"Yes," Ellis said. "I saw her watching John Knoblock all that time."

*****

William E. Utesler had worn a lot of hats in a lot of places in his fifty-four years. He was born in Iowa and had lived in Missouri, Nebraska, and Colorado before settling in Coffey County twenty years earlier. He had experience as a railroad foreman, still ranched with his son, and had been sheriff until his term expired last year, when he gladly stepped aside and became a deputy.

He looked down at little Roger Knoblock, playing by his papa's knee. He remembered the boy as a baby. Did he understand, have even the faintest idea, how much trouble his father was in?

"I was at the Knoblock farm on Sunday, the morning after the murder. John told me that Roger did not see his mother. He said that his little boy was with him but that he opened the door only a little ways into the kitchen and then closed it. He told his boy that his mamma had been killed and that he couldn't go inside," Utesler said. "He said he got a bedspread to put over his wife but decided it would be too much trouble to wash, so he got an old blanket instead. Then he got his gun, put in a shell, and looked through all the rooms for the murderer. He said that when his father-in-law, John Mozingo, arrived, he had the boy in one hand and the gun in the other, the boy having fallen asleep on the spread."

"Did you ask Mr. Knoblock what motive he thought the murderer might have had?" Rolston said.

"John said Aunt Min—that's Minnie Jaggers—asked him if it couldn't have been Blackie Stevens," Utesler said.

"Did Mr. Knoblock mention anything about the clothing scattered throughout the house?"

"He said a light pair of pants had been taken upstairs and that the pockets were turned wrong-side out. He also said that the blue pants, like the coat he had on, had been sent to the pressers. They were part of the only good suit he had, and the pants had been ruffled up."

Utesler recalled his conversations with John Knoblock in the days following the murder. How Knoblock said that when he saw the blood on the floor, he thought his wife was hemorrhaging because of her "sick" time. How his little boy had asked him, "What are we going to do for another mamma? Who will do our cooking?" How Knoblock told him he had found the razor used to slit Mrs. Knoblock's throat lying on the floor in front of the bureau in the downstairs bedroom under the boy's clothing.

"Johnnie Kellerman and Sam Shoup were both there when John told me about finding the razor Sunday morning. I saw it lying on the corner of the bureau and asked for some cotton," Utesler said. "I carefully wrapped it up to avoid spoiling the bloody fingerprints. I had either Harry Bradford or Clarance Williams take it in to Burlington."

"Tell us about the clothing you found in the yard, Mr. Utesler," Rolston said.

"I was in the yard, and I picked up what appeared to be women's clothing hanging in a catalpa tree. Some of it was real bloody, some of it not so bad. I put them in a gunny sack in the dining room. I asked Knoblock why they were out there, and he said at first, he was going to bury them, but then it occurred to him that someone might find them and it would look bad, so he hung them up in the tree."

"When did you next speak to Mr. Knoblock?"

"On Monday. He said he was sure that the murder was a nigger's work, and he wanted to see the Negro being held at Iola. A few days later, Mr. Maple, the Burns detective, brought Blackie in to see John. When John got there, he said, 'Hello Blackie, how you'all comin'?' And Blackie said, 'Hello, Mr. John. How's you'all coming?' and they talked for a while. 'What makes you think I killed your wife?' Blackie had asked him, and John didn't answer. 'Do you think I'd kill your wife because she gave me strawberries?'"

"Did you hear Mr. Knoblock tell Mr. Stevens that he didn't think the Negro killed his wife?" Rolston said.

Utesler shook his head. "I had left the room during part of the conversation and didn't hear John say any such thing. But finally, I asked John, 'Do you say he killed your wife?' and John said, 'I don't know.'"

"What was your reply, Mr. Utesler?"

"It wasn't very nice," Utesler said. "I'm not sure I should say it in court."

Giggles and snickering traveled through the crowd as the lawyers whispered among themselves for a few minutes, and then Rolston approached the bench and whispered what Utesler had said to Judge Richardson, who sighed. "Please answer the question, Mr. Utesler," Richardson said.

"I said, if a Black son of a bitch had killed my wife, I'd tell him so." A few ladies clutched their hankies to their hearts in shock, but most of the crowd sat at the edge of their seats with glee.

"And how did Mr. Knoblock respond?"

"He didn't say a word."

"What did Mr. Maple say during all of this?" Rolston said.

"He said to John, 'John, you talk an awful lot. Why haven't you put a reward for the arrest of the murderer?' And John told him, 'I feel I'll need all the money I've got to get out of this, and the little boy will need the rest.'"

W. C. Harris stood before his tobacco hit the spittoon. "Objection!"

"Overruled," Judge Richardson said.

"Did Mr. Knoblock offer you any motive for the murder of his wife?" Rolston said.

"John told me he had a five-, a two-, and a one-dollar bill in the house in a Peoples Bank checkbook, which were missing from the light pants pocket or the shoebox. Then he said he had remembered that he had spent some of the two-dollar bill and had given the change to his wife, but the five and the one were gone. John said he went to Madison with his pop, where they found a crazy man with six dollars in his pocket, and John said he had not missed the money from the house until after his return from Madison."

*****

"I heard John say that he came in with the groceries, saw his wife, dropped the groceries to the floor, and went to her," Charley Dewey said. The hotel man, who had never met the Knoblocks before the day of the murder, now found himself on the stand because he had tagged along with oil man Warren Ellis and Lee Hettick, a reporter with the *Gridley Light*. "John said someone ransacked the house upstairs, that the pockets on his pants were turned wrong-side out, and that the blood stains on the pants were probably made while the murderer was searching the pockets."

"Did he say anything was missing?" Rolston asked.

"He said nothing was missing."

"Did Mr. Knoblock share any thoughts on who might have committed this murder?"

"I heard him say he was glad he wasn't there when it happened, because he figured people would suspect him," Dewey said. "He also said that he didn't know who did it unless it was Blackie and that he couldn't think Blackie would do it."

"What made him suspect Blackie?"

"He said that Blackie asked him if he went to town every Saturday, and he replied that he invariably did."

"Did Mr. Knoblock tell you how the murder was committed?" Rolston asked.

"I heard John say that her throat was cut with his second-best razor and that he didn't know where the murderer got it, as it had been lost."

*****

Clarence Conrad knew John Knoblock well. They were about the same age, farmers in the same part of the county. They were also kin of a sort, because their wives had been cousins.

"I was there when John talked about finding the razor."

"Was anyone else with you?" Rolston asked.

"Lots of folks. John Kellerman, John Mozingo, John Mozingo Jr., Sam Shoup, Herman Jenkins, George Naylor, and the two Massey boys," Conrad said. "He said, 'We found the razor in the little boy's clothes' and that 'it only had a little blood on it' and that it 'must have gone through so fast the blood couldn't stick.'"

*****

Sam Shoup was one of those men who managed to look distinguished no matter what the occasion. He sat on the witness stand, wearing a nicely tailored suit, looking as dignified and respected as always. Shoup knew his words carried a great deal of weight in the minds of the folks of Coffey County, and he hated to say anything that would cause his friends the Mozingos more pain.

"Why were you at the Knoblock farm the Monday following the murder?" Rolston asked.

"Mrs. Mary Knoblock, John's mother, asked if my wife, Rose, could be with her at the farm on Monday," Shoup said. "I drove her over in my car."

"Were you asked to do anything, help out in any way, while you were there?"

"Mary Knoblock asked me to burn some rags," he said. "She pointed me toward a gunny sack in the dining room and asked me to burn them."

"Did you look inside the bag?"

"No. But it had a very bad odor," Shoup said.

"Did Mr. Knoblock know you were going to burn the bag?"

"I asked John where he kept the coal oil."

"Objection," W. C. Harris said, before he could even spit.

"Did Mr. Knoblock ask you what for?" Rolston said.

"Objection," W. C. Harris said again.

"No. He just told me where to find it," Shoup said.

"Where was Mr. Knoblock at the time?" Rolston said.

"Oh, eight or ten feet away. I took the bag behind the house, on the west side, and poured the oil over it and set it on fire."

"Objection!" W. C. Harris shouted. "The state isn't showing any connection between the defendant and Mr. Shoup's action of burning the rags."

"Strike the testimony," Richardson said.

File Type: Newspaper Clipping

The wits of John Knoblock's lawyers were
mobilized Friday afternoon to keep from
the consideration of the jury testimony
of several state's witnesses about certain
alleged relations between John Knoblock and
his sister-in-law. . . . If proven, probably
it would furnish the only motive the state
could establish which would explain why John
Knoblock might have murdered his wife.

"Seek Murder Motive: Knoblock's Relations
With Sister-In-Law Probed," *Emporia Gazette*,
January 16, 1926

Chapter Sixteen

Motive

Coffey County Courthouse
Burlington, Kansas
Friday, January 15, 1926

The Knoblock murder trial dragged on. John Redmond, Bill White, Glick Fockele of *The LeRoy Reporter*, and even the very odd Reverend A. C. Babcock continued to sit attentively throughout the trial, but the run-of-the-mill spectators showed signs of fatigue. As the state called witness after witness and picked apart their statements, the few still observant could see minds wander, toes tap, and hands cover yawns.

Redmond wondered what Knoblock was writing on all of those pieces of paper.

The courtroom door opened and the bailiff appeared, escorting Mrs. Bender to the witness stand. The crowd was jostled out of its stupor. The rumor was that the trial was about to take an interesting turn.

*****

Lethia Melvina Bender and her husband, Daniel, farmed what used to be the old Kimeto farm ten miles outside of Burlington.

She had known both the Mozingos and the Knoblocks for a very long time.

"I was walking to the Bethel Methodist Church. As I turned onto the road between the Knoblock farm and George Albert's corner, I saw Edna Mozingo in John Knoblock's car, between the corner and the bridge crossing the creek."

A few gasps escaped in the crowd.

"Mrs. Bender," Owen Samuel said in his best courtroom voice, "at what time was this?"

"About nine-thirty," Mrs. Bender said. "I was on my way to church."

"Where do you suppose they were going?" Samuel said.

"I assumed to the Mozingo farm," Mrs. Bender said.

"So you believe John Knoblock was taking his sister-in-law home?"

"I suppose so."

"Were they taking an exceptionally long route to get there?"

"No, they would have arrived at the Mozingo farm in just a few minutes. It's the shortest way to drive there."

"Were they behaving inappropriately?" Samuel said.

"No. He was driving his car, and she was sitting in the passenger seat."

"So what you're saying is that you witnessed, in broad daylight, Mr. Knoblock taking his wife's sister back to her own home via the most direct route, doing absolutely nothing inappropriate," Samuel said. "Why did you feel this was important?"

"I didn't, at the time. But then Mrs. Knoblock was murdered."

"Mrs. Bender," Samuel said, "Isn't it true you have been having some trouble at the Bethel church?"

Mrs. Bender stared at Owen Samuel.

"Well?"

She hesitated, then nodded. "Yes."

"The minister forbade you coming to church until you had apologized to some of the congregation, didn't he?"

"He did not!" Mrs. Bender snapped.

"No further questions," Samuel said.

*****

Maude and George Albert lived across the road from the Knoblocks, just east of the Knoblock farm and just west of Maude's family's farm.

"Every morning in the spring and summer, I usually see Mrs. Knoblock or some other member of the family doing work on the farm," Maude said. "I often saw Mrs. Knoblock in the yard or with the chickens. That's what was so strange. I was surprised not to see anyone out that morning."

"What's the first thing you noticed that morning?"

"I saw the car parked on the east side of the house. That was at about six-thirty or seven," Maude said. "I was expecting Skip Beatty, our egg man. I remember looking at my watch at nine-twenty, wondering when he would arrive. Beatty was there when the Knoblocks drove past. I remember because John waved at us, and he usually didn't do that unless Florence was in the car with him."

"Did you see John and Roger Knoblock return?" Rolston said.

"Yes, about one o'clock."

Owen Samuel approached the witness. "Mrs. Albert, you said that no one had been out in the Knoblock's yard the morning that Mrs. Knoblock was murdered."

"No, I said I didn't see anyone. Someone could have been out in the yard at some point, but I personally didn't see anyone."

*****

Were she to do it all over again, Minnie Jaggers would have kept her mouth shut during those early interviews by the sheriff and Ray Pierson. She had *thought* she was doing the right thing, telling them everything she saw and heard; she *thought* she was helping solve the murder of her late niece; she *thought* she was helping clear John.

"How long have you known John Knoblock, Mrs. Jaggers?" Rolston asked once the older woman was settled on the stand.

"Since he was in high school," Minnie said. "Seventeen or eighteen years now."

"When did you see Mr. Knoblock after the murder?"

"I stayed at my sister's house the night of the murder. Mrs. Mozingo's house. John was there the next day for dinner,[9] around one o'clock. He was in the dining room, along with Edna, my sister, and Vesta and possibly others, though I don't recall now who."

"And what did you see Mr. Knoblock do?"

"I was standing close to Edna when John reached out his arm toward Edna, like this—" Minnie reached out an arm, as if to place it on an invisible shoulder. "Edna scowled at him and moved away."

"A bit inappropriate, wouldn't you agree?" Rolston fished.

Minnie frowned at Rolston. "Absolutely not," Minnie said. "John was never anything but proper around my sister's girls, and they always conducted themselves appropriately."

Little had she known how her words would get turned upside down, how Pierson and that prosecutor, Joe Rolston, would twist what she said in those early days of the investigation. If she had just kept quiet, if she had just shaken her head when they questioned her, the state wouldn't be using her as proof positive that John was straying from his wife, even though she had never said any such thing.

"Were you at the Knoblock house at all?"

"The night of the murder," Minnie said. "I heard John tell someone that he had forgotten about the chickens in the incubator and that the incubator had burned, killing the chickens."

---

9 In Kansas, particularly in rural areas, it was and still is common for *dinner* to mean the noon meal and *supper* to mean the evening meal.

Minnie could almost see her words being pulled like taffy, massaged and twirled until a listener might think she believed John was the kind of man who set baby chicks afire and cheated on his wife. She glanced away from her kin, from their hard stares and rolled eyes.

"I understand you tried to convince Mr. Knoblock to have his fingerprints taken."

"Yes, but he refused, saying 'they might get a convict to swear it on him, like they done on Governor Davis.'"

"Did Mr. Knoblock say if anything was missing?"

"He said at first he thought some papers covering a matter between him and my brother-in-law, John Mozingo, had gone missing, but they turned up afterwards."

"Were you present when Ruth Mozingo asked Mr. Knoblock for the key to his house?"

"Yes," Minnie nodded. "I told Ruth not to go into the house until she had checked with the sheriff."

"What did Mr. Knoblock say?"

"That it was all right, as he and the sheriff were friends."

"Did you know Ruth was going to clean the house?"

"No."

"Did Mr. Knoblock know that Ruth was going to clean the house?" Rolston said.

"I don't know."

In her mind, she heard her own words and knew she sounded like she was saying that Ruth and John had planned out how to clean the house and winced inwardly.

She looked at her sisters, at Edna and Ruth, pleading with her eyes. Did they not realize how much she loved her niece and John and that darling little boy? How she cried for them? How hard it was to sew a proper burial dress for Florence? But she had, because it was all she could do. She could not bring her back. She could not give Roger back his mama. She could not give John back his wife. But she could give Florence one last bit of dignity by sewing a proper dress to wear into the hereafter.

After Rolston stepped aside, Samuel picked at every word she said.

"Mrs. Jaggers," Owen Samuel bellowed, "do you mean to say that you told John Knoblock in the presence of this murdered woman's father, her mother, her two sisters, and her little boy that he ought to make his stories hang together more?"

"Yes," she said, in a small voice. "I told him so. And he said he could not."

*****

Coffey County Courthouse
Burlington, Kansas
Saturday, January 16, 1926

John Redmond puzzled over how Ed Tolbert ended up in the courtroom. He was not subpoenaed, yet the prosecution had paid his travel expenses to be there. Redmond had heard the rumors of why Tolbert was in town, but he had also heard rumors regarding Tolbert's integrity. By the look on Ray Pierson's face, Redmond was certain that Tolbert would play an important role in undermining John Knoblock's image.

*****

Bill White took his seat next to John Redmond, a bundle of pencils at the ready. Rumors that the prosecution would question Ed Tolbert on the stand had been speculated upon for months, and his testimony was quite possibly more anticipated than that of John Knoblock's. Yesterday, the defense had successfully kept him off the witness stand. But as the *Gazette* reporter studied Owen Samuel and Joe Rolston, he thought perhaps John Knoblock would not be so lucky today.

*****

"Your honor, there is no point in questioning this man," Samuel argued. "He is an atheist, an infidel! His word means nothing on the stand. An oath is not binding if you don't believe in what you're swearing!"

Judge Richardson looked down at Samuel and said, "That is, indeed, a fine legal point, but as your own partner, a former judge, can tell you, there is a Kansas decision covering that very question."

Samuel looked back at Harris, who gave a slight nod.

Ray Pierson just sat at his table, smug.

"Your honor, we'd like to call Ed Tolbert to the stand at this time," Joe Rolston said, and Tolbert, a somewhat familiar face to the Pleasant Township community, crossed the room to the stand.

Before Rolston could say a word, Owen Samuel shouted, "Mr. Tolbert, it's true you are an atheist, isn't it? You have said on repeated occasions that you didn't believe in God?"

"Objection!" Rolston shouted, and Pierson leaped to his feet.

"No, sir, I did not," Tolbert answered, despite Rolston's protests.

"He's my witness right now, Mr. Samuel," Rolston snapped.

The little judge pounded his gavel and demanded order with a voice that would have commanded Lucifer himself to do the judge's bidding. "Mr. Samuel, you will wait your turn," the judge commanded. "Proceed, counselor."

"Mr. Tolbert, how do you know John Knoblock?" Rolston said.

"I lived on my mother's farm for nearly five years," Tolbert said. "Her place was two, two-and-a-half miles from where the Knoblocks farmed."

"And do you live there now?"

"No, I'm a foreman on the roads, building twenty-two miles from Colorado Springs."

"But while you lived in Coffey County, you had the opportunity to become acquainted with Mr. Knoblock, is that correct?" Rolston said.

"Yes, sir," Tolbert said.

"And during this time, you had conversations with him?"

"Yes, sir."

"Could you recount a particular conversation you had with him in 1922?" Rolston said.

"Objection!" W. C. Harris shouted. "This is irrelevant!"

The judge folded his hands and frowned. "We'll let the question stand for now. Answer the question, Mr. Tolbert."

"Well, sir, John and I were hauling kafir[10] corn, and we were talking, and John said that he had had relations with Ruth Mozingo."

"Objection! Irrelevant!" W. C. Harris spat.

"Overruled," the judge said.

"Relations?" Rolston said.

"Yes. He said he had had sexual relations with Ruth Mozingo," Tolbert said. "John also said that he knew 'Edna Mozingo was that kind of girl,' but that he'd only had sexual intercourse with Ruth Mozingo."

"Objection!"

"And you had another conversation about these matters in 1924?" Rolston asked.

"Objection! Irrelevant!" W. C. Harris shouted.

"Yes, sir," Tolbert said.

"Objection!"

"Could you recall that conversation?" Rolston said.

"Objection!" W. C. Harris said.

"Overruled! Sit down, Mr. Harris," the judge ordered.

"We were riding in a buggy, somewhere between Burlington and the Knoblock place," Tolbert said. "John told me that he knew how to keep a woman from having children, and he said he knew how to get rid of children before they came. He said he knew how to keep a woman from getting in that way."

---

10 Kafir corn, a sorghum crop, was once popular in Kansas for its drought-resistant qualities. It fell out of favor when farmers began to plant milo, which could be cut with combines. See http://www.kshs.org/kansapedia/kafir-corn/12108.

"Objection!"

"Overruled! I said to sit down, Mr. Harris!" Judge Richardson said.

"John said if his wife took out her preventative, he'd know she wanted to have children. I said, 'John, it was my understanding that those instruments sometimes killed women.' And John said, 'Ed, I'd rather kill her than see her raise a family.'"

The courtroom burst with shouts and noise. Judge Richardson pounded the gavel repeatedly until the roar gave way to silence.

"No further questions." Rolston sat next to Pierson, who sat back in his chair, his arms crossed over his chest, all but daring the defense to try to bring down Tolbert's testimony.

"Mr. Tolbert, you said Mr. Knoblock told you he'd rather kill his wife than let her raise a family," Samuel said.

"That's correct."

"That's a mighty threatening statement," Samuel said. "You must have been very concerned to hear a man say such a thing about his wife."

"Yes, sir," Tolbert said.

"Did you tell anyone of what he told you?" Samuel said.

"I think I told my wife."

"Anyone else?"

"I don't believe so."

"You heard a man threaten to kill his wife before he'd allow her to have a family, and you didn't tell anyone?" Samuel said.

"I don't recall for sure," Tolbert said. "But no, I don't believe I told anyone."

"Mr. Tolbert, were you subpoenaed to testify today?"

"Subpoenaed?"

"Did a sheriff in your county deliver an official document to you, requesting your presence at this trial?" Samuel said.

"No, sir," Tolbert said.

"Did you contact the prosecution because you heard about Mrs. Knoblock's death? Any of the men sitting at that table there?"

"No, sir."

"Did you contact Frank Hunter, our sheriff in Coffey County?"

"No, sir."

"Then how did you know to come here for this trial, Mr. Tolbert?" Samuel asked.

"Mr. Rolston there said he'd send me money if I agreed to come to the trial," Tolbert said.

"Mr. Rolston sent you money?"

"Yes, sir. He paid my mileage and what he called *witness fees*. I said I'd surely come for the trial if he was paying."

*****

"Sure, I remember that conversation," Harry Pennock told Rolston. "It was four years ago, in August or September. John Knoblock told me he didn't like his wife like he used to. Then he said, 'I got some sisters-in-law that'll sit on my lap. They'll do anything I want them to.'"

"Mr. Pennock, do you know the Mozingo girls?" Samuel asked after Rolston had finished questioning his witness.

"Yes, sir," Pennock said. "Mrs. Kellerman there is one of them, though she's married now."

"Did Mr. Knoblock ever say he'd ever had relations with his sisters-in-law?"

"No, sir," Pennock said.

"Did he ever imply he'd had intercourse with them?"

"No, sir."

"Then what, exactly, did he say?"

Pennock shifted uncomfortably in his seat. "Like I said, all Knoblock told me was that he had them so they would sit on his lap and do anything he wanted."

*****

"One morning, I think it was May or June in 1918, I was driving my team out by the Knoblock's old place,[11] the Pete Hahn place northeast of Burlington," Ralph Scott said. "Anyhow, I saw Mr. Knoblock chasing Mrs. Knoblock out the door, around the house and halfway to the road. The woman was screaming, and he had a butcher knife in his hand. I stopped my team and buggy and after he—Mr. Knoblock—caught up with her, he said to me, 'We was just a-foolin'.'"

"Do you believe they were 'just a-foolin''?" Rolston said.

"I couldn't say if they were fooling or not," Ralph said.

"Mr. Scott," Owen Samuel began, "There wasn't any reason why he couldn't have killed his wife with that butcher knife if he wanted to, was there?"

"Well, I had no objections," Ralph said.

"Did you tell the officers about this?"

"Yes."

"When?"

"Right before I was subpoenaed."

"Mr. Scott, is there any reason why you should look at those lawyers before answering questions?" Samuel said.

"I can look at who I please, can't I?"

*****

As Saturday morning progressed, the state engaged in a series of progressively confusing testimonies that were disconnected at best and unsuccessful at worst. Bill White took careful notes but knew much of what was being said was not worth the ink needed to print the words. Dr. Melvin Roberts, a physician from Gridley, spoke of the condition of Mrs. Knoblock's body lying on the undertaker's cot in the Knoblock kitchen. George Dornes was sure "Knobby" had left by nine-thirty, as he had seen fresh tracks turning from the Knoblock gate east onto the road. Joe

11 John and Florence Knoblock had briefly lived in northeastern Coffey County before returning to the Pleasant Township.

Rolston then called Garfield Anspaugh to the stand to testify that he had "seen John Knoblock park in front of Engle's produce house and saw him sit in his car for a minute."

Worst, though, was the testimony of Herman Volland, a general store merchant in Aliceville. Even the attorneys for the state weren't sure what they were trying to prove with Volland's testimony. After several minutes of questioning, the only thing Bill understood was that no one had been to the Knoblock house except a neighbor girl the evening before and a dog in the field they had discovered early the morning of the murder. Then E. O. Grant took the stand and testified to having seen John Knoblock and his little boy at ten-fifteen in the morning on the road into town—the same road Knoblock supposedly turned onto before nine-thirty in the morning, according to Dornes' testimony. Which meant that Knoblock and his son had only traveled about three miles in forty-five minutes. By car.

At eleven o'clock, Judge Richardson called a recess until Monday morning so that he and Woodrow, the court reporter, might catch the noon train home to Emporia. That afternoon, the bailiffs, Levi Heddens and Al Rickman, were to take the jurors to the Knoblock house so they might get a better sense of the place.

"You will visit the Knoblock house in the custody of the bailiffs," Richardson told the jury. "No one else—and that means *no one* else—should be there at the time or be with or near the jurors on the trip. Do not take notes. Do not draw diagrams. Do not discuss the condition of the house, the murder, or anything touching it. I hope I've made myself clear."

*****

That sunny January afternoon, as the judge, his wife, and the court reporter boarded the train to Emporia, twelve men and two bailiffs traveled into the countryside to see the site of Burlington's darkest crime.

File Type: Newspaper Clipping

[Dr. A. N. Gray's] testimony . . . was sufficiently sickening enough to satisfy the most morbid of curiosity seekers.

"State Rests Tonight," *Emporia Gazette*, January 15, 1925

Chapter Seventeen
Journalism

John Redmond's house
Burlington, Kansas
Sunday, January 17, 1926

John Redmond was pleased to be sitting in his own home, at his own table, in his own chair, eating a real dinner. The "grand bunch of old girls," as Bill White called them, of the Burlington Women's Relief Corps[12] were taking advantage of the crowd of hungry court-watchers to raise funds for the corps, and each day during the noon recess, they served a venerable feast of hot beef or pork, gravy, pickles, bread, butter, mashed potatoes, jelly, vegetables, pie, and coffee for thirty-five cents. But because of deadlines and press times, the reporters for the dailies spent their lunch hours eating five-cent candy bars and phoning in newspaper copy to their pressrooms. The judge had no sympathy for the reporters at the press table; the other day, after phoning in his story, Bill White hastened to the lunch counter and got a big sandwich, a piece of pie, and some other food in a sack and hurried back to the courtroom. Just as he was about to take a bite

---

12 The Women's Relief Corps serves as the Auxiliary to the Grand Army of the Republic, an organization originally founded for Civil War veterans (http://www.suvcw.org).

of his sandwich—and Redmond's mouth twitched a smile every time he remembered the moment—Judge Richardson reminded Bill that the courtroom was not a lunch room, and Bill disposed of his lunch and returned to the press table a hungry man.

The W.R.C. was not the only organization benefiting from *State of Kansas v. John Knoblock.* The *Daily Republican* was printing and selling more copies of the paper each day of the trial than in any previous day in the paper's history. However, getting those papers produced in a timely manner took a Herculean effort. The *Daily Republican* was printed early in the day, so papers could be delivered to some outlying communities via the morning trains. The courtroom, unfortunately, did not consult with the paper before setting up a schedule. So each evening, Redmond wrote the lead to the story, then changed the details as they came up during the day. But Saturday had proven to be full of surprises. The judge had ruled that the jury would disregard the testimony of Mrs. Bender and Mrs. Albert. But even that hadn't slowed the prosecution down once the judge had ruled that Ed Tolbert's testimony would be allowed. Three different headlines for the story had been set that morning, and changes were made to the story twice after the paper got on the press.

Perhaps he'd write about that after writing the main lead for tomorrow's paper.

*****

John Knoblock sat in his in-laws' parlor, watching his son play. Not even the warmth of the fire could take the chill out of the cold, drizzly January afternoon. John was cold, cold to the bone, cold in the soul. Today was Sunday, and Owen Samuel and W. C. Harris had assured him that the state was essentially finished with presenting their evidence. They insisted he needed to stay positive, that he had an excellent chance of winning. But as he watched his son play, he wondered if this would be his last Sunday as a free man.

File Type: Interview
Subject: Marjorie Barrett, daughter of Velma
and Orville Haehn, friends of the Knoblocks
Date: June 9, 2009

Marjorie: John Knoblock didn't murder his
wife. He was best friends with my dad and
was a very nice man.

Diana: What did you hear about the Knoblocks
growing up?

Marjorie: Charles [Knoblock] and John Mozingo
always believed John Knoblock was innocent.
John Mozingo asked Roger [Knoblock], "When
did you see your mother?" and he said he saw
her standing on the steps that morning. No
matter how many times they asked him, Roger
always said the same thing.

Chapter Eighteen
Defense

Coffey County Courthouse
Burlington, Kansas
Monday, January 18, 1926
9:00 a.m.

In an attempt to keep entry to the courtroom civilized, Judge Richardson had instigated a new rule: all courthouse doors were to remain locked until precisely nine o'clock. He had also hoped the foul weather would keep some away, but the morbidly curious braved the muddy, slippery roads to hear what W. C. Harris and Owen Samuel would say in John Knoblock's defense. As a result, throngs of people hoping to score a seat in the courtroom milled around the soggy grounds of the courthouse, anxiously checking their watches and the courthouse doors.

At the appointed hour, the doors to the courthouse swung open, and the masses lined up, single file. When the last seat was filled, the courthouse doors were shut in the faces of the disappointed.

*****

After A. P. Patterson, the county engineer, returned to the stand to refresh the jury's memory on the layout of the kitchen, the state called its final witnesses to the stand. Dr. Harry T. Salisbury was a well-known face in Coffey County, having practiced medicine in the area for more than thirty years.

"Dr. Salisbury, did you conduct the autopsy of Florence Knoblock?" Rolston asked.

"Yes, two days after her funeral, when the body was exhumed. I was assisted by Dr. Manson," Salisbury said. "We were trying to determine whether or not Mrs. Knoblock had been raped and whether or not she had been pregnant."

"Had she been raped?" Rolston said.

"I don't think so," Salisbury said.

"Dr. Salisbury," Owen Samuel asked, "You say that Mrs. Knoblock was not raped—"

"No, I said I didn't think she had been raped. She could have been raped, but there was no evidence of it."

"Was Mrs. Knoblock pregnant?"

"She was not pregnant nor were there signs of a recent pregnancy."

*****

"I've practiced in Burlington for fifteen years," Dr. David W. Manson told the court. "I've known both John Knoblock and his wife since they were children."

"Did you assist Dr. Salisbury in the autopsy?" Rolston asked.

"I did," Manson said. "We examined Mrs. Knoblock's body for signs of rape."

"Was Mrs. Knoblock raped?"

"I could not find any signs of rape. I do not think she was raped. I didn't notice any bruises on the body or on the insides of the legs," Manson said.

"Is it true that Mr. Knoblock approached you with the request to perform an illegal abortion on his wife?" Rolston said.

"Objection!" W. C. Harris bellowed. "Any conversation between the doctor and my client is privileged information."

"Sustained," the judge said.

"Dr. Manson, can you say, without a doubt, that Mrs. Knoblock was *not* raped?" Owen Samuel asked.

"I cannot say for certain that rape wasn't committed," Manson said. "I can only say there was no discoloration that would have been there if she had been raped before her death. There were no signs of a struggle. However, she might have been raped when she was past the point of struggling."

*****

After the state rested at nine forty-five that morning, the judge declared a thirty-minute recess. John Redmond took advantage of the opportunity to tidy up the lead for Monday's paper. "ABOUT READY TO HEAR JOHN KNOBLOCK'S SIDE" would be today's headline, followed by "State Finishes Presenting Case Against Knoblock" in one column and "Mr. Samuel Will Give Defendant's Side of the Case" in another.

"So far, not a word has been said by either side concerning the absence of Sherman Stevens, better known as Blackie or Deacon Stevens, the Negro who was under arrest for several weeks," Redmond wrote. "The attorneys for the defense issued a subpoena for him, and it had been rather expected that the state also would want him here for emergencies. But so far, as has been made known, his whereabouts are unknown to either side."

*****

The courtroom was silent. Owen S. Samuel, attorney for the defense, swept his eyes over the visitors in the court before fixing them on the twelve men in the jury box. It was time to sow the seeds of doubt in the minds of the jurors.

"Gentlemen of the jury," Samuel said in his best courtroom voice, "allow me to present to you what the defense expects to prove—and disprove—during the remainder of this trial."

Samuel stepped toward the jurors while gesturing to his client. "We will show that John Knoblock is thirty-four years old and that his wife, Florence Emma Knoblock, was thirty-one at the time of her murder. That Knoblock is a Coffey County boy, born on a farm, who has spent his entire life in this county. For years, he lived as a next-door neighbor to the Mozingo family. He and Florence attended the same school. At no time did she ever go with any other boy or young man but John Knoblock, nor did John Knoblock ever go with any girl other than Florence Mozingo."

Samuel softened his voice into a gentle, compassionate tone. "Their attachment for each other was the subject of much comment, and many folks said it was a real love match."

*****

John Knoblock's pen scribbled furiously across one of the sheets of paper provided by his attorneys. The writing steadied him; the movement gave him a sense of calm and control. For several days, Ray Pierson and Joe Rolston pointed fingers and called him names. He could almost ignore it; he could almost believe they were talking about anyone but him. But now the trial was most assuredly about him, and Owen Samuel stood in front of a courtroom full of people, attempting to bare John's heart and intentions for everyone to inspect. It was one thing for folks to accuse him of wrongdoing. It was another for folks to look at him, hear him, see him, and still believe that he killed his wife.

The jury had to believe him if he told the truth, he thought. The truth was all he had left.

*****

John Redmond discreetly glanced at his watch and sighed. Owen Samuel was just getting started, and he'd barely allowed

John Knoblock to grow into a young man in his account, much less move forward to the point where the man's wife was murdered. Should the paper include the statement in its entirety and save any testimony for the next issue? Should he summarize the defense? Redmond continued to write copious notes. He would decide later.

*****

"John Knoblock was never alone with either of the Mozingo girls, except when going back and forth from the Knoblock home to the Mozingo home or from the Mozingo's to his home, and then only with full knowledge and consent of his wife. He was never—" Samuel punctuated the word *never* with his hand, "—alone with them at night or under circumstances where they even could be suspected of anything wrong."

*****

This was the longest opening statement presented by the defense in any trial in the state of Kansas, Bill White thought as his mind drifted. Unlike John Redmond, he couldn't imagine recording Samuel's entire speech in the *Gazette*. None of Samuel's statements mattered unless he could prove them with testimony anyway. Bill switched his attention from Samuel's words to Samuel's hair. Samuel appeared to be training his black hair into a coiffeur that followed the top of his head over the back to his neck, leaving it long enough to form a sort of black collar necklace. Interesting. Perhaps he ought to write about that.

*****

"No such conversation as described by Ed Tolbert took place in 1924 or at any other time, and John Knoblock never used any rubber instrument or anything like Tolbert said he had told him he did," Samuel said. "Nor had there been an abortion and Knoblock never thought of one. In fact, Tolbert's story is—" Samuel stressed the next two words "—*not true*."

*****

It was fair to say that Owen Samuel's speech would take up all of the available room in Tuesday's paper. Perhaps, Redmond thought, he could run it in its entirety, and on Wednesday add pages to allow for all of the copy from the actual testimony. In the back of his mind, he compared the figures for the cost of the added page against the figures for the number of papers the *Daily Republican* was likely to sell.

*****

"John Knoblock honked the horn as he drove up to the house, took some things out of the car and set them on the porch, then set the boy on the porch. He picked up the egg case with the groceries and went in the east door," Samuel said. "He saw the form of his wife on the floor, dropped the case, and went to her. He touched her arm and saw she was cold."

*****

Bill White studied John Mozingo, the defendant's father-in-law. The tall, angular farmer had remained straight-faced throughout the trial so far, except to periodically whisper to Knoblock's attorneys. Curious, Bill thought. He'd never noticed that Mozingo's head was pear-shaped before.

*****

"The evidence will show that after the officers and the bloodhounds came from Emporia, the dogs went to the dresser and razor box and sniffed at them, then went out of the dining room door right past the defendant, paying no attention to him," Samuel said.

*****

Yes, the newspaper could afford to add an extra sheet to Wednesday's edition, Redmond thought. It seemed important to include the defense's intentions in their entirety, for the sake of posterity.

*****

Bill tuned out Samuel and attempted to capture some of the most prominent figures in the courtroom in brief caricatures. "A postmortem examination on [former] Judge Harris," Bill wrote, "will probably disclose the fact that under his tonsils lay a large elastic sack which holds more than a pint of tobacco juice." Bill smiled at the image and decided to hold on to it for the paper.

*****

"The attorney general's investigator, John Stewart, went to Pueblo, Colorado, to get a statement from Carl Goodrick, a neighbor of Knoblock's. He presented Goodrick with a fake telegram from Sheriff Frank Hunter, which ordered Stewart to arrest Goodrick for Florence Knoblock's murder unless he signed a statement that he was at the Knoblock home early on the morning of May 30 and saw Florence lying on the floor and that Knoblock had killed her before he left home that day," Samuel said and watched the courtroom snap back to attention.

"Objection!" Joe Rolston called out.

Samuel didn't skip a beat, continuing in the hypnotic flow of his story, describing the murder scene, the lies, the underhandedness of the law.

"Knoblock has no motive because he loved Florence, and she was his sweetheart. And because the state couldn't find a motive, they arrested the defendant, claiming a means to clear him. They still can't find a motive because there isn't one. Even her folks believe in his innocence.

"And that, gentlemen, is what the defense sets out to prove to you during this trial."

*****

Owen Samuel and W. C. Harris were not pleased to learn that two of their key witnesses were nowhere to be found. George Eaton, the man from Kansas City, Kansas, whose bloodhounds allegedly pointed the way to Blackie Stevens, did not show up as ordered that Monday, and Carl Goodrick's subpoena was returned marked "Not Found."

"Your honor, we request a bench warrant be issued for George Eaton," W. C. Harris said shortly after the noon recess.

"Sheriff Hunter, see what you can find out about Mr. Eaton," the judge ordered.

*****

After court clerk Jennie Caven reported on the status of Carl Goodrick's subpoena, the elderly Mrs. Margaret Winchester was called to the stand.

"Of course I knew Florence Knoblock's voice," said the woman. "And the morning she was murdered, I heard Florence talking over the phone to Ray Knoblock at the bakery. Our phone is on the same party line as the Knoblocks'."

"What did you hear her say?" Samuel asked.

"She told him that 'John is here and will talk to you.'"

"What else did you hear, Mrs. Winchester?"

"Nothing else, really," she said.

"Did you hear John Knoblock say he was going into town?" Samuel said.

"No."

"At what time would you say that was?"

"Eight o'clock, or a little later."

*****

The owners and employee of the Burlington Bakery could have been very strong witnesses in John Knoblock's favor, Redmond thought, had they not mostly been related to John Knoblock.

The defense first called Lavon Stewart, co-owner of the bakery since 1924.

"I'd known Florence Knoblock for a year and a half," Lavon said. "Of course I knew her voice over the phone. She called about nine o'clock on Decoration Day."

"Did you look at a clock or a watch?" Samuel said.

"I knew the time by the stage of the baking."

"And what did Florence say?"

"She asked for Ray, who came and talked over the phone."

Lavon Stewart's still-warm seat was taken by Ray Knoblock, a partner at the Burlington Bakery. Ray Knoblock also happened to be John Knoblock's first cousin.

"I spoke with Florence on Decoration Day," Ray said. "We were discussing compound and then she said, 'John is coming to town and will talk to you.'"

"And at what time was this?"

"About nine o'clock," Ray said. "I was sure it was nearly nine by the stage of the bread. It had been put in at seven and the dough was put on the bench just as she called."

Jake Knoblock, another cousin, was Burlington Bakery's newest employee, having started his position less than three months before Florence Knoblock's murder.

"I was there on Decoration Day," Jake said. "I heard Ray talking on the phone at about nine o'clock that morning. I heard him say he hadn't placed Florence and John's order because he didn't know if they wanted lard or compound and whether they wanted fifty pounds or one hundred pounds."

"And how did you know the call came at nine o'clock?"

"By the bread," Jake said, as if it should have been obvious.

*****

Despite his partner's two-hour presentation on everything the defense hoped to prove during the *State of Kansas v. John Knoblock*, W. C. Harris knew the defense had only one true goal: to convince the jury that it simply wasn't possible for John Knoblock to kill his wife. To persuade the men of reason, they would use logic. To win over those with a sentimental streak, they would appeal to the heart. To accomplish both of these goals, the defense would flood the court with witnesses—dozens of witnesses who saw John Knoblock the morning his wife was murdered, dozens more who would attest to his affection for his wife. After all, how could a man who was seen by half of Coffey County be at home killing the woman he loved?

*****

Skip Beatty, the neighborhood egg man, was at the home of Maude and George Albert, the Knoblocks' nearest neighbor, the morning of Decoration Day.

"Sure, I saw John Knoblock pass by at about nine-thirty or ten," Beatty testified. "He was heading east, and he had his little boy with him."

"How far apart are the Albert and Knoblock homes?"

"About a quarter-mile."

"Did you see Mr. Knoblock at his house?"

"I didn't see him until he and his boy drove past George Albert's home. They both waved as they drove by," Beatty said.

Elmer Anderson was a teamster who hauled gravel for the county. He knew John Knoblock. He knew most of the country folk for that matter, having lived in the county for forty-three of his fifty-two years.

"Sure, I saw John Knoblock that morning on Decoration Day," he told the jury. "He walked past the K-T Oil station."

"At what time?" Harris said.

"I'd say between eleven and eleven-thirty. He was alone. Didn't have his boy with him then."

Bill Phillips, a house-moving contractor, lived on the west edge of Burlington and saw John Knoblock and the boy in a car coming east a little before ten o'clock. "I was walking west toward my house. When I got home, it was ten minutes of ten by my watch, which I set with Mosher's regulator[13] that morning."

"What made you look at the time, Mr. Phillips?" Harris asked.

"My father-in-law was very sick. I checked the time because I knew he would need his medication."

"Where were you when Mr. Knoblock drove past you?"

"Just west of the Katy track, near Cole's store."

*****

"I live next door to John Knoblock's parents, in the house at the corner of Eighth and Yuba," Eva Sharr said to the jury. "I have two boarders—Mary and Katherine Bon, who stay with me so they can attend Burlington High School."

"Do you know the Knoblocks, Mrs. Sharr?" Harris asked.

"I've known Florence and John for years," she said. "They often visited me at my home when they were in town to visit John's parents."

"Were you at home the morning of May 30?"

"Yes," Mrs. Sharr said. "I saw John at about ten o'clock. He went into his father's house with eggs, milk, and strawberries.

13 In the United States, the railroads were responsible for creating Standard Time Zones for the sake of scheduling train departures and arrivals. Regulator clocks maintained official Standard Time (http://americanhistory.si.edu/ontime/synchronizing/zones.html).

He left his son in the car. Roger's grandma, Mrs. Knoblock, came out to talk to Roger while John was in the house."

"Did you talk to John Knoblock that day?"

"At about five after one, maybe ten after, John phoned me. 'Where's the folks?' he asked. His voice was familiar, but I didn't immediately recognize it, so I said, 'Who is this?' and that's when he said, 'This is John,' and I told him that his folks had gone to the Decoration Day program. Then he said to tell them that 'Florence is murdered.'"

"Did you go out to the Knoblock farm that day?" W. C. Harris asked.

"I went out to the farm that afternoon, getting there at two-thirty or three o'clock. I saw the mixed bread in an aluminum kettle on the porch. The bread had obviously been mixed in the morning."

"How did you know that?" W. C. Harris said.

"I've been baking bread for twenty-seven years," Mrs. Sharr said. "I know what bread looks like after it's been mixed."

"Did you see John Knoblock that afternoon?"

"I saw him when I arrived," she said. "He looked and talked like he had been crying."

"Were you at the farm when the bloodhounds arrived?"

"John Knoblock and John Mozingo were standing on the porch when the bloodhounds came out of the house. The dogs paid no attention to him."

*****

"Yes, I know John Knoblock," said Marvin Engle, who ran Engle Produce and Feed in Burlington. "I bought cream and eggs from him about once a week. I saw him on Decoration Day. I handled the eggs he brought with him and talked to him."

"How did he seem?" Harris asked.

Engle shrugged. "Natural, I guess. Nothing unusual or unnatural about him that morning. He left his stuff and went out, coming back later for the check, which Ernest Bates had made out."

*****

"Sure I know John Knoblock," Henry Smith said. "He's renting a field next to mine. He stopped in to my hardware store and told me about cattle breaking into the wheat. My side of the fence needed fixing, so I hired him to fix the fence that afternoon. I sent out two rolls of wire by him."

"At what time did Mr. Knoblock come by your store?" Harris asked.

"Between nine and ten that morning," Smith said. "He was in the store between fifteen and thirty minutes."

*****

John Kellerman felt the swirl of butterflies in his stomach as he approached the witness stand. Eight months had passed since his sister-in-law's murder. Eight months of grief, anger, worry, and heartache. As he walked by the defense's table, he saw two men—his father-in-law, John Mozingo, and his brother-in-law, John Knoblock—the latter of which had aged twenty years during those eight months. The state claimed they were looking for justice; but if anyone asked Kellerman, he would tell them the greatest injustice of all was accusing an innocent man of the most awful sorts of wrongdoings as he grieved over his dead wife and worried about his little son. Kellerman would have done anything to help his wife's family and had even hired a private detective not long after the murder, someone separate from the Burns Agency detective and the sheriff's men. But even that wasn't enough to prevent this trial.

Kellerman sat, adjusted the trousers of his suit, and allowed himself to be sworn in. He was, by nature, an honest man, with an honest and kind face. He could only hope the jury would agree.

*****

"Mr. Kellerman," Owen Samuel began, "You are married to Florence Knoblock's sister, is that correct?"

"Yes, sir," Kellerman said. "Ella and I were married three years ago in October."

"And you work for Burlington Hardware Company?"

"Yes."

"Did you see John Knoblock at the Burlington Hardware Company on Decoration Day?"

"Yes, sir," Kellerman said. "He and Roger entered the store around eleven a.m. George Crotty was also there that morning. John asked about some wire. He was there for fifteen or twenty minutes, then left for a short while before returning about a quarter to noon. I went with him and Roger to the Pioneer Hardware and Music Store and returned to the store just about the time the whistle blew."

"Where did Mr. Knoblock go after that?"

"He went to Hoffmans Mercantile Co. and then drove west at about a quarter past twelve."

"When did you first learn about Florence Knoblock's murder?"

"After dinner. The Mozingos phoned my wife. We stopped by the Mozingo house to pick up Vesta and then drove to John and Florence's farm. That was between two and two-thirty."

"What did you find at the Knoblock farm?"

Kellerman blew out a breath. "First we saw my in-laws, then John. He was crying. I looked into the kitchen and saw Florence there. Then I looked into the bedroom. Afterwards, Sam Shoup and I drove out to Hartford to tell Frances McCormick—that's another of Florence and Ella's sisters—what happened."

"When did you return?" Samuel asked.

"It was about five o'clock that evening. Roy Jones, the undertaker, was there then, helping take care of Florence's body," Kellerman said.

"What did Mr. Knoblock do then?"

"I was with him the rest of the evening. There was a report of three Negroes seen in Hartford, so we drove out to Hartford to investigate. We drove back around nine o'clock. We went into the house together, along with Orville Haehn and Reverend Neden."

"Was Mr. Knoblock ever alone in the bedroom during that time?" Samuel said.

"No, sir. We all moved from room to room together, locking up the house except for the dining room door. John's parents, Martha and Erky Woods, Alice Naylor, and my wife were left in the dining room, and I think they all stayed the night."

"And Mr. Knoblock?"

"We didn't get to bed at all that night," Kellerman said. "We returned to John's house around six or six-thirty Sunday morning. My wife mentioned that Roger would need some fresh clothes before we left for her folks' home. Ella, Sam Shoup, John, and I all went into the bedroom to get a few clean things for the little boy to wear. John reached for a pair of overalls on the floor and then a shirt. That's when he saw the razor lying on the rug."

"Did you see him pick up the razor?"

"No, I did not."

"What did you do that morning?"

Kellerman thought about their foolish efforts to search the county for Blackie Stevens.

"We drove to Lebo, Olivet, and Osage City on the report of Negroes seen going that way from Lebo. We stopped in Lyndon and talked with the sheriff there. We turned up nothing and drove home," Kellerman said. "I think we got back in time to eat dinner at the Mozingos' home a little after one o'clock."

"Mr. Kellerman, who was present at that dinner?" Samuel asked.

"The Mozingos, the Shoups, Pete Jenkins, one or two of the Massey boys. I don't think Clarence Conrad was there for dinner, but he was there afterwards."

"Did you hear Sam Shoup and John Knoblock discuss the razor at that time?"

"No, sir, I did not. I don't think it happened."

"Did you hear Mr. Knoblock say that he would not take the evidence to the men working at his house?"

"No."

"Did you hear Mr. Knoblock say that he wouldn't give any information to the men with the bloodhounds?"

"No, I did not," Kellerman said.

"Did you hear Mr. Knoblock tell the undertaker that he wanted Florence Knoblock's eyes photographed because he had heard that the photograph would show her murderer?"

"Well, I—"

"Objection!" Joe Rolston called out. "Completely irrelevant."

W. C. Harris spit a stream into his cuspidor. "It is absolutely relevant, as it shows that Mr. Knoblock was interested in finding his wife's murderer."

"The objection is sustained," Judge Richardson called out.

"Your honor!" W. C. Harris stood, fists braced on the desk in front of him.

"There is a rule of law more ancient than either of us," Judge Richardson said to his predecessor, former Judge W. C. Harris, "which plainly says that self-serving declarations are not available for defense. The objection is sustained."

As the defense attorney sputtered, Judge Richardson casually glanced at the clock in the courtroom. "Let's adjourn for today. Court will resume at nine o'clock in the morning."

*****

Coffey County Courthouse
Burlington, Kansas
Tuesday, January 19, 1926
9:00 a.m.

"Your honor, George Eaton, the Kansas City bloodhound man, has failed to appear. Again," Owen Samuel reported immediately after the doors to the courtroom opened.

"Sheriff Hunter? Did you reach Mr. Eaton yesterday?" Judge Richardson asked.

"Yesterday morning he said he would come straightaway if one hundred dollars was wired to him to cover his expenses," Hunter said.

"Which we did," Samuel said.

"Which we did," the sheriff agreed. "After which, we couldn't reach him. And the next thing we heard was that he left Kansas City, Kansas, for Kansas City, Missouri, and he wouldn't return home until evening."

"This is ridiculous," the judge said. "This is a criminal case. He does not have the luxury of deciding when he's going to show up." Judge Richardson folded his hands in front of him. "I'm issuing a bench warrant. Sheriff, have one of your men travel to Kansas City to apprehend Mr. Eaton."

*****

Sam Shoup wondered how many more times he and his wife would have to make themselves available for John Knoblock's trial. Colder weather was expected that evening, and there were chores to see to before the rain and sleet moved in. Yet he was in this courtroom, answering questions he'd answered a dozen times before.

Shoup adjusted the cuffs in his coat sleeves, placed his hands in his lap, and directed his gaze toward Knoblock's defense attorney, as if granting Owen Samuel permission to begin.

"Mr. Shoup, were you in the company of John Knoblock the Sunday morning after the murder?" Owen Samuel asked.

"Yes."

"And did you enter the first-floor bedroom that morning?"

"I went in, along with John Kellerman and his wife and John Knoblock. Johnnie's little boy needed clothes. I was in there when Johnnie picked up the overalls and shirt for the boy."

"And did you see the razor at that time?"

"The razor was laying on the floor, open. The blade was turned back a little. We left it there," Shoup said.

"What did you do then?"

"The clothes were taken to the Mozingos, and Roger was dressed. We were in the Knoblock house only a few minutes."

"Mr. Shoup," said Fred Harris during the cross-examination, "Did you tell anyone about the razor?"

"I didn't mention it to anyone, and I didn't hear any of the others mention it."

"Do you realize that your testimony today is different than the testimony at the preliminary hearing?"

"Objection!" Both Owen Samuel and W. C. Harris stood simultaneously.

"The state is hoping to impeach Mr. Shoup for his varying statements in different examinations," Fred Harris, the prosecutor from Ottawa, said in his most matter-of-fact voice.

Shoup cocked an eyebrow.

"Sustained," Judge Richardson said.

When Sam Shoup was dismissed, he stood, calm and confident. Nothing would come of the prosecution's threats. They wouldn't dare touch him.

*****

Dr. Albert N. Gray was back on the witness stand. "Mr. Knoblock was restless, very talkative, and anxious," Dr. Gray told the jury. "I arrived at the house at about two-twenty and had the opportunity to observe him for an hour to an hour and a half. He appeared to be suffering from shock following the loss of his wife."

"But Dr. Gray," said prosecutor Fred Harris, "Couldn't these same symptoms be caused by anxiety or guilt?"

"Yes, they could."

*****

Ella Mozingo Kellerman hardly slept the night before she was called to court. Be confident, she told herself as she sat in the courtroom, waiting for her name to be called. You know the truth, tell the truth. Seconds later, the bailiff escorted her to the stand.

"I saw John Knoblock sitting there, crying," Ella said. "I saw him cry several times throughout that afternoon."

"And how long did you stay at the Knoblock house?" Owen Samuel asked.

"Until six-thirty the next morning, along with Charles and Mary Knoblock, Mrs. Shoup, Ann Naylor, and others, I believe."

"Had you gone into the downstairs bedroom on Saturday afternoon?"

"Yes," she said. "There was clothing all over the floor. Eight or twelve pieces including John's yellow shirt, which had been worn, Roger's clothes, and some white things."

"How did the room appear the next morning?"

"The same things were there in exactly the same places Sunday morning."

"Had you been in the rest of the house?" Owen Samuel said.

"John Knoblock suggested going upstairs to get cloths to clean up the kitchen. He and the undertaker went upstairs with me to get the cloths out of the east room. I saw a pair of gray trousers wadded up in the bottom of a chair. I heard John say his blue trousers on the floor upstairs with the pockets turned out belonged in a closet downstairs. John sat on the bed and cried for two or three minutes before we returned downstairs."

"Was that the only time you ventured upstairs?"

"I went up a second time with the undertaker, Eugene Stone, and others and went into the east room to find Florence's clothes. No one entered the west room."

"Did you see anything on the dresser in the downstairs bedroom that evening?"

"An old razor box, but it was empty," Ella said.

"Did you see John Knoblock enter the downstairs bedroom alone at any time that evening?"

"John never went into that bedroom again at all after five that evening that I saw."

"But the next morning, you entered the bedroom," Samuel said.

"We entered the bedroom. John Knoblock, my husband, Mr. Shoup, and I. John Knoblock picked up his son's clothes, and all of us saw the razor on the floor. We left it there."

"But Mrs. Menard claims that on Saturday, she and two other women stood in the room and talked for at least fifteen minutes," Samuel said, "and that they didn't see a razor under the clothes."

Ella didn't know why she let Stella Menard get under her skin, but every time the woman's name came up, she could feel her blood boil. That busybody liked having people fluttering around her, and she would tell whatever she had to—truth or fib—to ensure it happened. Ella took a calming breath and answered John Knoblock's attorney.

"Mrs. Menard was not in that bedroom for fifteen whole minutes," Ella said sternly.

"But what about the two other women?"

"I saw the showgirl; she was tall and slender, with a light complexion. She wore a red hat."

"Did she enter the bedroom?"

"The showgirl never entered the house while I was there," Ella said.

"What about the other woman?"

"I never saw the middle-aged heavyset woman Mrs. Menard described."

"Did you see Mrs. Menard engage in a conversation with the coroner, J. O. Stone?"

"No, I did not."

"Are you calling Mrs. Menard a liar?"

Ella took another deep, steadying breath. "Mrs. Menard has told many people that she was a longtime, close personal friend of my late sister. The truth is, the afternoon Florence was murdered, Mrs. Menard asked me who Florence was."

*****

Her husband having been recalled for a few more questions on the stand, Ella sat next to her sisters and waited. Soon, Kellerman was excused and a recess was called. The courtroom doors opened, and the jurors were led down the hallway to the basement. After the jurors passed through, the rest of the visitors in the courtroom spilled into the hallway, chattering loudly as people do when a picture show or church service lets out. Ella felt a hand at her elbow and was relieved to see her husband standing at her side.

Last to exit the courtroom were her brother-in-law, father, and Harris and Samuel. She gave John Knoblock's hand a squeeze as they met in the hallway. "It will be all right, John, you know it will," she said. He squeezed her hand back and said nothing.

The WRC women had provided another wholesome lunch, but Ella could only pick at it. "Do you think they're done with us yet?" Ella asked her husband, who sat next to her, picking at his own plate.

"Who knows?" he said, then considered her question. "No, I don't. They only asked questions about the razor. There is still much of the story left to tell."

*****

Sure enough, Ella found herself describing the appearance of the Knoblocks' dining room to a lunch-laden sleepy-eyed jury just after the noon recess. "There was hair on the dining room floor," Ella said. "It was short. Some of it was gray, like

John's hair, and some of it light, like Roger's. The hair was in the northeast corner of the dining room. I swept it into the kitchen and left it there."

*****

Unlike the Mozingos and the Knoblocks, Velma Mae Truelove Haehn had been afforded the opportunity to grieve in private. Velma and Florence had been good friends—close friends—and Florence's absence, even now, eight months later, left a hole in her heart as fresh as when Velma first set foot on the Knoblock farm and saw for herself that the news was true.

"I'd known Florence for fifteen years," Velma said. "I was her closest friend, and we visited back and forth often."

"How did Florence and John seem, as a couple?" Samuel asked.

Velma thought about when John and Florence were married in Ottawa, Kansas. How she and several others had taken the train to Franklin County to celebrate their happiness with a shivaree. They had found the happy couple hiding out in a cattle shed. "They got along fine," she said. "Florence always seemed very happy after her marriage."

"And John?"

"John and I never spoke of his feelings toward his wife, but he always treated her with respect and kindness."

"You said you visited the Knoblock home on occasion?"

"Many times, both when they lived east of town and in their home west of town. John seemed devoted to her."

"You went to the Knoblock farm the afternoon of the murder?" Samuel said.

The place had looked wrong, all wrong, with all of those people trampling down the grass in the field.

"Yes," she said.

"And how did John seem to you then?"

"Excited and grieving," Velma said.

*****

"I've known John Knoblock all my life," Orville Haehn said. "And I've seen John and Florence together since their courting days. The Kellermans, the Knoblocks, and the wife and I were all friends, and we visited back and forth."

"How would you describe the relationship between John and Florence Knoblock?" Owen Samuel asked.

"There was never a quarrel between them," Orville said. "I never was in a more loving home."

"Did you go to the Knoblock house after the murder on May 30?"

"Yes, I did," Orville said. "He looked real downhearted. I was with him practically all evening. John was only in the house once, and then it was with John Kellerman, Reverend Neden, and myself. We went in to lock up the house. I remember because while we were in there, John broke down and cried when he saw his wife's hat."

"Did you happen to notice any milk buckets while you were there that afternoon?"

"Sure I did. I noticed one of the cows needed milking, so I took the buckets and milked the cow," Orville said.

"And what was the condition of the buckets?"

"One of the milk buckets had a little milk in it. So did the separator."

"Mr. Haehn, did you lock the doors yourself?" asked the prosecutor Fred Harris.

"No, I held the flashlight while each door was locked."

"Did you go into the bedroom?"

"No, we locked the bedroom door from the hall under the stairway."

"But what about the windows?"

Orville thought about it for a moment before answering. "I know we locked the doors, but I don't remember whether the windows were locked or not."

*****

Arch C. Brown, a deputy sheriff of Greenwood County, had made the long trip from Hamilton to be at the courthouse that morning. He remembered that poor, balled-up man he helped return to the asylum in Oklahoma. Did Brown think John Weber was capable of murder? He had learned a long time ago that a man could do just about anything, given the right motivation. But no, he didn't think the man walking down the highway with nothing but socks to protect his feet had killed the Knoblock woman.

"Deputy Brown, do you recall the occasion of the murder of Mrs. Florence Knoblock?" Samuel said.

"I do," Brown said.

"Do you recall picking up a crazy man near Madison shortly after that murder?"

Before Arch Brown could open his mouth to answer, one of the prosecutors objected and all of the lawyers began yelling at each other. Brown watched them huddle like football players discussing a play before approaching the bench. Less than a minute later, the huddle dispersed.

"You may step down, Deputy Brown," Judge Richardson said, and Brown stepped into the hallway to study the train schedule before returning to Hamilton.

*****

Reverend Joseph Neden looked exactly as one expected a young member of the anointed to look: simple, tidy, wearing a white shirt with a turned-down, starched collar and no tie.

"I arrived at the Knoblock farm between nine and ten o'clock that night," Reverend Neden said. "I went into the house with Orville Haehn, John Kellerman, and John Knoblock. Together, we moved from room to room, locking the kitchen and then the bedroom by way of the dining room."

"Did you ever see Mr. Knoblock enter the bedroom?" Samuel said.

"Not while I was there."

"Who turned the keys?"

"I don't honestly remember. I just remember moving around the house, carrying a Coleman light."

"Reverend Neden," Fred Harris asked, "Who locked the windows?"

"I can't say that I remember anyone locking the windows."

"Is it possible that someone from your little foursome could have stepped away for just a moment?"

"I don't believe so," Neden said. "I think I would have noticed."

"But it's not impossible, is it?"

"No, I suppose it's not impossible."

*****

Rosa Knapp had spent much of the morning shifting uncomfortably on a hard, metal folding chair in the hallway of the courthouse, simultaneously dreading the waiting and hoping she was never called to the stand. When the bailiff finally came for her, she wasn't sure whether to be horrified or relieved. She didn't know why she was even testifying. If what she had seen mattered, then Mr. Knoblock wouldn't be on trial right now. Some other fella would have been caught.

"We live four miles west of the Knoblocks, on the same road," Rosa said. "When we were on our way home, we passed Mr. Knoblock and his boy. They were in their car, heading east."

"And where was this?"

"About three miles east of the Knoblock farm," Rosa said. "When we passed the Knoblock place, I saw a man wearing dark clothing standing on the front porch on the east side of the house."

"Miss Knapp," Fred Harris began, "at the preliminary hearing, you said you weren't sure if he was colored or white."

Rosa felt her heart racing. Had she remembered wrong? She hadn't thought so, but all of the lawyers and all of the sheriff's men had asked her so many times that she wasn't certain anymore. "That's true."

"But just now you said he was dark."

Rosa let out a breath she didn't realize she had been holding. "He was wearing dark clothing," she said. "I couldn't tell if he was a Negro or white."

*****

Dora Goodrick sat on the metal folding chair outside the courtroom, waiting for the bailiff to escort her through the heavy courtroom doors.

Today was the day, Mr. Samuel had told her. Today, she would be asked to testify about the man rumored to have been pursing Florence Knoblock.

It wasn't a rumor, thought Dora, but she didn't correct John Knoblock's attorney. Florence didn't have it in her to lie, and even if she did, she wasn't lying that day as she stood in Dora's kitchen, tears in her eyes, begging Dora's advice.

There was too much fear, real fear, for Florence to have been lying.

Dora knew she couldn't tell anyone about the day Florence was murdered. It was too late for that. She and hers would come out looking guiltier than the murderer. But maybe if she testified to what she knew, what Florence had told her about the man she had seen out in the yard, about the man who was trying to court her despite Florence being a married woman, the law and the jury could put two and two together and figure out they had the wrong man on trial.

The bailiff called on her, and she took her seat on the witness stand.

"Mrs. Goodrick, could you tell us about a conversation you had with Florence Knoblock in March before she was murdered?"

"Florence told me that she had heard a peculiar noise and had seen a man standing in her house and was very much afraid—"

"Objection!" Rolston shouted, and as Dora's heart pounded, the attorneys on both sides of the courtroom began to argue and after a huddle, turned to the little judge with the big voice.

"Objection sustained," the judge said, and Dora was asked to step down.

Dora shook with disbelief as she exited the courtroom.

*****

Mrs. Rose Shoup, Sam Shoup's wife, was called to the stand.

"I'd known Florence for twenty-three or twenty-four years," Mrs. Shoup said. "I occasionally visited them in their home, and certainly I saw them at church socials and fairs. John always seemed very affectionate toward her."

"And how did Mr. Knoblock seem the afternoon of her murder?"

"I arrived at the farm around one-thirty or so," Mrs. Shoup said. "When I went to him, he put his hands to his head and started to cry and walk away."

*****

W. C. Harris suspected it was unlikely the judge would allow testimony regarding Blackie Stevens, especially if the evidence about the bloodhounds was deemed inadmissible. But until Judge Richardson bellowed a resounding no, he and Samuel would offer up the testimony of any and every witness who'd ever seen a colored man in Coffey County.

Warren "Warnie" Yoho, a young farmer living just north of Yates Center, testified to seeing a Negro coming down the road just north of Yates Center. "He was a colored man wearing overalls with a bib, a faded blue jacket, and a hat that would have been gray if it was clean," Warnie said. "He was better than six feet tall. I'd say he was chocolate colored. Glen Weide was with me."

Next Warnie's pal Glen Weide was called to the stand. "Warnie and I were going to town on horseback when we saw a fairly heavy Negro walking north of Yates Center. He wore faded khaki pants, a blue shirt, and a dirty gray cap."

Warnie's father, John Yoho, also saw the colored man coming north on the highway. "He wore yeller khaki pants, a khaki shirt, and he had a bad swing to his right foot," Yoho said. "I saw the same man in the county jail, and folks said he was Blackie Stevens. I saw him walk across the room. He walked the same way. He was very black, weighed about a hundred and seventy-five pounds, and was about five-foot-six, maybe five-foot-seven inches tall."

Marie Fosnight testified to seeing a colored man go by the old Willett home on Friday night.

Bill Crotty claimed he saw Blackie Stevens a quarter-mile from Crandall at about seven-thirty Friday night. "He was heavyset, about five-six or five-foot-seven, with that peculiar walk."

"There was an old frame house north of my place that we used to keep the cobs in last year. It had two windows on the south boarded over," said George Albert.

"When did you notice the boards were missing?" The state objected to the question. The judge declared he would reserve ruling until later and told George Albert to answer the question.

"Five or six days later," he said. "I noticed that a nail wasn't much rusted, which meant that the board had only recently been knocked off."

*****

After building a foundation for the possibility of a Negro in the vicinity of the Knoblock farm on the day of Florence Knoblock's murder, Owen Samuel and W. C. Harris set out to discredit any proof conjured up by the prosecution.

Charles Griffith was a nineteen-year-old boy who worked at the Royal Cleaners for Charles Knoblock, who happened to be John Knoblock's brother. He testified to cleaning and pressing a blue serge suit for John Knoblock the Monday afternoon before the funeral.

"No, I didn't see any blood on the pants," Griffith said. "Bloodstains can be cleaned out with water, but I didn't notice any signs that someone had tried to clean the pants."

*****

"Currently, I raise chickens," said David F. Ray, the man hired by John Kellerman just days after the murder. "But before that, I was a detective for two years, and I studied fingerprints."

"Did you visit the Knoblock place after the murder?" Samuel said.

"John Kellerman requested that I go. That was on the Monday after."

"And what did you see?"

"I saw a notice on the gate about not entering, but I drove in anyway. I looked around the rooms in the company of both John Knoblock and John Kellerman. I found a thumbprint, called a *smear* because the lines were obliterated. Then I went to the bedroom and saw prints of fingers where the ends of the fingers had touched under the stairway. I also saw marks on the bedstead that looked like swipes and not prints. There weren't any lines on the mark on the bedspread, but the prints of three fingers of a right hand were on the drawer of the dresser. The bloody prints on rags on the dresser weren't distinguishable."

"Is that all you saw?"

"Those are all the fingerprints I saw," Ray said. "I saw lots of blood in the kitchen, some in the bedroom on the dresser, a little on the dining room floor, which was almost in front of the kitchen door. I looked at the furniture in all of the rooms and didn't find any other prints."

*****

Dr. A. B. McConnell, a practicing physician, testified to being called in to examine John Knoblock in the county attorney's office. "I saw no marks, scratches, or bruises on him," he said.

*****

Leroy Hurt had farmed in Lyon County for fifteen years before becoming Emporia's police chief. "The city of Emporia acquired the bloodhounds and has used them several times before the Knoblock murder. They were trained. They had almost two months' worth of experience and practiced daily. The dogs would follow a man during practice."

"When were you called to Coffey County?"

"Sheriff Hunter called Sheriff Crumley, who is Lyon County's sheriff. Sheriff Crumley, the dogs' manager George Wilson, and I went to Coffey County together."

"Objection," Fred Harris said. "The dogs have not been qualified under the rule of law."

"Sustained," Judge Richardson said.

*****

Bill White watched John Mozingo give his son-in-law a gentle pat on the shoulder as Mozingo left his seat behind the defense table and approached the witness stand. By all accounts, Mozingo was well respected in this community, and many had argued that John Knoblock's greatest defense was having Mozingo's steadfast support throughout this ordeal. The fact that the Mozingo family signed for ten thousand dollars of Knoblock's twenty-five-thousand-dollar bond meant more to many folks than any fingerprints or hearsay.

"We went to the house immediately after John called us," Mozingo said. "John stood on the porch, a gun in his hand. I asked him, 'What's the matter?' and he didn't answer. I asked him again. 'Florence is murdered,' he said, and he stood there, crying. He was pretty white."

"What happened next?" Samuel said.

"I went directly into the house and saw—" Mozingo's voice broke for a moment "—my daughter on the floor in the blood. The blanket was up over her body and halfway over the pillow. I turned it back, removed the pillow, pulled the blanket up and replaced the pillow. There was blood on much of the floor, spread out around the head, and it had run south and east of the stove and as far as the oil stove. The oil stove had a tea kettle on it, over the east burner, which was still burning. The kettle was almost dry. There was a kettle with dough on the west end of the oil stove."

"Was it dough or starter[14]?" Samuel asked.

"I saw no *starter*," Mozingo said with impatience. "I saw bread dough. I *know* the difference between the two."

"Go on," Samuel said.

"I saw two stove lids on the floor. One was under the shoulder near her head, and the other was under Florence's left ankle. I turned around and noticed the north door was almost but not quite shut and not locked. I opened it and saw that the screen door was hooked on the inside."

"What was Mrs. Mozingo doing during this time?"

"She was very excited and was phoning people," Mozingo said. "Later, I went to the west part of the house. I saw the black mark on the white spread and the things on the floor."

"Did you see an empty razor box on the dresser?"

"I didn't notice. I am not sure what was on the dresser."

14 According to the K-State Research and Extension, *starter* is a form of yeast, typically made by combining flour and water, then exposing the mixture to air to attract wild yeasts, which then cause fermentation. The starter is then used to make bread dough. "You Asked It: Tips from the Rapid Response Center," *K-State Research and Extension Newsletter* 3, no. 2 (February 2005): 4.

Mozingo swallowed. "I didn't see that Florence's clothes were up until the Coroner's Jury[15] was there and the blanket was raised. That's also when I noticed the pieces of broken dishes on the floor."

"Mr. Mozingo, did you spend much time with your daughter and son-in-law?"

"We often visited back and forth with them. Their farm was on the same section as ours. They got along fine. I never heard of any trouble. John seemed a good, affectionate, and kind husband and was always considerate of Florence."

"Had their relationship changed over the years?"

"When they first married, they lived with John's parents for about a year. Then they lived east of Burlington. When they lived east, we still visited back and forth. I didn't notice any difference in his demeanor toward her then and no change in the whole nine years they were married."

---

15 The Coroner's Jury was called to officially declare the cause of death. Members of the Jury called in Florence Knoblock's case included George King, Sam Shoup, Joe Rolston, Fritz Koch, John Redmond, and Steven A. Grubb. *Daily Republican*, June 1, 1925.

File Type: Newspaper Clipping

The dwindling crowds are accounted for by the fact that the trial, as a spectacle, has changed. Last week, when the state lawyers and witnesses were depicting the defendant as a blood-thirsty, murderous scalawag, the good burgers of Burlington were ripping their vest buttons off to get inside and listen to the fun. This week, when lawyers for the defense are painting him as an honest, respectable, home-loving, church-going citizen, the audience may be sympathetic, but it certainly is bored.

"Knoblock on Stand : Murder Trial Defendant Tells Story To Jury," *Emporia Gazette*, January 21, 1926

Chapter Nineteen
Uncommonly Affectionate

Coffey County Courthouse
Burlington, Kansas
Wednesday, January 20, 1926

Bill White greeted the familiar faces lining the hallway as he approached the courtroom that Wednesday morning. An army could have moved into his hometown of Emporia overnight and occupied the town without firing a shot, Bill thought as the county sheriff, the city police chief, and the officer formerly in charge of the city's bloodhounds all sat on cold metal folding chairs in a hallway in Coffey County.

Leroy Hurt, the police chief of Emporia, was the first person called to the stand that Wednesday morning. His attempts to describe how the dogs behaved after sniffing the crime scene then trailing out the dining room door were so peppered with sustained objections that it was hard to sort out what was and wasn't allowed for the jury's consideration.

"Only Sheriff Crumley, Officer Wilson, and I were in the house when the dogs went into the bedroom at around four-fifteen," Hurt said. "The day was fair, and it had rained the night before or maybe that morning, which made ideal conditions for trailing. A dog can still trail a scent for ten to twelve hours after the fact. When the bloodhounds were about a quarter of a mile from the house, I saw the tracks."

*****

Frustrated with the judge's response to the testimony regarding the bloodhounds so far, the defense switched tactics, abandoning science and investigation for reason and sentiment. It was time to let the Mozingo women take the stand.

*****

Her husband had been right, Ella Mozingo Kellerman thought as she was recalled to the stand. There were still more questions to be asked, more of the story to tell. What would they want to know this time?

"Mrs. Kellerman, did you attend dinner at your parents' home the Sunday following the murder of Florence Knoblock?" W. C. Harris asked.

"Yes."

"Was Mrs. Jaggers there that day?"

"She didn't eat dinner with us, but she was there afterward," Ella said.

"Did she and John Knoblock talk about rewards and fingerprints?"

"No, they did not."

"Did she and your sister, Ruth Mozingo, discuss cleaning up the Knoblock's house?"

"No, they did not."

"Did you at any time, witness John Knoblock attempt to put his arms around Edna Mozingo?"

"No such thing happened."

"Did you call your mother the morning of May 30 to tell her that you had been trying to call Florence Knoblock that morning and couldn't reach her?"

"No, I did not."

"Did you attempt to call Florence Knoblock that morning?"

"No, I did not."

*****

"He called shortly after dinner that Saturday," Mrs. Mozingo, Florence Knoblock's mother, said. "At first, I couldn't recognize his voice until he said who it was. He said to come over. John and I went to their place at once."

"And how did John Knoblock appear?"

"He was white as he could be. He cried several times," Mrs. Mozingo said. "I've known John Knoblock for almost seventeen years. He and Florence married November 8, 1916. John was always kind and affectionate to her down to the time of her death."

*****

Before calling Ruth Mozingo to the stand, the defense read the deposition of Steven A. Grubb, taken while the former sheriff and current deputy sheriff was hospitalized in Emporia.

"I've known John Knoblock nearly all his life," Mr. Samuel said as he read Grubb's words, "and so far as I know, John's reputation was that of an honorable, upright, and moral citizen. I never heard anything against him until after the murder. I saw Dr. Gray wipe his bloody hands several times on the blanket while examining Mrs. Knoblock. I also heard Aunt Min suggest to John Knoblock that the murderer may have been Blackie Stevens."

*****

Bill White studied Edna and Ruth Mozingo with the discerning eye of an American male. The looked a great deal alike; pretty, he thought, average in height, slender without being skinny. Both were endowed with a feminized version of their father's prominent nose. While they were raised in the country, these were not naïve country milkmaids. Both Edna and Ruth had the polish and tasteful clothing that came from working in a city, and in fact, both women had been working in Topeka throughout the past year.

Ruth Mozingo would turn twenty-four that April. She had taught school for four years, spending her summers working in Topeka until she moved there permanently in 1924.

"Edna and I came down to Burlington with our uncle, Pete Jenkins, late that Saturday night," Ruth told the jury. "We had been in town for a little family reunion at my parents' house the week before Florence was killed."

"How did John and Florence seem then?" W. C. Harris said.

"The same as usual," Ruth said. "John and Florence never quarreled or had misunderstandings. He was always very kind and affectionate."

"Were you ever alone with John Knoblock?"

"No, I was not," Ruth said.

"Did you ever sit in his lap?"

"No!"

"Were you ever intimate with him in any way?" W. C. Harris said.

"No!" Ruth said. "Absolutely not!"

"Did you talk to John Knoblock about cleaning the house?"

"No, I did not."

"Did you ask him for the key to his house?"

"I asked him for the key, but we didn't discuss why I wanted it."

"Were you present when the house was cleaned?"

"I was there, along with my uncles George Smith and Pete Jenkins, Mr. and Mrs. Hursh, Mr. and Mrs. Haehn, and my sister Edna. I gathered up clothing. I didn't scrub any marks or move anything else. No one cleaned anything in the bedroom. The men were in the kitchen. Any cleaning that was done was by them."

Like her younger sister, Edna had also taught school, boarding with various community members during those years before moving to Topeka with Ruth in 1924.

"I saw John and Florence when I was home during the weekends when I was still teaching school," Edna said. "John always seemed to respect Florence and was kind and affectionate. I never saw unkindness, quarrels, or misunderstanding between them."

"Were you ever alone with John Knoblock?" Samuel said.

"No," Edna said, "except for when he drove me between my parents' home and his home or when he drove me into town."

"Were you physically intimate with him?"

"No."

"Did he ever attempt to kiss or hug you?"

"No."

"Did he attempt to put his arms around you in the dining room the Sunday after your sister was murdered?"

"No," Edna said. "That never happened."

*****

Aside from their client's testimony, which would be last, the defense was in its final afternoon of witnesses. Owen Samuel and W. C. Harris had carefully considered the order in which to call each witness. First, they would remind the jury that Blackie Stevens, another likely suspect, was seen by many witnesses around town. Then they would show that the bloodhounds led the police directly to the Negro. And last, Samuel and Harris wanted the jury to feel no qualms about Mr. Knoblock's goodness. That way, if the court continued to deny the evidence pertaining to the bloodhounds—and as far as Samuel and Harris were concerned, that in itself would practically be a crime—the jury could still count on Mr. Knoblock being too good of a man to do something as heinous as beat his wife with a stove lid and slash her throat with an old razor.

"I saw Blackie Stevens in the county jail on the first Wednesday of June. He looked like the Negro I saw walking by my home the Friday night before the murder," said Bert Johnson, a ranch hand who worked Warren Crandall's ranch south of Burlington. "I can't say for sure it was the same man, but I noticed that he walked a little crippled, and the man in the jail walked the same."

"We saw the Negro pass by the house around six that Friday night," said Mrs. Johnson, after she took her husband's place on the stand. "He looked and walked like the man in the jail."

"A Negro came in to the Crandall store just after six o'clock," Mrs. Clara Beall said. "Then he left and headed north."

"He had black button shoes, dark pants, a gray shirt, and a gray cap," said twelve-year-old Ivan Beall. "He bought candy and cookies."

"I saw the nigger walking with a limp in his right foot go by, wearing a light shirt, dark pants or overalls, and he wore a cap and carried a bundle," said Mrs. Matie Vick. "He headed east from here toward the main road to Burlington."

*****

Sheriff Samuel T. Crumley had only been sheriff of Lyon County for five short months when he received the call from his counterpart in Coffey County. "The phone call from Sheriff Frank Hunter came around two forty-five that Saturday afternoon," Crumley said. "We started for Burlington with the bloodhounds and arrived at about four-ten. We went into the house with Sheriff Hunter. George Wilson, the officer in charge of the bloodhounds, came into the house as well."

George Wilson was a tall and handsome man with striking blue eyes, a shock of black hair, and a kind face. He couldn't help but feel that he was on trial, that he was going to be asked not about what his dogs did but whether or not he had done things correctly. What would it mean, if the courts decided he had not? What about the other men he'd helped capture with the bloodhounds? Would they also be found innocent because of something he did wrong?

"I was a policeman in 1925," Wilson told the jury. "I was in charge of the city's bloodhounds beginning the first of April and had almost full charge."

"Had you ever worked with bloodhounds before?"

"No, I had not," Wilson said. "I tried to take them out for an hour or two each day. I had someone make a trail for them to scent."

"Were the dogs able to pick up the trail?"

"Always. And follow it."

"Objection!" said Fred Harris, for the state. "The defense has not proved these dogs competent!"

The judge tapped his fingers together for a moment. Men behind both tables stilled, waited.

"Sustained," the judge said finally. "The jury will disregard all testimony regarding the bloodhounds."

George Wilson walked away from the witness stand, feeling like a failure.

*****

Mrs. Emma Randolph had served the District Five courts[16] as a stenographer for more than two decades before retiring last year. She was the widow of a lawyer and was as comfortable in the courtroom as any lawyer or judge. To find herself on the witness stand was an unusual experience, however, and the sixty-year-old woman held her official notes tightly as she was sworn in.

"Mrs. Randolph, you were the stenographer who recorded Owen Samuel's interview of Stella Menard, correct?" W. C. Harris asked.

16 In 1925, District Five included Chase, Coffey, and Lyon Counties (see Revised Statutes of Kansas [Annotated] 1923). Today, Coffey County is part of District Four.

"Yes."

"And you served as the stenographer for John Knoblock's preliminary hearing, correct?"

"Yes."

"Could you please read back to us what Mrs. Stella Menard said regarding John Knoblock?"

"Mrs. Menard said, 'I think John Knoblock is wild.'"

"And could you please read Mrs. Menard's remarks with regards to the condition of the house?"

"Mrs. Menard said, 'I couldn't say whether there were any clothes on the floor in front of the dresser or not.' And later, she said, 'I didn't see blood on the kitchen floor.'"

*****

Orville Haehn was recalled to the stand. "One of the Mozingo girls called and said they were going to clean up the Knoblock house the day after the funeral and would appreciate some help. So we went."

"Did you see any signs that said not to disturb the house?" Samuel asked.

"There was some sort of sign on the bed and on the dresser, saying 'Do Not Molest' or 'Do Not Touch' or something to that effect. So we left the dresser and bed alone."

Orville's wife, Velma Haehn, also returned to the stand. "I did some sweeping at the house and helped Edna pack Florence's clothes. Neither Edna nor Ruth did any washing, and they didn't touch the bed."

"What were the men doing?" Samuel asked.

"All four men scrubbed the kitchen while I was upstairs. Young Johnnie Mozingo was out in the garden picking strawberries and cherries."

"Did you not see any signs asking that no one disturb the house?"

"I saw a sign on the bedstead, but not on the bed or in the kitchen."

"Why did you stop cleaning?"

"A phone call came to quit cleaning up, and so we stopped." Velma said.

Alfred Hursh, a neighbor of the Mozingos and the Knoblocks, was also at the Knoblock house the day after the funeral. "Johnnie Mozingo asked me and my wife to go over and help clean up. Young John was in the dining room, and the rest of us men swept and scrubbed the kitchen."

"Was anyone cleaning in the bedroom?" Samuel asked.

"I didn't see anyone cleaning the bedroom."

"Did you see any signs forbidding you to disturb the property?"

"There was a sign on the outside door and one on the bedroom. But like I said, none of us touched the bedroom that I saw," Alfred said.

"I don't recall seeing any signs," Alfred Hursh's wife, Elizabeth, said when she took the stand. "No one did anything in the bedroom or washed anything. The bedclothes were already off the bed when I looked in there."

Herman Peter Jenkins, known as Pete to his friends and family, was the only one of his siblings who never married and was quite comfortable in his bachelorhood in Topeka. That didn't mean that family wasn't important, and when his sister Mary Mozingo called and choked out that her daughter Florence had been murdered, he wasted no time driving his nieces Edna and Ruth back to Burlington that very night.

"Yes, I was at the dinner the Sunday after Florence's murder, but no, I didn't hear any conversation about the razor, and I didn't hear my sister Minnie talking to John about fingerprints and rewards and such," Pete said.

"Did you help clean the Knoblock house the Wednesday after the funeral?" Samuel asked.

"I was there. I drove into the yard about the same time as Orville and Velma Haehn."

"And what did you do?"

"I cleaned and scrubbed the kitchen floor."

"Did anyone clean in the bedroom?"

"No one did any washing or scrubbing in the bedroom. There was a sign saying not to disturb the marks on the bedspread or something like that. So I took the bedspread off, carefully folded it up with the sign inside, and put the spread in a drawer to keep it safe."

Young John—John Mozingo Jr.—was then called to the stand. The fifteen-year-old boy testified to being at the Knoblock house the Wednesday after the murder. "I didn't do any washing," he said. "I was outside picking strawberries and cherries, and I carried some boxes to the girls upstairs."

"Did you see anyone else cleaning?" Samuel asked.

"Only the men were cleaning in the kitchen," he said. "No one was in the bedroom that I saw."

"Did you see any signs around the house?"

Johnnie shrugged. "I saw some signs, but I don't remember what they said."

*****

Next W. W. Sanders Jr., a shoe salesman at the Kennedy Mercantile Co., was called to the stand. He attempted to testify that the shoes worn by Blackie Stevens matched up with the tracks found after Florence's murder, but all of the questions were objected to and all of the objections were sustained.

*****

W. C. Harris could see that the attention of both the jury and the crowd was waning. They were holding out to hear John Knoblock tell his story. But first, the defense sought to establish that John Knoblock had a good reputation and loved his wife. That Wednesday afternoon, Harris and Samuel bombarded the court with witnesses, respected citizens in all shapes and sizes, to testify to the goodness of John Knoblock and John's relationship with his wife.

"John and Florence lived with us the first year they were married," said Mary Knoblock, John's mother. "The seemed very happy and got along all right then and right up until Florence's death. John treated her kindly and with affection. I never heard of them having any misunderstanding."

"How did John seem after his wife's murder?" Samuel asked.

"He was crying," she said.

"I can't even find the words to express it," John's father, Charles Knoblock said. "John and Florence got along better and different from anyone else. They seemed very affectionate and to care only for each other."

"How did John seem after learning of his wife's murder?" Samuel asked.

"He was pale and nervous and deathlike in color," Charles said.

"I worked at the Knoblock farm for four weeks in 1923," said Lucy Isch. "He treated Florence all right and they seemed happy. I never heard any hard or harsh words. He seldom went away from home."

"I worked at the Knoblocks' quite a bit." It was Charles Goodrick's turn to take the stand while his wife, Dora, sat in the hallway. He looked at John, a man who, just a few short months ago, had been farming land to the east, his wife by his side. "John treated Florence with kindness and affection and never said anything out of the way. And John was quite a home boy."

"I've known John Knoblock practically all my life," said Dr. J. W. Thimes, a dentist in Burlington. "He is a peaceful, law-abiding citizen."

Orville Haehn's father, Jacob Haehn, was another highly respected longtime farmer of the county. He, too, testified to Knoblock's good reputation. So did Mrs. L. M. Grimsley, Knoblock's landlady; Amos Paxson, the Pleasant Township trustee; Mort and Pearl Sanders, farmers in the Pleasant

Township; Noble Nesbitt, the vice president of Peoples National Bank; M. A. Limbocker, president of Peoples National Bank; Henry Young of Star Township; Henry Hatch, another highly respected farmer in the Pleasant Township; Elvin Cleaveland, who had lived in the Pleasant Township since 1884; the former sheriff William Utesler; and Hayward Theobald, who had known Knoblock for eighteen years.

"So far as I could see," said Maude Theobald, another farm wife who had known the Knoblocks for fourteen years, "his treatment of Florence was kindly and affectionate."

File Type: E-mail

From: Sharan Hamman
To: Diana Staresinic-Deane
Date: April 24, 2008

Carol and I were interested when Mark told
us you had found a folder with clippings on
Knoblock's murder in the Emporia Library. For
some unknown reason this murder seems to
keep popping up in the last year. On May
26, 2007 I was talking to someone and that
person told me from out of the blue that
they knew who killed Florence Knoblock. The
person told me they wouldn't tell me who
it was because there were still distant
family members of the killer living in the
area. The person told me that this person's
parents knew who did it but never told so
this person would not tell either. The
person said it wasn't Florence's husband who
killed her it was a neighbor. This person's
parents had seen a man ride up on a horse
and tie it to the fence by the road. He
got off the horse and after a while they
saw him hurriedly get back on his horse
and ride off. It wasn't until they heard
that Florence was murdered that they knew
what they had witnessed. They said it was a
neighbor that had killed her. This person
also told me there was a footprint found but
I never remember hearing about that. This
is what I recall of the conversation. I
never thought someone would tell me 82 years
after Florence's death that they knew who
killed her.

Chapter Twenty
The Judge

National Hotel
Burlington, Kansas
Wednesday, January 20, 1926

Judge Isaac T. Richardson believed in democracy and the law almost as staunchly as he believed in God, but even he was ready for the Knoblock case to come to an end.

He missed his wife.

He was tired of living out of a hotel room.

And there were still forty-three cases left on the docket.

He was also tired of listening to the yammering of the former judge, W. C. Harris, a man who spent the better part of 1924 trying to get Richardson, then a probate judge, disbarred for alleged inappropriate conduct in the courtroom. What was most puzzling was that Owen Samuel continued to work with Harris, despite Harris' suggesting that Samuel was in on the alleged shenanigans.

Because this trial was proving to be the equivalent of a live theater performance in Burlington, he was also spending an inordinate amount of time coaching Coffey County's citizens on courtroom decorum. With the exception of John Knoblock's immediate family and John Redmond, the local newspaper man, he had strictly enforced the rule that all witnesses were to remain out in the hallway. Yet they frequently stood on their metal folding chairs, their faces and ears pressed against the glass in hopes of catching a glimpse of the goings-on in the trial. That is, Richardson thought with a snort, when the witnesses showed up. And then there was the constant shoving. He spent the better part of his lunch recess admonishing Elmer Ward, one of the spectators, for muscling his way through the crowd. Irritated that he'd go through the afternoon on an empty stomach, the judge ordered the sheriff to arrest anyone caught shoving.

But inappropriate behavior wasn't limited to the ignorant, thought Richardson as he changed into his pajamas. He ordered the attorneys for both the prosecution and the defense to surrender their newspapers, as the jurors could easily read the large headlines from their seats. Richardson had even had to tell Bill White, a man who was regularly assigned to cover trials, to get rid of his lunch.

The Supreme Court's decision last year to order a new trial for *State v. Scott*, another case in which a husband was accused of killing his wife, had proven to be a constant headache. While he agreed with the Supreme Court's decision—particularly with regard to throwing out the judge's orders to consider negative testimony about the defendant to have more weight than positive testimony—both the state and the defense used the precedent set by *State v. Scott* as a reason to object to almost every statement made by almost every witness. And he didn't even want to think about Owen Samuel's hundreds of offers to prove that his evidence was admissible every time Richardson sustained an objection made by the state.

After the trial had adjourned for the day, Richardson spent the better part of two hours dictating his instructions to the jury to May Larson, his stenographer. Even he, a man of the law, thought they were ridiculously lengthy, but another outcome of the Supreme Court's decision with regards to *State. v. Scott* was the decision that the judge had failed to give proper instructions to the jury. Richardson would not make that mistake.

Yes, Richardson thought as he settled in with a copy of that day's *Daily Republican*, he was ready for this trial to come to a close.

File Type: Author's Personal Notes
Subject: Telephone Party Lines

In his own testimony, John Knoblock said that
Florence would have gone to town with John but
chose to stay home when John asked if Roger
could go with him. Grandma Winchester, who
lived in George King's household, testified
to hearing Florence talking to the bakery.
If there were several households on the
same party line, then perhaps someone other
than Grandma Winchester could have heard
Florence telling the baker that John was
going to town that morning.

The fates were on my side at the Coffey
County Historical Museum. They only had one
phone book from before 1941, and that was a
directory from 1925. I copied every single
page of that little booklet, including the
instructions on how the party lines worked.
I looked up George King's number, since
I knew that was where Grandma Winchester
lived: 962.

The directory included instructions on how
the ringing codes for rural lines worked.
"The first figures designate the signal. The
last two figures, the line. Thus 10-34 would
mean the 10th signal on the 34 line." The
signals, it turned out, were a series of
long or short rings, almost like Morse code.

Now that I understood the line was 62, I
scanned every single page in the phone book
and made a list.

George King was at 962. E. J. King was at
862, R. C. King at 762. The Knoblocks were
at 2062. Someone named R. M. Livingston was
at 2362, W. W. Wood was at 1062, George
Albert, the Knoblock's neighbor to the east,
was at 1862. John Mozingo was at 662, and
C. E. Zink was at 2462. Three more numbers
were assigned to people in town, and 1262
was assigned to Sam Shoup. The Goodricks
were not listed in the book.

Chapter Twenty-One
Tracks

Coffey County Courthouse
Burlington, Kansas
Thursday, January 21, 1926

At last, George Eaton, the Kansas City man who brought the second set of bloodhounds to the Knoblock house after Florence's murder, was escorted to the stand.

"Mr. Eaton, could you please describe to us the qualifications of your dogs?" Samuel asked him.

"The dogs I brought here were Old Bess, my six-year-old bitch, and Tom, who is a young dog," Eaton said. "Bess is of genuine English strain and is an excellent dog with a record of many captures. Tom at that time had about six months of training and not much experience. But Bess, she's an extra-fine dog."

"Can bloodhounds scent a trail even if there are many people around?"

"If the dogs are given the proper scent—in this case, if the dogs got a good scent in the house—it wouldn't make any difference how many people had been in the field."

"Mr. Eaton, where did your dogs pick up the scent?" Samuel asked.

"We picked up where the Emporia dogs left off."

"Objection, your honor," Fred Harris said. "As the Emporia dogs were not proved competent to follow humans, the testimony pertaining to Eaton's dogs picking up where the Emporia dogs left off proves the dogs were not qualified as well."

The judge looked at all of the men standing and sitting at the two tables in front of him. "Objection sustained," the judge said.

"Mr. Eaton, did you see a razor in the bedroom the Sunday you visited the Knoblock house?"

"I saw a closed razor under the dresser," Eaton said. "I picked it up by the little end and gave it either to the county attorney or Sheriff Hunter."

*****

"Roger Knoblock was taken to my home the afternoon of the murder," said Maude Albert, the neighbor who lived just east of the Knoblock farm.

"Did Roger say anything about his mother that afternoon?" Samuel asked.

"He said he kissed his mamma good-bye that morning," Maude said.

"Objection! This line of questioning is wholly incompetent," Fred Harris said.

Judge Richardson took a deep breath. "Bailiffs, please take charge of the jury. Counselors, you will join me in my chambers."

Fred Harris, Joe Rolston, Ray Pierson, W. C. Harris, Owen Samuel, and A. H. Woodrow, the court reporter, fell in line behind Judge Richardson, who led the parade to his chambers.

"Woodrow, close the doors." The judge sat in the chair behind his desk. Once the others were settled, the judge said, "All right. Let's hear it."

Ray Pierson opened his mouth, but Owen Samuel beat him to the punch. "We are trying to present a vital piece of evidence," Samuel said. "Even though the boy is four years old—"

"And therefore not a competent witness," Fred Harris interjected.

"And possibly not a competent witness," Samuel agreed, "the statements made by the little boy to a competent witness are admissible as evidence. *Res gesta.*"

"Prosecutors?" The judge turned to the three men on the other side of the room.

"First, the testimony does not directly relate to the tragedy. Second, Maude Albert *asked* Roger Knoblock what had happened that morning. His statement was not a spontaneous one. It was drawn out of him. And little children can easily be confused when asked questions."

The judge leaned back in his chair. "There are very few Kansas decisions touching on the testimony of or pertaining to children." Richardson tapped his fingers together. "But in this case, I am inclined to agree with the prosecution. Objection sustained."

*****

Irritated but not yet defeated, Harris and Samuel temporarily set aside the issue of little Roger Knoblock to call several witnesses regarding the tracks found going to and from the Knoblock farmhouse.

"The closest tracks I saw were about three-quarters of a mile from the Knoblock home," W. W. Sanders Jr. said when he was recalled to the stand. "They were the ones I said fit with the Negro's shoes."

"Objection," Fred Harris said. "The defense has shown no connection between these tracks and the Knoblock murder."

"Sustained," Judge Richardson said.

Next, Thomas E. Hunt, another farmer living northwest of Burlington, was called to the stand. "I found footprints north of the catalpa grove and some near the toilet," Hunt said, referring to the outhouse.

"And how far is the toilet from the house?" Samuel asked.

"Forty or fifty steps."

"Were these the tracks the bloodhounds followed?"

"Objection," Fred Harris said.

"Sustained," the judge said. "The defense would be wise to remember that any reference to the Emporia hounds is inadmissible."

"Did you notice any other tracks?"

"I followed tracks from the depression to the catalpa grove toward the Knoblock house and then tracks away from the house to the depression. I examined them closely. I even put three stakes around the track near the toilet. I saw the same tracks down by the creek. But there, it looked like he crouched down and crawled in places. He must have, because a man standing up could be seen from two houses nearby."

"Mr. Hunt, how far would you say the tracks on the creek were from the Knoblock house?"

"Five miles or so," Hunt said. "They were the same as the tracks I saw by the depression and the catalpa grove."

Earl Griffin, another farmer, took the stand. "I was with Tom Hunt that Sunday," he said. "We both saw the footprints along Otter Creek, going down the creek."

"Could you tell which direction the tracks were going?"

"They were going away from the Knoblock house," Griffin said. "They looked like a man was crawling or stooping in places, which he'd have to do to stay out of sight."

Lou Volland hadn't been subpoenaed, but when Sheriff Hunter arrived with a request from the court to make an appearance, he didn't waste any time. "I was at the Knoblock place the day of the murder," Volland said. "I saw the tracks headed from the old house on George Albert's place to the creek and then to the Knoblock house. Then there were tracks going from the Knoblock house northeast toward the creek, where they kept going."

"Could someone making the tracks be seen?" asked Fred Harris.

"Yes, sir, in some places, a man could be seen for some distance."

*****

Dr. David Manson, the Knoblocks' family physician, returned to the stand. "I was the family physician when Roger was born," Dr. Manson said. "Mrs. Knoblock suffered from painful menstruation. I prescribed the gold instrument[17] to relieve the pain."

*****

Owen Samuel was ready to make a last-ditch effort to introduce little Roger Knoblock's testimony, but he needed to talk with John Knoblock first.

"John, I want to call Roger to the stand," Samuel said.

John Knoblock was dressed in his best clothes. He wore a blue suit, a light blue shirt, and a dark tie. His thick gray hair was starting to silver, making him look far older than his thirty-four years. His son, Roger, was sitting in his lap, playing with John's horn-rimmed glasses.

"He's just a little boy," John said, running his hand over Roger's hair.

"He may be your best chance," Samuel said.

John took his glasses back from his son and put them on. Roger looked up at his father with curiosity.

"Yes. Fine then."

Owen Samuel stood. "Your honor, the defense would like to call Roger Knoblock to the stand so that he may tell his story."

"Objection," Fred Harris said.

Judge Richardson looked at the little boy, sitting in his father's lap, clutching his father's tie. "Mr. Samuel, I appreciate

---

17 Likely an intracervical device made of gold (e-mail from Jennifer Nieves, archivist at Contraception History Museum at Case Western Reserve, May 6, 2009).

what you are trying to do for your client," he said, "but the possibility of an error in a case so important as this by a child so young and so timid as Roger has shown himself to be by his conduct in this trial—I'm sorry, but I won't allow it."

Out of the corner of his eye, Samuel saw John relax a bit. He was sure the judge saw it, too.

"Very well, then," Samuel said. "The defense calls John Knoblock to the stand."

File Type: Interview
Subject: Helen[18]
Date: July 2008

Helen: Why are you interested in the
Knoblocks?

Diana: I'm working on a book about the murder
of Florence Knoblock.

Helen: Are you related to the Knoblocks or
the Mozingos?

Diana: No, I've never knowingly met anyone
in either family, actually. The story just
sort of fell at my feet.

Helen: John Knoblock did not kill his wife.

Diana: Did you hear stories about the
Knoblocks growing up?

Helen: My grandmother said she knew he
didn't do it. [pause] My grandparents were
out working in the field that morning. They
saw a man ride his horse up to the house
and go inside. A while later, he left. My
grandparents didn't know Florence had been
murdered until the afternoon, when word was
out and the Knoblock's yard was full of
people.

Diana: Did your grandparents know who the
man was?

---

18 Not the interviewee's real name.

Helen: Yes. [pause] He was a neighbor.

Diana: Did they tell the sheriff?

Helen: This was a prominent man. My family was very scared of him. He had influence.

Diana: Did your grandmother tell you his name?

Helen: [pause] Yes. [pause] This man had been bothering Florence Knoblock for a while. My grandmother said Florence was very upset about him. He thought he was a real ladies' man, but she wasn't interested in him. Florence had asked my grandmother for advice on what to do about him at one point.

Diana: Did the police ever suspect him?

Helen: My grandmother said that the detective was on the right track, but after he left, the sheriff and the county stopped looking at him.

Diana: If your grandmother didn't want anyone to know she knew, why did she tell you? Why not take the secret to her grave?

Helen: [pause] My grandmother was going to tell after he died. But his son still lived in the area, and she didn't want to embarrass him. Then the son died, but the killer's grandson still lives in the area. She didn't want to ruin his life for something his grandfather did.

Diana: But why tell you, then?

Helen: She was afraid he was capable of doing it again, and she wanted me to steer clear of him. My grandmother said a lot of people suspected him back then, but no one wanted to cross his path. He had influence.

Diana: I don't suppose you'd tell me his name?

Helen: He died in the fifties. He lived in the neighborhood. And when he was young, he had a broken leg that never healed right, so he limped all his life.

Diana: Did he have a history of violence or issues with women?

Helen: He was sort of a—He thought he was a ladies' man, but he was a Dr. Jekyll/Mr. Hyde type. He could put on a good face, but he could turn into a monster.

Chapter Twenty-Two
Recollection: John Knoblock's Testimony

Coffey County Courthouse
Burlington, Kansas
Thursday, January 21, 1926
10:30 a.m.

I was born in Coffey County and lived here all my life. I will be thirty-five next month. I went to Fairfield Rural School and part of one year in Burlington High School.

I met Florence Mozingo in school. I went with her for about seven years before we got married. I never went with no other girl and she never went with no other man. We got married on November 8, 1916, in Ottawa. We had one child, Roger, who will be five years old on January 30.

When we first married, we spent one year on the Barker Ranch, where my folks were living. After that, we lived northeast of Burlington for two years, and we moved back to the old neighborhood, to the house where my wife was murdered.

On May 30 last year, I got up around six-thirty in the morning. My wife and Roger also got up around then. I milked three cows in the lot first thing. The red white-faced cow had a ten-day-old calf, and I only milked her occasionally to keep her bag from swelling. Roger came to the cow yard with a tin cup and I gave him a cup of milk. After I turned the cows out, I separated the milk. I took the cream to the house and the milk to the hogs.

Florence had been taking care of the little chickens while making breakfast. We had an incubator in the dining room with a hundred eggs in it. They began to hatch on Thursday and finished hatching on Friday evening. On Saturday morning, Florence brought in some chicks and put them in the old house. She asked me if I thought forty chicks would be too many for one hen. She had some dead chicks wrapped in a paper on the stove. She usually burned the dead chicks.

I ate breakfast, then went out to feed the hogs some corn and slop them. I came back to the house, and Florence cut my hair in the dining room in front of the table. I got my razor down from the shelf in the kitchen and shaved while Florence cut my boy's hair. I put the razor back after I finished shaving.

I turned the horses into the pasture and came back into the house to help Florence get the eggs ready for town. The eggs were in the cellar, and Florence went into the cellar ahead of me and we cleaned up the eggs.

Roger had dressed, except for a shirt and pants, and came down into the cellar, too.

While eating breakfast, he had asked if he could go to town with me. I told Florence that if it was all right with her for him to go, it would be no bother.

I had brought the car up to the house early that morning, maybe an hour and a half or two hours before Roger and I headed into town. The ground was muddy, and I brought the car up because it would be easier to load the car by the house.

I heard Florence talking on the phone. She had called the bakery and asked for my cousin Ray and asked if the lard had been ordered. She asked how much and then told Ray that I would be in to see him. She gave me a list of groceries to get.

We loaded the eggs into the car after bringing them upstairs and put strawberries and a can of cream in the car to take to my folks. I went inside to get ready to go to town. I changed out of my work suit and hung those overalls under the stairway. I put on a clean shirt and clean overalls. Florence had prepared Roger to go.

I kissed Florence good-bye.

Florence kissed Roger, and he climbed into the car. I went around to the other side and got in. Florence was standing in the doorway. She told us to hurry back. I said I would and made a funny face at her.

That was the last time I saw her.

We expected to get back early, so I left the gate open and drove out into the public highway. I made the first track on the highway. That was at about nine-fifteen.

The first people we saw were Skip Beatty and Mrs. Albert. They were in front of the Alberts' house. I believe I waved to them, and they waved back. Then we saw E. O. Grant in a lumber wagon with sideboards. We saw Chris and Rosa Knapp two or three miles east of our home and Bill Phillips just west of the Katy track. Elmer Anderson was in his farm yard and Cole's daughters were near the store.

The first place we stopped was at my folks' house. We left some eggs and strawberries with my mother. That was at about ten o'clock.

Then we went to Marvin Engle's produce house on the second block. Roger stayed in the car while I took in the cream. I did not sit in my car after stopping in front of Engle's. I got out and unloaded.

Then I went back to the car, collected the sprayer, and took it into the tin shop to be repaired. I was there maybe five minutes.

Roger went along with me when we went to the bakery, where we saw Lavon Stewart and my cousins Ray and Jake. I bought Roger an ice cream cone and talked to Ray about ordering a hundred pounds of lard and talked with Jake about cattle. Roger and I went back to Engle's to pick up the egg case and the cream can and the money we got for them, then we went back to the tin shop, where they were soldering the handle on my sprayer. We waited for them to put in the rivets, and I paid them.

We went into Burlington Hardware, which is George Crotty's place. George and my brother-in-law, John Kellerman, were both there. We weren't there long—about ten minutes—and then we went up the street a few doors to Smith's hardware to see about wire for Smith's end of the pasture fence. I agreed to put on the wire for three dollars, and he would furnish two spools of wire and staples. Roger and I went back to Crotty's place to see about some more wire, but they didn't have any in stock, so John Kellerman, Roger, and I went to Pioneer.

After the noon whistle blew, Roger and I went to Hoffmans' store, where we saw the meat cutter, Mr. Hoffmans, and Mr. Pollock. We bought things on Florence's list: two pounds of lard, tea, some meat, butter, and a sack of meal. We were there maybe ten or fifteen minutes.

We drove down the alley and stopped behind Smith's, where Henry Smith helped fix the wire in the car.

We went out to Third Street, then to Neosho Street, and drove out of town, heading home.

Our mailbox is at the crossroads by our house. We stopped there first, looking for mail. I'd forgotten it was a holiday.

We went home. It was about one o'clock. The gate was still open, and there weren't any new tire tracks. Roger honked the horn as we drove up to the house. I got out of the car right at the house steps and unloaded the cream can and the empty buckets. I didn't hear or see my wife.

I went to the other side of the car and got the groceries and set them down. I lifted Roger out of the car. I opened the screen door and went into the house with the groceries in the egg case.

I saw my wife lying on the floor, first thing after entering the kitchen. I dropped the groceries. Florence was lying there on the floor. My little boy must have seen her. She was lying there on the floor, her dress was up to her waist, and her feet were far apart. At first, I couldn't imagine what the matter was. I went to her and touched her on the arm. Then I saw the black pillow on her face. I picked up the pillow and saw her throat had been cut. I saw the blood on the floor.

I went to the bedroom and got the gun. I saw the dresser drawers were open, and there was clothing all over the floor in front of it. An old yellow shirt and some of Roger's clothes were on the floor. I noticed an empty razor box on top of the dresser.

I got the gun, put a shell in it, and took a hurried look around the house. Then I laid the gun on the table and called my wife's mother and told her to come at once but to be prepared for an awful shock. Then I phoned the sheriff.

Roger was standing by the door, crying.

I didn't want to leave my wife naked like she was. I saw the quilt, but I thought the blood would ruin it. Then I got the blanket and folded it once and laid it over her from her feet to partway over the pillow.

I went out to the east porch and waited until my in-laws arrived. They were the first ones there and asked what was the matter. I went into the house with them. My father-in-law went to Florence's body and picked up the pillow. He then raised the blanket and put the pillow back down over the blanket.

There was lots of blood. Blood all over, running against the base of the range, and a lot under the oil stove.

I think the Shoups came next, then the sheriff and the coroner. They came in. I don't remember what was said. More and more people kept coming from then on. I was in the dining room for a while. Roger laid down on the quilt. The sheriff did some phoning.

Dr. Gray and the county attorney, Ray Pierson, came and went into the dining room. Pierson made some remarks, and I turned around and went out of the room when they turned the blanket back.

The next thing I remember, I was outdoors, where Dr. Gray was telling people how it had been done. That her throat was cut and her head mashed in. I heard talk of men going around to search for the murderer. After that, I asked the sheriff if he didn't think we should have bloodhounds. The sheriff asked the coroner if the dogs from Emporia were any good.

What I remember happening next was the coroner's inquest.

Aunt Min had asked if I supposed that nigger murdered Florence. I thought maybe, as he had been there two weeks before and had visited the house before. See, there had been three workmen who boarded at our house when the bridge was being built about three years ago. Blackie sometimes came up, and we gave him apples and such. The next time I saw him was two weeks before Decoration Day, on a Friday. I thought I saw him in the morning, but he moved past the farm. When he came over that afternoon, he visited a while. He asked several times about when I went to town. I told him I generally went on Saturday afternoon, but when it rained, I sometimes went in the morning. He drove the disk one round then helped do some chores in the house. Florence fixed some strawberries for him, and Blackie ate while I shaved.

The night of my wife's murder, I stayed around the place until evening, talking with lots of different people. I was there when the undertaker, Eugene Stone, came. I think Mrs. Stone was with him. I only went into the kitchen when I was called.

The undertaker and Ella Kellerman and I went upstairs to get some cloths to mop up the kitchen floor. We went into the east room and got some rags out of a box in the closet. The west room belonged to Mrs. Grimsley, who owns the house. She stores some things in there. A pair of blue serge pants was lying on the floor in there. The undertaker went in there and looked. The pockets were turned wrong side out. No one picked them up.

Eugene Stone went upstairs again late in the evening to get some clothes to put Florence away in. My father-in-law and Ella Kellerman went with him. Then they went downstairs into the bedroom to get stockings and such.

After getting the clothes, I went back outdoors. There were still lots of people out there, and I talked to many of them. John

Kellerman asked me to get a tub. I got the tub from the cellarway and gave it to the undertaker.

John Kellerman told me the undertakers wanted to take Florence's body to town. Both Eugene Stone and Roy Jones were there. They wanted to take the body to town, because it would take a long time to prepare her body there in the kitchen. I told them to take her body to town.

I left home before sundown. I went looking for the sheriff and told him about Blackie. I couldn't find him, because he was out with the hounds. John Kellerman suggested we talk with the Deputy Sheriff Olinger instead.

We came to town. John Kellerman did some phoning. We were at the Crotty store for a while and got some flashlights and went back home. Bill Crotty was with us. It was quite late, but there were still a number of people there. We locked up the house—Orville Haehn, John Kellerman, and the minister and I. We locked everything except the kitchen and the dining room. We didn't go into the bedroom that night. But the house was locked so you couldn't get upstairs or into the west part of the house. The north kitchen door was unlocked when I found it; the first time I touched it was when I locked it that night.

After locking up the doors that night, we went to Hartford in Sam Shoup's car, because someone phoned that three Negroes had been arrested at Hartford. We went to Hartford to see if one of the Negroes was Blackie. We saw Bill Utesler and Sheriff Hunter there. I told Bill I was glad he was on the job.

We got gasoline and returned to Strawn,[19] getting there about one o'clock in the morning. We stopped and talked quite a while

19 The town of Strawn existed from 1872 to 1963, when much of the town was evacuated to make way for the John Redmond Reservoir, which would help control the dangerous floodwaters that regularly swept across Coffey County. Many of the buildings were moved or disassembled in order to reuse building materials. Many Strawn citizens moved to New Strawn, which was built along U.S. 75, just north of Burlington. Verla I. Keith, ed. *Strawn, Kansas USA, 1872–1963: 91 Years Worth Remembering*, 1969.

about the Kansas City bloodhounds. We got back to Burlington about three in the morning.

In Burlington, we went to several places. We were in front of the Nickel Plate Café and Williams boardinghouse, where we tried to persuade a man who owned an airplane to fly to Kansas City immediately and bring down the bloodhounds.

Later that morning, Ella said we needed to get some clothes for Roger. We went into the bedroom—John Kellerman, Sam Shoup, and Ella and I—to get the clothes for Roger. There was a pair of the boy's suspender overalls and a shirt on the floor. I picked them up and then saw the razor on the floor under them. All four of us were there. An old yellow shirt and some other clothes were on the floor in front of the dresser, about two feet in front and a little to the side. All four of us saw the razor. No one touched it.

We went outdoors and over to the Mozingos at about seven o'clock. If we got any breakfast, we got it there. We told about finding the razor.

From there, Sam Shoup, John Kellerman, Florence's uncle Pete Jenkins, and I all went to Osage City to see if they could find the Negroes. We went through Strawn and Lebo. Lebo hadn't heard anything. We went to Osage City and were there for twenty minutes or maybe half an hour. We went to Lyndon and stayed there about a half hour before heading back home. We didn't stop anywhere on the way back, just headed straight for the Mozingos' house, arriving at about one o'clock. We ate sandwiches and were there about an hour.

That evening, I went back to my house and found Bill Utesler, Clarance Williams, and Martie Bradford there. The house was unlocked. Bill was outside and some folks were inside. I have no idea who all had been in and out of there since I had left that morning. I saw the razor in the dining room. Martie Bradford came carrying it out between his fingers. Utesler had asked for some cotton, saying he wanted to wrap it up. That was the last I saw of it before the trial.

The funeral was held that first Tuesday in June.

I did not tell the sheriff how the murder was committed.

I don't remember telling the sheriff that it was up to him to figure out where the razor was.

I think I may have said it looked like Florence's body had been dragged across the floor.

I was at the courthouse when the Negro, Blackie, was there in the presence of the Burns Detective, Bill Utesler, T. H. Olinger, and Sheriff Hunter and Ray Pierson part of the time. I did not have a conversation with Blackie in the courthouse as told by Sheriff Hunter. I did speak to Blackie when I came in, but Blackie didn't ask why I thought he killed Florence, and I didn't say that I didn't think he killed her.

I didn't say that my wife was standing at the cabinet when she was hit, though she probably was.

There was no money on the dresser, but probably there were some beads in the tray Florence kept pins and such in.

I didn't say to anyone I hoped they'd catch Blackie and hang him.

I didn't say to anyone that I was glad I wasn't at the place when Florence was killed.

I did not say to anyone that there were blood stains on the pants. Yes, I took the pants and the matching coat from the house Sunday night about nine o'clock when I locked the house. I took them to my parents and the next day took them to the cleaners. That was my best suit, and the only one fit to wear to my wife's funeral.

I had never been intimate with Ruth Mozingo or any woman other than my wife. I did not tell Ed Tolbert that I had done so. I also did not tell Ed Tolbert anything about a rubber instrument to prevent having children, and I did not say I would rather kill Florence than to have her have a large family. I never even rode into town with Tolbert.

I never told Harry Pennock that I had my sisters-in-law sit on my lap and that I could do anything with them I wanted to.

I also never chased my wife around with a butcher knife. I'd never even seen Ralph Scott until this trial. I definitely didn't know him in 1918.

I did not try to put my arm around Edna Mozingo during dinner at her folks' home. I've never put my arms around any girl except Florence.

Ruth did ask me for the key to the house.

I was examined by Dr. McConnell in the county attorney's office.

I did not talk about fingerprints or rewards with Aunt Min.

From the time Florence and I married, we never had quarrels, difficulties, or animosities at any time. No man could love his wife more than I did mine.

*****

Everyone in the courtroom was silent, their heads turned to stare at the quirky, nervous man as he told his story.

"Mr. Knoblock," W. C. Harris said gently, "Did you kill your wife on May 30, 1925?"

"No, sir," Knoblock said emphatically. Then he put his face in his hands and sobbed.

File Type: Interview
Subject: Robert[20]
Date: July 9, 2008

John Knoblock. He was the man who killed
his wife, then tried to blame a colored man
for it, right? This is just hearsay, but I
heard that John Mozingo was a gambler and
in a lot of things he shouldn't have been,
and Knoblock had so much dirt on him that
Mozingo had no choice but to help him get
off.

—A current Coffey County citizen, during a
phone interview

---

20 Not the interviewee's real name.

Chapter Twenty-Three
Unhappy

Coffey County Courthouse
Burlington, Kansas
Thursday, January 21, 1926
5:10 p.m.

Ray Pierson looked around the courtroom in disgust. How could any of these people possibly be buying John Knoblock's story? Fortunately, the prosecution had devised a strategy for rebuttal. Knoblock could cry all he wanted to, but the final testimony the jury would hear would be in regards to the unhappiness of his late wife.

"I saw Mrs. Knoblock at the Ladies Aid meeting at the Winchester's in April," Dora Goodrick said when she returned to the stand. "She seemed despondent and appeared sad. At times, she had an awful sad look and at times seemed as happy as anyone else."

Mrs. Bender testified to seeing Florence Knoblock in town prior to her death by Garrett's grocery store. "I've known her for years," Mrs. Bender said. "She didn't look happy. She had a troubled look."

Maude Albert also testified to seeing Florence looking very unhappy at the Ladies Aid meeting at the Winchester's on April 30, 1925. "She looked so unhappy, like something else was on her mind."

Finally, the state called Grace Goodrick to the stand. The girl had been one of the last people to see Florence alive, as she and her dog had walked down the hill to the Knoblock farm to visit for an hour the Friday afternoon before Florence was murdered.

"She seemed like she was trying to be pleasant, but it seemed forced. As if she wasn't feeling well," Grace said.

The state rested.

File Type: Newspaper Clipping

There is an undercurrent of sentiment against convicting a man on purely circumstantial evidence, which was all the prosecution offered in this case, and Owen Samuel made a wonderful plea for mercy, based largely upon possibility of error in circumstantial evidence, and told them that it were better that 99 guilty men should escape than that one innocent man should be punished for a crime he did not commit.

"No Verdict Yet After 5 Hours," *Daily Republican*, January 23, 1926

Chapter Twenty-Four
Deliberation

Coffey County Courthouse
Burlington, Kansas
Friday, January 22, 1926

Charles Strickland and the eleven other jurors followed the bailiff, Levi Heddens, into the courtroom like a dozen ducklings trailing a mama duck. Strickland was used to sharing space, seeing as how he was the youngest of ten siblings, but even he was ready to go home after eleven straight nights of sharing a room with the bailiff and eleven other jurors.

Strickland took his seat, the eleventh juror's chair, after Judge Richardson walked into the courtroom and announced they could be seated. The courtroom was especially full today, as the judge had announced that everyone, including the witnesses, would be allowed to watch the closing statements from both sides. Strickland looked out at the room full of now-familiar faces and wondered if they had any better sense of John Knoblock's guilt or innocence than he did.

Judge Richardson pulled out a stack of typed papers and turned toward the jury. As he read his instructions, he was careful to make eye contact with each man, giving weight to every word.

"Gentleman of the jury, in presenting to you the instructions herein following, the court is impelled to admonish you to see that the majesty and purity of the law is vindicated," the judge said. "It may not be necessary for me to remind you that upon the honest and impartial and rigid enforcement of the laws of the land, depends the life of the citizens and proper enjoyment of all their rights. The certainty of punishment is one of the surest remedies for the prevention of crime. Without a just, rigid, and impartial enforcement of the laws of the land, none of these rights are secure."

Strickland was aware of his heart beating as the magnitude of judge's words settled over him. "The rights of the defendant," the judge continued, "are sacred to him and you are bound to be especially careful that an innocent man shall not be punished and disgraced, that no injustice be done to him, and that he may have the benefit of every reasonable doubt of that just presumption of innocence which the law not only mercifully but wisely and justly clothes and invests him."

Strickland glanced at his fellow jurors and saw that the sense of what they were being asked to do was washing over them, too. He looked out at John Knoblock's kin, wondered about them as they rallied around a man accused of killing their sister, daughter, mother, and niece.

"Instruction number one," the judge read, "the information in this case charges, that within Coffey County, Kansas, and on or about the 30th of May, 1925, the defendant, John Knoblock, then and there being, did then and there unlawfully, feloniously, willfully, deliberately, premeditatedly, and with malice aforethought, kill and murder one Florence Emma Knoblock, then and there being, by striking her in the head with instrument and instruments, or by cutting her throat with a sharp instrument, the names of said instruments and a more particular description of said instruments being unknown, which said instruments the said John Knoblock, the defendant, then and there, in his hand and hands had held."

As the judge read through each of the carefully worded twenty-three instructions, Strickland turned to study the accused. John Knoblock sat behind the defense's desk, wearing the same suit but a different shirt as he did while offering his own testimony. His little boy, Roger, sat in his lap. As the judge described the crime Knoblock was accused of committing, tears streamed down the broken man's face, and his little boy, who only saw that something was not right with his father, reached up to pat his face and give him comfort.

"It now becomes the duty of the Court to admonish you that all testimony regarding the Negro, Blackie Stevens, is stricken from the record and taken from your consideration," the judge said. "You are further admonished that during the progress of this trial considerable evidence has crept in to your hearing, from the witness stand and other sources, pertaining to the bloodhounds in connection with this tragedy. Concerning this, you are instructed that all testimony and all reference to bloodhounds is stricken from the record and removed from your consideration."

Strickland thought the lawyers—a whole herd of them, between Knoblock's men and the state's men—looked like they were chomping at the bit to get to their speeches. When the judge finished with his instructions, Joe Rolston began his final arguments as to why Strickland and the others should vote to take John Knoblock away from his little boy and lock him up for the rest of his life.

*****

John Redmond sat in his chair in the courtroom, watching the large crowd of John Knoblock's family, witnesses, and everyday people who muscled their way into the courtroom to hear Joe Rolston, Owen Samuel, W. C. Harris, and Fred Harris argue their sides. He gave the four men high marks for their oratory skills. Not a soul slipped out before the last word was spoken by Owen Samuel, and everyone was riveted, with the exception of little Roger Knoblock, who sat on his father's lap and spent quite a bit of time playing with his father's horn-rimmed spectacles, putting them on his little face and peering at the jury over them and generally amusing himself.

At six forty-eight that evening, the case went to the jury.

*****

Many who followed the trial and were present for the closing arguments expected the jury to come back with an acquittal that evening. Owen Samuel had closed his speech with several examples of injustice done by convictions on circumstantial evidence and made one of the strongest pleas for mercy ever heard in the Coffey County courthouse, bringing most of the courtroom, including several jurors, to tears.

Redmond, ever the newspaper man, had already written three stories with three different headlines, ready for wherever the jury would stand by press time on Saturday.

*****

John Knoblock remained at the courthouse, surrounded by family and friends. He instinctively tried to still his twitching hands but decided it no longer mattered. The jury would decide what the jury would decide now, whether he appeared nervous or not. It was all he could do not to scoop up his son and run out the door.

*****

Twelve solemn faces sat around the little jury room. The judge's instructions were reread, and Oliver Kelly was selected foreman. The first vote showed ten in favor of conviction, two in favor of acquittal. The jurors continued to discuss and argue until ten o'clock, when the bailiffs removed them to their sleeping quarters in the courthouse basement.

*****

Coffey County Courthouse
Burlington, Kansas
Saturday, January 23, 1926
9:00 a.m.

At nine o'clock on Saturday morning, the jurors were marched back to the little jury room. John Redmond had reclaimed his desk in the courtroom and made notes on his observations. The courtroom was nearly empty as compared to Friday, but John Knoblock was there, along with John Mozingo and several other family members, and friends stopped in throughout the day to visit with him.

It must have been terribly hard, especially for a man as nervous and fidgety as Knoblock, to wait around the courthouse for the jury's verdict, thought Redmond. When friends stopped in to cheer him up, Knoblock was visibly relaxed. When they left, he was visibly anxious, and put in the better part of an hour pecking at a typewriter just to give his hands something to do.

At half-past nine, the jury sent the judge a note requesting more information and clarification. The judge confirmed that yes, the evidence regarding tracks around the grove of catalpa trees was allowed for consideration, but no, he couldn't tell them whether John Knoblock gave his theory on how the murder happened before or after Dr. Gray did. They would have to determine that for themselves based on the evidence.

Saturday's *Daily Republican* ran with the main headline, "Knoblock Jurors Still Are Deliberating," and the subhead of "No Verdict Yet After Five Hours."

*****

The second and third votes showed eleven jurors were in favor of conviction, while Charles Strickland continued to hold out. With all of the testimony they'd heard from both the prosecution and the defense, there was only one piece of the puzzle the jurors continued to argue: did John Knoblock describe how he thought his wife was murdered before or after Dr. Gray announced how Florence Knoblock died? The general feeling was that a man who said he'd only touched his wife's arm before calling the sheriff wouldn't know if his wife, who was lying on her back, had been hit in the back of the head.

At the request of the judge, A. H. Woodrow made a hurried search through the testimony and found only two statements by witnesses fixing the time.

The sheriff said it was before the doctor arrived at two-thirty.

John Knoblock said it was after he heard it from the doctor.

The jury took another ballot. The vote was back to ten and two.

*****

At five o'clock that night, the jury was allowed a two-hour recess for their supper. John Redmond returned to the newspaper office, only to find that the word around town was that Knoblock had been acquitted.

"The jury is in recess right now," Redmond said. "Where is this rumor coming from?"

"From us, apparently," Maude Redmond said. "I followed it back to the source, and he said he saw the headline right here when he stopped in today."

John Redmond thought about the proof sets of each version of the story, depending on the outcome. He laughed and rubbed his eyes. "I suppose I should write about that in Monday's paper," he said.

*****

The fifth vote was also ten and two. During the sixth, Charles Strickland's was the only remaining vote for acquittal.

"We need to see the testimony regarding John Knoblock's statements about how his wife was killed," Oliver Kelly, the foreman, said. The other jurors agreed, and the request was put to the judge. At nine o'clock that night, the judge recessed them until Monday morning, with the orders that they were not to discuss the trial in any capacity until then.

*****

Coffey County Courthouse
Burlington, Kansas
Monday, January 25, 1926

John Knoblock returned to the courthouse Monday morning, along with Roger, his parents, and his in-laws. His stomach was upset, he hadn't slept, and he fought to keep his hands from twitching uncontrollably. Harris and Samuel advised him to look relaxed, but he thought that was easy for them to say as no matter what the outcome, they would be paid and would return to Emporia. They assured him there was still a good chance of an acquittal, but the rumors circulating in town weren't as comforting. They would appeal, Samuel told him, if the outcome was "unfavorable." *Unfavorable*, Knoblock thought. A word you might use to describe the weather when it rained too hard after a crop was planted, not a word used to describe being convicted of murdering your wife and then spending the rest of your days in jail while someone else raised your boy.

*****

John Redmond returned to the courtroom Monday morning to learn that the judge had delivered the requested testimony to the jury, and at ten o'clock, they resumed their deliberations. No further requests for testimony were made. At press time, the jury was still deadlocked. At ten minutes past eleven, the jurors reported that they had stopped discussing the evidence, and there didn't appear to be any chance of an agreement being reached.

Judge Richardson asked them to make another earnest effort at reaching a verdict.

*****

At one-forty in the afternoon, after eighteen votes, the jury returned to the courtroom. John Knoblock and his attorneys took their seats; the prosecution took theirs. Redmond could feel his skin prickle with the anxiety filling the room.

"What say you, jurors? Have you reached a verdict?"

Oliver Kelly stood. "We have, your honor," he said. "We, the jury empaneled in the above entitled cause, disagree."

File Type: E-mail

From: Floyd Decker, nephew of juror Frank
M. Decker
To: Diana Staresinic-Deane
Date: August 8, 2008

Floyd: I do remember that our family was a
little apprehensive during that time, that
a murder could be loose in the area, because
of the remote area where we lived. As I
recall, by the people I was talking with, it
generally was felt that John Knoblock was
the murderer.

Chapter Twenty-Five
Strategy

Coffey County Jail
Burlington, Kansas
Wednesday, January 27, 1926

John Knoblock's stomach twisted in knots as he sat on the cot in the little cell in the brick jail just outside the courthouse for the third time since his wife's murder. Sheriff Frank Hunter had hauled him in on Judge Richardson's orders. John's father-in-law had protested loudly and angrily, as the county still had Knoblock's bond money, but Hunter only shrugged and told Mozingo to call their attorneys and have it out with the judge.

"I've spoken with W. C. Harris, and he's arranging for your release." Mozingo spoke through the cell door bars to his son-in-law. "The judge had you picked up because he didn't think the original bond covered you until the next trial."

"They think I'm going to run," John said.

"No one thinks you're going to run," Mozingo said. "It's a technicality. You'll be out in no time. I promise."

*****

Daily Republican **office**
Burlington, Kansas
Friday, January 29, 1926

John Redmond looked up just in time to see Owen Samuel, Samuel's wife, and Samuel's two-year-old son step into the *Daily Republican* office. Redmond motioned for them to have a seat.

"We're just passing through town," Samuel said. "We're on our way to Joplin for a visit."

"What brings you by the *Republican*?"

"We've just filed a complaint at the courthouse on behalf of our client," Samuel said. He handed Redmond a copy of the complaint.

Redmond skimmed it over quickly and looked up at Samuel. "What did Ray Pierson have to say about this?"

Samuel grinned. "I appear to have missed him," he said. "It seems that he was on his way to Emporia just as we were on our way to Burlington."

Redmond reread the complaint. He reached for his paper and a pencil. "Would you care to make a statement for the paper regarding why you believe Blackie Stevens should be rearrested and tried for Florence Knoblock's murder?"

*****

Coffey County Courthouse
Burlington, Kansas
Saturday, February 13, 1926

Despite the anger churning his gut, Ray Pierson appeared calm as he filed a motion to dismiss the case against the Negro, Blackie Stevens. He was disgusted by the audacity of the two attorneys from Emporia and was determined to shut down their complaint at the hearing in front of Judge Rudrauff on Wednesday.

"I am moving to dismiss the action, because there is no reason to do otherwise," Pierson told Redmond for the paper. "Blackie was held in our jail for six weeks, and despite strenuous efforts, there was no evidence connecting him to Florence Knoblock's murder."

"But Ray," Redmond said, "Isn't it true that Harris and Samuel could proceed with the preliminary hearing without you?"

"I'm following the decision of the Kansas Supreme Court in the Pete Foley case, which you'll find in the 102nd Kansas reports on page 66," Pierson said. "The court held that the county attorney doesn't have to participate in a preliminary hearing, but if he does, he has full control and may dismiss the action. I'm exercising my ability to dismiss the action."

*****

Coffey County Courthouse
Burlington, Kansas
Wednesday, February 17, 1926

As Redmond wrote up Wednesday's piece on the Stevens case, he decided to stick to the facts: the hearing regarding the complaint against Blackie Stevens was postponed until next Wednesday. There was no reason to mention that Ray Pierson looked as if he might succumb to apoplexy when he learned the postponement was because Harris and Samuel, the instigators in the whole new mess involving Blackie Stevens, were too busy to make the trip to Burlington.

*****

Offices of Harris & Samuel
Emporia, Kansas
Tuesday, February 23, 1926

Owen Samuel and W. C. Harris formulated their strategy. In
the event they would not be able to move forward with a case
against Blackie Stevens, they needed to have an alternative plan
or plans in place. First, they would demand a change of venue.
Second, they would ask for a continuance. And if neither of
those options worked, Samuel and Harris would ensure that the
jury selection process was as painful and difficult as possible.

*****

Coffey County Courthouse
Burlington, Kansas
Wednesday, February 24, 1926

The hearing of the motion to dismiss the case against Blackie
Stevens was postponed until Friday, February 26. Owen Samuel
and W. C. Harris called Ray Pierson that morning to let him
know they were unable to make the trip to Burlington, because
it was raining hard in Emporia.

*****

Coffey County Courthouse
Burlington, Kansas
Friday, February 26, 1926

John Redmond wondered what stars had to align to finally
bring together Owen Samuel, W. C. Harris, Ray Pierson, and
Judge Rudrauff. John Knoblock and Mr. and Mrs. Mozingo
were present, along with a handful of friends and relatives, but
nothing as compared to Knoblock's trial last month.
    "The case against Blackie Stevens will be dismissed for lack
of evidence," Judge Rudrauff said.
    "We accept the motion," Owen Samuel said, "because we
are now filing a complaint on behalf of John Mozingo, accusing

Blackie Stevens of the murder of his daughter, Florence Knoblock."

"On what grounds?" Ray Pierson barked.

"Section 19-717. The prosecuting witness—that would be John Mozingo—may hire counsel to assist the county attorney—that would be you, Ray—and the county attorney—again, you—cannot dismiss the action over the objection of the associate counsel—that would be me—until his reasons are submitted in writing for objecting the dismissal."

Ray Pierson sputtered as Owen Samuel went on for fifteen minutes about the proposition. "However," Samuel said, "under the law, there is nothing for me to do but to dismiss the case if the county attorney—that's you, Ray—has the nerve to request it."

"Oh, I have the nerve to request it," Pierson said. Redmond thought Pierson's chest puffed a little as he said it.

"Very well, the case is dismissed," Judge Rudrauff said, and Samuel and Harris moved into the next phase of their strategy.

*****

Coffey County Courthouse
Burlington, Kansas
Tuesday, March 2, 1926

Redmond didn't think anyone was surprised when John Knoblock's attorneys filed a motion for a change of venue on his behalf. The petition, which was filed with Miss Jennie Caven, the clerk of the Coffey County district court, stated that Knoblock wanted his trial moved to either Lyon or Chase County to ensure an impartial jury could be found. The county attorney, however, said he would oppose the motion. This was also not a surprise.

*****

Daily Republican office
Burlington, Kansas
Monday, March 15, 1926

As John Redmond proofed Monday's edition of the *Daily Republican*, he wondered how many more column inches he would allow the paper to dedicate to legal documents pertaining to the Knoblock murder. Today "J. Knoblock Would Compare His Finger Prints With Murderer's—Asks Court Order to Get Prints" filled two entire columns on the first page. John Knoblock requested that not only his fingerprints be taken but also all of the evidence covered in fingerprints—the doorknob, a dresser drawer, and various articles of clothing, be available at the next trial with a fingerprint analysis completed.

Redmond wondered why John Knoblock was just now conceding to have his fingerprints taken. But even more, Redmond wondered why the sheriff's office hadn't arranged it a long time ago.

*****

Coffey County Courthouse
Burlington, Kansas
Thursday, March 18, 1926

"No new evidence has been submitted to show any prejudice against the defendant in Coffey County, and at the former trial, very few jurors said they had any prejudice or had formed any fixed opinions," Judge Richardson said during the hearing to consider a change of venue for John Knoblock's trial. "I mingled with the crowd during recesses during the last trial, and I found no bitterness or prejudice against the defendant. In fact, in general, people expressed a hope that he be given a fair trial and that justice, and no injustice, be done."

Richardson looked at each of the attorneys—Joe Rolston, Fred Harris, and Ray Pierson for the state, Owen Samuel and

W. C. Harris for the defense—and then at John Knoblock. "The publication of the evidence in the *Daily Republican* will accentuate the difficulty in getting a second jury in Coffey county, but it will be more difficult to secure a jury here or anywhere at this season because of farm conditions and because more people have undoubtedly formed opinions or come in contact with the case. But the fact remains, the case should be disposed of in the county of origin unless it should appear that a fair and impartial trial cannot be had."

In a glance, Richardson could see the parties involved were beginning to comprehend his decision: Ray Pierson attempting to not appear triumphant, John Knoblock clenching his hands so they wouldn't spasm, John Mozingo's shoulders slumping in defeat.

"In some cases, courts have found it necessary to call out the National Guards to protect defendants from the public, and yet still, a fair trial was held. The first trial was remarkably orderly, and the crowds seemed anxious to have a fair trial, showing no bias or prejudice or malice toward the defendant. However, should the process of securing a good, eminently fair jury prove difficult, there is still plenty of time to continue the hearing and grant a change of venue."

Richardson shuffled to the next piece of paper in the pile. "As for the list of items taken from the home. Where are these things now?"

"All of the articles mentioned that were not brought into the trial are still at the state penitentiary at Lansing," Fred Harris said. "All of these articles are available to the defense."

"We want to be informed as to when the defense goes to the Bureau of Identification to investigate these items so that we can be present," Joe Rolston said.

"Absolutely not," W. C. Harris said.

"Nor is it necessary for the state to be present," the judge agreed. "The defense is under no obligation to include the state in their investigation."

*****

Coffey County Courthouse
Burlington, Kansas
Tuesday, April 6, 1926

Their hopes of moving the trial to another county temporarily on hold, Samuel and Harris moved to the next phase of their strategy—delay the trial. On April 6, they filed a carefully worded application for continuance on the grounds that two key witnesses—the wayward coroner, J. O. Stone, and the showgirl, Mrs. Lavelle, who supposedly witnessed the conversation between Stone and Stella Menard—were both missing, and their testimony was key to the defense.

Two days later, Judge Richardson denied the motion.

*****

On Thursday, April 15, the first thirty-six men in the jury pool appeared for duty. John Knoblock's second trial was underway.

File Type: Newspaper Clipping

There must be some satisfaction to John Knoblock, under the circumstances, when the same persons signed a $25,000 bond three times, and especially when those who signed it include the father of the woman he is charged with murdering, and the names of others of her relatives and old neighbors.

"John Knoblock Placed In Jail Two Hours Wednesday Afternoon Quickly Gives New $25,000 Bond," *Daily Republican*, January 28, 1926

Chapter Twenty-Six
Commemoration

Goodrick Farm, seven miles west of Burlington, Kansas
Saturday, April 17, 1926

Dora Goodrick stood at the edge of her porch, allowing herself to be enveloped by the warmth of the sunshine and the scents of springtime. The fields were beginning to green, and wild buttercups and violets sprinkled color across the landscape. It was the kind of day that held promise, Dora thought, exactly the kind of day Florence Knoblock would have appreciated had she been alive to celebrate her thirty-second birthday.

The Knoblock farm—Dora couldn't think of it as anything else, despite the Knoblocks' having rented it from Mrs. Grimsley the entire time they lived there—sat empty, the fields left to grow back to a natural state once the last of the garden was harvested in the fall. She wondered if old Mrs. Grimsley would rent that house out again. She wondered if anyone would dare live there.

Dora believed in the wonders of God; she knew that such a beautiful day was certainly one of His making, and she knew there were mysteries in the way He moved through herself and others. Yet as much as she wanted to believe there was some higher purpose for Florence's passing, as much as she wanted to

believe there was some reason John Knoblock was being tried
for her murder when the man likely responsible didn't have a
worry in the world, she couldn't help but wish that God would
leave her a little sign to deepen her understanding.

"I'm ready, Mama," Grace said as she stepped through the
front door. Charles pulled the car up to the front steps, and the
two women climbed in to the Ford. This year, Dora and Grace
would commemorate Florence Knoblock's birthday by testifying
at John Knoblock's second trial.

File Type: Author's Notes
Subject: Visit to Knoblock Farm, Pleasant
Township, Coffey County, Kansas
Date: July 11, 2008

   Days earlier, I had been in touch with L.
J. Bahr, the current owner of the property
on which the Knoblock house stood. He was
only the second owner since the Knoblocks
lived there, having purchased the property
in 1990 from Chris and Dorothy Schif. "You're
more than welcome to go there," he said.
"There's not much to see. It was gutted and
turned into a hay barn a long time ago."
   "Is it safe to go inside?" I asked.
   "Well, it's unlocked. Take a look for
yourself," Bahr said.
   "Are there any other buildings there?" I
asked.
   "There used to be an old barn and a chicken
house, but they were both torn down a long
time ago," he said.
   "Do you think I'll need a letter of
consent or anything, in case anyone asks
why I'm poking around with a photographer?'
   "My daughter owns the house just across
the street to the east. I'll let her know,
just in case," Bahr chuckled. "Too bad
Dorothy Schif isn't around. She and her
husband owned the place before I did, and
she knew all kinds of history. But she died
a few years ago."
   A week later, Stephan Anderson-Story and
I pulled up to the gates that led to the old
house. Stephan was a college student, an art

major, and an amazing photographer, and I chose him both because he's good and because doing so allowed me to equally offend all of my professional photographer friends.

Despite the menacing sky, the place was beautiful. The grass was chest high, lush, and green, dappled with wild flowers. Cows had trampled down narrow paths around the house, which we followed, watching where we stepped the entire time.

"If I were a cow, I think I would be very happy here," I said, watching the wind ripple across the grass.

Up close, the house looked battered, older. The wood siding was bare to the grain. Vertical boards covered the windows, though the doors remained accessible and still wore their screens. We gingerly approached a door and peeked inside.

"It's stripped down to the studs," Stephan said.

The house had been gutted so thoroughly that not even the lathing remained. The floorboards were still there, running diagonally across the building, but many were loose or broken, and the rest were covered in hay and muck.

"I had hoped at least the walls would still be there," I said. "Color, wallpaper, something."

"Yeah, me too," Stephan said.

A few fat drops of rain splattered on my head. We both looked up. The rain stopped.

Stephan began to shoot pictures, and I walked around the building, amused to find hoofprints in front of the doors and windows. I stood in front of each doorway and noted I could clearly see both roads that passed by the farm. Had I been standing on either porch, I easily would have been visible to anyone passing on the street. Rosa Knapp certainly could have seen a man standing on the porch, as she had testified at both of John Knoblock's trials.

Joe Bahr said the chicken house and the barn were both to the north. Sharan Hamman, Florence's great-niece, sent me a photo from when the barn was still there, and I knew it was a good distance from the house. There also was an outhouse in 1925. The buildings were spaced out, but perhaps someone could have hidden behind them, walked around them, stayed out of sight.

According to the *Daily Republican*, the bloodhounds headed north, away from the house, and followed the creek northeast to Sam and Rose Shoup's farm, where they showed interest in a stack on the Shoup property. Along the way, they found a bloody stick, thought to be a piece of stove wood, and a bloody stone.

I studied the grass. Around the house, the grass would have been cut. But surely the field would have been left a meadow toward the creek. The grass would not have been chest-high on May 30, but it would have been very damp after a night of rain. Anyone walking through it would have been wet and muddy.

Even if Knoblock had killed his wife, I wondered, why would he run to the creek,

which was nearly a half-mile from the house,
and then to the Shoup property, whose border
was another three-quarters of a mile away?
If he had killed his wife before going to
town, that would mean that he left his son
on the property, possibly in the car, while
killing her and then leaving a trail and
blood more than a mile long before—what?—
walking back, getting in the car where his
son was waiting, and heading to town?

It just didn't seem plausible.

Chapter Twenty-Seven
Change of Venue

Coffey County Courthouse
Burlington, Kansas
Tuesday, April 20, 1926

The defense and the state examined one hundred and fifty-one jurors out of a potential pool of two hundred and twenty-five jurors.

Only six passed.

"Council, please approach the bench," Judge Richardson said, and Joe Rolston, Fred Harris, Ray Pierson, Owen Samuel, and W. C. Harris stepped forward.

"What do you think our chances are of securing a jury here in Coffey County?" the judge asked.

"Absolutely impossible," Owen Samuel said. "It is absolutely impossible to get a fair and impartial jury here at this time."

The judge nodded. "Your official statement, then?"

"Something like two hundred and twenty-five men had been called as jurors, and one hundred and fifty-one were actually examined, and only six sit in the box tentatively, against eighteen challenges. The defense believes that conditions in Coffey County are such that the minds of the people are made up and opinions formed so that a fair and impartial trial cannot be had. The defendant, therefore, renews his two applications for change of venue and asks the court to regard them as presented and to change the trial to Chase County."

"Is there a special reason for Chase County instead of Lyon County?" the judge asked.

"The *Emporia Gazette* also covered the trial, and it circulates throughout Lyon County," W. C. Harris said.

"But the *Gazette* is not delivered north of the Missouri Pacific line in Lyon County," Joe Rolston said.

"What say you?" the judge asked Rolston, Harris, and Pierson.

After a brief conference, Fred Harris said, "The attorneys for the state have considered the informal application for change of venue. They are extremely anxious to try the case in Coffey County, but under the showing the last four days, they can't conscientiously consider offering objections to the application. To continue here would unduly increase the expense on Coffey County, as it appears it will be impossible to secure a jury in this county."

Judge Richardson nodded.

"The court concurs in this conclusion that it is practically impossible to get a satisfactory jury here, and the change of venue is granted."

*****

Up until the moment Judge Richardson spoke the words, John Knoblock had lost all hope that anything would ever go his way again. Even now, he was almost afraid to believe it. He almost jumped when his father-in-law slapped a hand on his shoulder. A fair trial. He might have a chance.

File Type: Author's Dream Journal
Date: August 2008

    I sat at one of the large library tables
in the Coffey County Historical Museum.
The tables were pushed together to form a
large square. There were people behind me,
standing at my shoulders, but I couldn't
see who they were. The only other people I
could see clearly were an elderly man and
an elderly woman who sat on the other side
of the square of tables. They wore grim
expressions and did not speak. Their hands
rested on something brown on the table.
    As I sat there and watched, they pushed
the brown object halfway across the table.
I reached for what appeared to be an old
leather satchel, with monogrammed initials
stamped across the flap. I looked at the old
man and old woman curiously. The old man
inclined his head toward the bag, willing
me to open it.
    I could feel the faceless, nameless people
behind me leaning over as I opened the flap
and peered inside. I pulled out a clump of
red hair.

Chapter Twenty-Eight
Emporia

The city of Emporia was nestled between the Cottonwood and Neosho rivers in the center of Lyon County. Though it sat on the edge of the scenic Flint Hills, Emporia itself claimed only a handful of sled-worthy lumps of soil and a sense that the entire city sat on a flat plain that tilted slightly to the southwest, making the park overlooking the Neosho River behind the Kansas State Teachers College the highest point in the city.

Emporia offered a curious combination of the intellectual and the commercial without straying far from the county's agricultural roots. It was home to three institutes of higher education: Emporia Business College,[21] the College of Emporia,[22] and the recently renamed Kansas State Teachers College,[23] which was the first and most highly respected normal schools west of the Mississippi. The city's prime celebrity, William Allen White, was one of the most respected figures in Midwestern America and brought the likes of Teddy Roosevelt and Mrs. J. P. Morgan calling at his door. There was a YWCA, a YMCA, the state's

---

21 Now defunct.
22 Now defunct.
23 The Kansas State Normal school was founded in 1863. It was renamed Kansas State Teachers College in 1923, then Emporia Kansas State College in 1974, and received its current name, Emporia State University, in 1977.

oldest library, and thirty blocks of paved streets in town; Sixth Avenue, which stretched from the Coffey/Lyon border to the Lyon/Chase border, was also paved. The Santa Fe Railroad had recently completed a $100,000 passenger station that housed a hundred officers and employees, and the city's newest hotel, the $400,000 Broadview Hotel, graced the corner of Merchant and Sixth Avenue.

Just over twelve thousand people lived in Emporia, and another fourteen thousand were scattered around the county, living on farms and ranches and in little towns with populations of less than three hundred. It was from these outlying areas, especially those north of the Missouri Pacific railroad line, that the Court hoped to find enough qualified jurors to provide a fair trial for John Knoblock.

*****

Judge Richardson was happy to be back in his own town. It was a luxury, he realized, to be able to walk or drive just a few blocks to get to work, and he much preferred sleeping in his own bed than in a hotel room. The Lyon County Courthouse was located at the corner of Fourth Avenue and Commercial Street, a marvelous structure with a grand stone arch at the entrance and a large dome that stood above all of the other buildings on Commercial Street. Its only disagreeable feature was its location. A mere five hundred and thirteen feet separated the building from the railroad tracks, and only a dozen feet of sidewalk and a small patch of grass kept the building from sitting in the street. On warm days, the windows were opened and noise from the outside often drowned out the proceedings inside.

John Knoblock's trial would start in a little over a week, Judge Richardson thought as he sat on his own porch, taking in the neighborhood. Two more witnesses had gone missing, meaning that the state and the defense would have to do without the testimony of Blackie Stevens, the coroner J.O. Stone, the neighbor Carl Goodrick, and now the former court reporter, A. H. Woodrow.[24] Still, one hundred and four subpoenas had been served already, and Judge Richardson expected there would be more.

*****

John Redmond packed his bag and closed his typewriter into a case. Arrangements had been made with the phone companies in both Burlington and Emporia to ensure he was able to get the story back to Coffey County as promptly as possible. As he had printed in today's paper, if anyone had questions about legal language or the trial, they only needed to stop in to the newspaper office and Maude would relay the question to him when he checked in. John Redmond believed in transparency in government, even if the *Daily Republican*'s excellent coverage of the first trial was a primary reason John Knoblock's second trial was being held in another county.

*****

Lyon County Courthouse
Emporia, Kansas
Wednesday, May 5, 1926

Redmond had a way with words, but even he found it hard to describe the tension that flooded the Lyon County courtroom. A room full of stags fighting over the one doe of justice? Roosters clawing for charge of the coop? Whatever the case, Redmond thought, the crowd of attorneys were going to make the first trial look like a sham battle by comparison.

24 Woodrow left Emporia and moved to Iowa after being charged with stealing paper from Chase County while serving as a court reporter for the Fifth Judicial District. He denied stealing anything but admitted to owing more than $500 in bills ("May Dismiss Woodrow Case," *Daily Republican*, May 5, 1926).

The defense was not happy to learn the prosecution had picked up a new attorney. Lon McCarty, a former county attorney for Lyon County, was selected because of his familiarity with the folks in northern Lyon County, and it was thought that he might help expedite the jury selection process.

The case was called.

The state announced it was ready.

The defense announced it was ready.

"How do you plead?" Judge Richardson asked.

"Before the defendant pleads, we would like to object to the state's use of Fred Harris, Joe Rolston, and Lon McCarty in this trial," W. C. Harris said.

"On what grounds?"

"Chapter 19-702 says the county commissioners have no authority to hire outside attorneys to assist the county attorney," W. C. Harris said.

"Chapter 139 of the Session Laws of 1925 grants authorities to commissioners to hire help," Fred Harris said.

"Overruled," the judge told the defense.

"We move that the case be dismissed on the grounds that John Knoblock had twice been compelled to plea, had been tried once and a second trial started, and no new information has been presented," W. C. Harris said.

"The hung jury in January makes this trial necessary," Fred Harris said.

The judge sighed. "Overruled." He looked at the defense. "Are there any other motions you'd like to suggest?"

"No, your honor."

"Very well, how does the defense plea?"

"Not guilty, your honor."

*****

Lyon County Courthouse
Emporia, Kansas
Friday, May 7, 1926

Judge Richardson was convinced there were more cars lacking mufflers in Emporia than any other city in Kansas. Or possibly the United States. Or maybe even the entire Earth.

The judge rubbed his temples as Lyon County Sheriff Sam Crumley reported on his efforts to contact the additional sixty prospective jurors drawn just before nine o'clock the previous night. Ninety-four jurors had already been examined in the first two days of the trial, and the jury was not yet secured.

Another loud car drowned out the sheriff.

"Sheriff Crumley," the judge said, "Is there not a law about driving cars without mufflers down Commercial Street? Can't your men enforce it? The attorneys and the jurors have been shouting over the noise for two and a half days now."

"I'll assign an officer to it, but I can tell you, your next docket will be very full," Crumley said.

The sheriff's next words were drowned out by a passing train.

*****

After three days of watching the jury selection process, Bill White decided it had been worth his time purely out of amusement. The attorneys claimed they were devoting their questioning to "searching the minds" of prospective jurors, but many jurors demonstrated they didn't have a whole lot occupying their minds.

A ripple of laughter rolled through the crowd as a prospective juror, sleeping peacefully with his mouth wide open, began to snore. Judge Richardson excused him shortly thereafter.

"It cost me nine dollars to report to jury duty today," Carl Schroeder, an employee of Bradfield Oil said. "I get twelve dollars a day at work and only three as a prospective juror. And no, I don't think I can start out with the idea that Knoblock is innocent until the state proves him guilty."

Excused.

"But I think Knoblock is guilty," said W. L. Marsh, a man who wanted to get back to his chicken ranch and cow in Americus. Excused.

"The only thing preventing me from being a good juror is my bad hearing," W. L. Peterson said.

"Do you have problems with hearing in both ears?" Fred Harris asked.

"What?" Peterson said.

"Both ears?" Harris shouted.

"No, just the left," Peterson said. "What I don't understand is why we're expected to presume a man is innocent until he's proven guilty. A man wouldn't have been arrested in the first place unless he were guilty, right?" Excused.

"Maybe I'd convict a man for stealing watermelons on circumstantial evidence, but not for first degree murder," said G. Henry Anderson. Excused.

"Well, yes, of course I'd expect the defendant to prove he's innocent," said A. W. Walker. Excused.

"I couldn't convict a man of murder on circumstantial evidence," said George H. Moore. "If I did, I might send an innocent man to the penitentiary. I'd rather let a guilty man go free." Excused.

"But I'm too busy at home to serve on a jury," L. A. Pendergraft argued.

"You see those nine other men sitting in the jury box? They're in the same fix," the judge said. "Have a seat."

Jack Davis' name was called, but the man was nowhere to be found. "Sheriff, locate Jack Davis," the judge ordered.

F. C. Betts made the journey from Allen to answer the jury summons, only to discover the court had intended to summon Walter H. Betts, a repairman from Admire.

Betts broke out in a smile and turned toward the door.

"Mr. Betts, since you're already here, please have a seat," the judge said.

Betts stopped smiling.

"I think it's wrong to convict on circumstantial evidence," said Charles Cowden.

Excused.

After another half-dozen men were excused for their inability to accept circumstantial evidence as grounds for conviction, one of the bailiffs caught the judge's attention.

"One of the excused jurors went outside and told the other prospective jurors that if they just explain they don't like circumstantial evidence, they won't have to serve."

Bill White thought Judge Richardson looked like he was going to walk out of the courtroom and beat on someone with his gavel.

"I see," Judge Richardson said, through slightly gritted teeth. "From now on, jurors who have been excused will sit in the courtroom and wait until we dismiss them all."

*****

John Knoblock sat in the courtroom, surrounded by his in-laws and his parents. He was especially glad to have his mother and mother-in-law nearby. He knew his father and father-in-law would fight for him, but Mrs. Knoblock and Mrs. Mozingo brought comfort, and after watching all six attorneys sort through the odd bunch of men who would judge him, he needed comfort.

John looked at Mary Mozingo, studied the deep lines that creased her face. She looked so tired, he thought. So did his own mother. All of the lawyers, his and even Fred Harris and the others for the state, had tried to make the questioning less harsh. Instead of saying *murdered* or *killed*, they said *tragedy happened* or *crime was committed*. Owen Samuel said that they did that for the whole family, out of respect, but he knew, deep down, they did it for the mothers. John figured even lawyers had mothers.

Friday turned into Saturday, with the constant rain and the rumble of the trains making the transition from one day to the next almost seamless. Sometimes John focused and paid attention to what the jurors were saying. Sometimes he wanted to laugh. Sometimes he feared for his life when he heard their answers. And sometimes, he didn't feel much of anything at all. But then he looked at his mother and his mother-in-law and saw that they felt everything. Yet there they were, trying to comfort him.

*****

Thirty-one more names were drawn for jury duty. Judge Richardson was beginning to wonder if the jury selection process would last longer than the trial. His back ached and he was tired of sitting on the bench. He gave in to the urge to get up and walk around before the pain overwhelmed his concentration on the matters at hand. He was beginning to think it wasn't so wonderful to be back on his home turf.

He was also quite annoyed with the college students—both from the College of Emporia and the Kansas State Teachers College—who treated the courtroom like a zoo or a sporting event. One young man wore white knickers, a loud sweater, and golf hose to match.

*****

"But I'm a citizen of Canada," said Paul Pykiet of Bushong. Excused.

"Irwin Sietz isn't here," the bailiff said, and the judge ordered the sheriff to seek him out.

"I've read everything I could find about the case," said Harry J. Taylor of Admire.

"But do you have an opinion?" asked Fred Harris.

"Oh, yes," Taylor said. "Want to hear it?"

Excused.

"I don't want to serve on the jury," said Matt Reid, a forty-five-year-old farmhand living near Allen.

"It doesn't work that way," said Fred Harris.

"But I don't understand what any of these court terms mean," Reid said.

Excused.

"I don't believe in circumstantial evidence," said William Nichols of Bushong.

Excused.

L. D. Gibson, a well-dressed young farmer from Admire, was next. "I have an opinion."

Joe Rolston sighed. "How long have you had that opinion?"

"I formed my opinion on circumstantial evidence," Gibson said.

Excused.

Glenn Hunter, another young farmer from Admire, went for a triple excuse. "I have an opinion, I don't believe in circumstantial evidence, and my wife's brother is related to a witness."

Excused.

The sheriff returned, escorting Jack Davis, the first of the wayward jurors, into the courtroom.

"But I have cattle to care for," Davis said.

"Do you know of any reason you shouldn't serve on the jury?" the judge asked Davis.

"Yes, sir, I don't like it."

"There are eleven more men just like you," Judge Richardson said. The judge looked up at the attorneys. "We'll pass him."

The sky grew dark, and the attorneys examined Louis W. Davis, their last prospective juror of the evening. Before he could answer his first question, the air filled with the booming sounds of guns and the dark sky flashed with the lightning of artillery.

Several men dropped for cover.

Judge Richardson yelled for the sheriff to find out why a full-scale war was breaking out at the corner of Fourth and Commercial.

The sheriff, exasperated, returned a few minutes later. "The American Legion men are advertising the show 'Who Won the War.'"

Before court adjourned, the judge called the bailiffs aside. "Please," Judge Richardson said, "tomorrow morning, take the eleven men already selected for the jury to the YMCA to bathe."

*****

On Monday morning, eleven more men were summoned to jury duty. Some of them had been previously excused. All eleven were examined. Before using their last peremptory challenge to remove L. O. Hodgson from the jury, Harris and Samuel conferred with John Knoblock and his family outside the courtroom for ten minutes.

At last, a jury was assembled.

S. C. White and Arthur Kirkland were from Bushong.

A. Q. Thornbrugh was a farmer and carpenter from Miller.

Robert Castle and Earl Stonebraker lived in Admire.

Edward Haas was from Allen.

O. B. Rhudy was a farmer living in Allen.

James Heironymous was a farmer living near Admire.

H. K. Gage lived in Reading.

W. C. Showalter was a painter and decorator in Bushong.

J. R. Bennett was from Miller.

John Mundy was from the Waterloo Township.

*****

At two-twenty that Monday afternoon, prosecutor Fred Harris began his opening remarks.

File Type: Interview/Psychic Reading
Subject: C. J. Sellers, psychic
Date: September 12, 2008

Author's Note: Almost nothing about this
murder is easily available on the Internet.
The only information C. J. Sellers requested
was the victim's name, and she did not even
ask how it was spelled.

C. J.: I have to tell you, my experience
with communicating with murder victims is
that they won't tell you things that can't
be verified somehow.

Diana: I'd just like to know if I'm on the
right track.

C. J.: I'm getting a sense of a pattern.
This person walks through an alley way or
a passage, singing or humming. I can hear
laughter coming out of the store. I get the
sense that he passes by here regularly and
often. I'm getting images of the murder
scene. I'm seeing . . . she had an admirer.
Someone who showed up on her doorstep. He
tricked her into getting past the door.
Like he made her think he was someone else.

[pause]

C. J.: Somewhere in this, a man whose name
starts with "D" fits in, but he's not the
murderer. It's a weird name. Not a normal
name, like David or Daniel. I'm seeing a

wooden handle of some sort. Not like a hammer, but similar.

[pause]

C. J.: He had no remorse. He was sociopathic. They're telling me that he was married and just went on with his life, walking the same paths over and over again. He never looked back and never paid for what he did.

[pause]

C. J.: The word I keep getting is *monster*.

Author's Note: Could the D stand for "Deacon," Blackie's other nickname? Could the handle be the handle to the iron stove lid (often wood)?

Chapter Twenty-Nine
Encore

Lyon County Courthouse
Emporia, Kansas
Tuesday, May 11, 1926

John Redmond looked around the courtroom and drew a conclusion. The testimony was the same. It was the people who were different.

If the people in this courtroom were a fair representation of Lyon County, then Lyon County—and Emporia especially—was full of disrespectful people who didn't care that a man's life was on the line. Or that a little boy could end up an orphan.

It took all of Redmond's concentration not to stare at the college students, who acted as if they were watching a show. Most of the college kids were inappropriately dressed for court, the girls wearing flapper dresses in broad daylight, the boys dressing in golf pants and sweaters. And they were rude, especially those kids from the College of Emporia.

Any man on the stand deserved to get a fair trial, and even John Redmond could admit that Knoblock was not able to get a fair trial in Burlington. He didn't think it was because most people inherently thought John Knoblock was innocent or guilty, but because the outcome of the trial was too important. Everyone in Coffey County wanted justice for John Knoblock. But what they wanted more was the peace of mind only a conviction could bring. If Knoblock walked, even if Knoblock really were innocent, it still meant there was a killer out there—a man so deviant, he would slaughter a woman in broad daylight.

Redmond sighed and looked out the window to the gray, misty day. It was best for Knoblock to have an impartial jury. But was it right to be surrounded by all of these indifferent people?

*****

Looking at the crowd of college kids scattered around the courtroom, Judge Richardson remembered exactly why he left teaching to read the law. They sat around the room, slipping in during the recesses after their own classes were done for the day, behaving in a disruptive manner, and dropping wads of chewing gum on the floor. After he dismissed the jury for their dinner at a quarter of two, he used an old teacher's trick and sat quietly, making eye contact with every college student—especially the ones from the College of Emporia—until the room was silent and everyone was paying attention to him.

"We have important business here," the judge said, his authority all the more potent as he spoke quietly. "This is a murder trial, not a movie or a vaudeville show. A man is on trial for his life, or at least for a crime for which conviction would mean life in the penitentiary. With this trial, the state of Kansas is attempting to ascertain who committed the crime."

Judge Richardson stared at a pair of young women who promptly stopped whispering when they realized they were under scrutiny.

"A rustle of a piece of paper or the squeak of a seat may detract a juror's attention and make a vast difference in his interpretation of evidence."

The room grew still.

"Persons who wish to hear the trial must be in the room at five forty-five in the morning and one-fifteen in the afternoon and stay until intermission. If you are sick and must leave, certainly we won't stop you. But if you are sick and you feel that you can't sit through the trial until an intermission, please do not come."

Someone sneezed and everyone turned to stare at the culprit.

"We are not making these rules just because we can," the judge said, "but because it is for the best interests of the case."

*****

Lyon County Courthouse
Emporia, Kansas
Wednesday, May 12, 1926

After spending two weeks in Burlington to cover the first trial, Bill White was impressed and not a little surprised by how rapidly the second trial was proceeding. The prosecution was nearly finished with its witnesses. At that rate, the testimony might conclude before the week was out.

Despite the seriousness of the occasion, Bill White could still see the humor in some of the courtroom's realities. John Redmond, his gray-haired counterpart from the Burlington paper, had gawked at the coeds as they took their seats. "This is the biggest array of flappers I ever saw in a courthouse," Redmond had said. Looking around the courtroom, one could spot the native Emporians, as they were the only ones *not* gawking at the coeds, being used to seeing scores of college girls stepping off their campuses on any given day. Bill White was surprised the jurors, mostly young, virile men from the countryside in the northern part of the county, were able to focus with so much femininity in the room. But one look at those ragged faces, squinty eyes, and unbuttoned collars proved that the men were taking jury duty seriously.

Bill White was also amused to know the judge had had it out with the mayor regarding the traffic noise. The mayor had told the judge the city would not pay to put a police officer on the street to stop every noisy vehicle that tried to pass by the courthouse. "You're welcome to appoint a special bailiff," the mayor had said, "but it will be on Coffey County's dime." The judge had determined that would be a dime well spent and appointed a bailiff to arrest anyone with a noisy automobile.

*****

Redmond didn't bother to record every word spoken during the trial as it was much like the previous trial, only more organized. Both the state and defense had a better sense of what would and wouldn't work and had reconfigured their arguments accordingly. Stella Menard's testimony was cut short; Ed Tolbert's story lost some of its punch outside of Burlington. Only a handful of new witnesses had been introduced. Charles Kimball, a man who had known John Knoblock since childhood, claimed to witness Knoblock's statement to the sheriff regarding the possibility that Blackie Stevens was the killer.

Changing tactics from the previous trial, the state introduced a previously unmentioned fingerprint expert named Fred Howard, a police officer from Independence, Kansas, who testified that he couldn't find any usable fingerprints at the murder site. Redmond wondered if the state switched to this line of argument to plant in the jurors' minds the notion that just maybe those unreadable prints really were John Knoblock's, which was a much stronger argument than confessing that the prints they had weren't his.

The state rested at four-ten that evening.

*****

Lyon County Courthouse
Emporia, Kansas
Thursday, May 13, 1926

The bailiff who was supposed to ticket noisy cars had left his post.

"Is there no relief from this noise?" Owen Samuel asked.

"When I was a judge," W. C. Harris said, the words edged with a jab toward the judge who had displaced him, "I once had an offender hauled into the courtroom. He was never a problem again."

Judge Richardson called the sheriff, who called Charles O'Brien and assigned him the task of arresting anyone who violated the noise ordinance.

*****

Little Roger Knoblock, now five years old, reached up to take his Aunt Ella's hand. He followed her to the witness stand, where she picked him up and held him before the court.

"Your honor," Owen Samuel said, "we would like to submit Roger's testimony. Not under oath, but we feel his story needs to be told."

The attorneys began to argue, and the little boy turned his face into Ella Kellerman's neck, pressing himself close to block out the words.

"He is too young," Fred Harris said for the state. "He couldn't possibly understand the nature of an oath."

Judge Richardson looked at the shy little boy with his faced buried at his aunt's collar. "In such an important proceeding," he said gently, "I cannot permit a child so young to testify."

Ella Kellerman whispered into the little boy's ear, stroked his back. His head came up as she took him back to his father, who gave him a piece of paper and a pencil.

Roger scribbled for a little while, then turned in his father's arms and fell asleep.

*****

File Type: Author's Dream Journal
Date: October 2008

    I stood in a field. It was nighttime, but
the moon was bright and my surroundings
were visible, albeit bathed in a silvery
light. I was standing on the Knoblock farm,
though it no longer looked like the farm I
had seen in person. I was near the bottom of
the hill, close to Otter Creek, looking up
at the house. I could see cows and a chicken
coop, a barn, and an outhouse.
    I suddenly realized I was standing behind
a man wearing a plaid shirt. The moonlight
glinted off of his hair. Was it gray? White?
Blond? And I realized he was staring at the
house.

Chapter Thirty
Will the Bloodhounds Save Him?

Throughout the early days of May, a photograph distributed by the Newspaper Enterprise Association was printed in newspapers across the country. A decent-looking fellow wearing a dark suit, white shirt, and light-colored tie held a young boy on his knee. The headlines varied, but whether the story was run in Michigan's *Ironwood Daily Globe* or the *Iowa City Press Republican*, Indiana's *Logansport Pharos Tribune* or Maryland's *Morning Herald*, each story asked the same question: Will testimony about the bloodhounds save John Knoblock?

*****

Lyon County Courthouse
Emporia, Kansas
Friday, May 14, 1926

Owen Samuel was convinced that the confusion over the evidence regarding the bloodhounds was the biggest reason the jury in the first trial was swayed against John Knoblock. Samuel knew Fred Harris would say that the state successfully argued that the Emporia bloodhounds were not qualified trailers, but

Samuel preferred to believe that the defense had simply failed to prove that they were.

The state didn't have much of a case against John Knoblock. But Samuel also knew it would be better if the defense could make John Knoblock look more innocent. W. C. Harris and Ray Pierson had made the trip to Lexington, Kentucky in March to take the depositions of the kennel owners who sold Emporia the bloodhounds. Much to Harris's delight, the owner of Rookwood Kennels was a man by the name of Captain Volney G. Mullikin, a Spanish American War veteran who began working with bloodhounds when he was a chief of police. Mullikin and his dogs were renowned, credited with the capture of over a thousand lawbreakers and the discovery of countless missing persons. Proving the Emporia dogs came from such breeding and training just might tip the scales in their favor.

*****

At four forty-five that evening, Judge Richardson dismissed the jury at the request of the prosecutor, Fred Harris, who thought it best to have the judge rule on the competency of the evidence before confusing the jury with more information.

W. C. Harris and Ray Pierson had taken depositions for two people—Captain Mullikin and Mrs. Louise McSpirritt, his bookkeeper and stenographer.

"King Rustler and Queen Rosalind were sold by Rookwood Kennels to the City of Emporia police department," W. C. Harris read. "The city paid one hundred dollars for King Rustler and two hundred dollars for Queen Rosalind."

Harris went on to outline the ancestry of the dogs, their training, their condition, and their ability in trailing criminals. "Captain Mullikan said he had trained Rustler for a year in the way all bloodhounds are trained and vouched for the hound's reliability. He said he had used him in one case, and the criminal had been apprehended. Mullikin testified he had only had Rosalind for four weeks, but she had come to him as an apparently trained dog."

Ray Pierson then began to discuss his cross-examination. "The trainer said he could only swear to the ability of the dogs when they left him and that 'they might have lost their noses after they left.' He also testified that even a person inexperienced in handling bloodhounds could put them on a trail and work them satisfactorily. However, a 'green' handler could also ruin a good dog. Mullikin testified the conditions in the Knoblock case were favorable to trailing. He said the rain the day before the tragedy, which had left the ground damp and moist, would assist the dogs, as moist ground held a scent longer than dry ground."

Pierson turned to the next page. "Mullikin testified that the dogs must have been satisfactory to Emporia, because no complaint had been received from the police. I then asked if he had heard from anyone regarding the dogs, and Mullikin admitted having received a letter from someone in Emporia asking about the qualifications of the dogs, but he said he did not remember who it was from and he did not answer it."

After the depositions were read, George Wilson, the former police officer who had been in charge of the dogs in 1925, was called to the stand.

"I worked the dogs in the north part of town on trails made by people who would drop something, like a handkerchief or a coat or a pair of gloves, and then walk or run a distance," Wilson said.

"How old was the oldest trail the dogs followed?" Samuel asked.

"About three hours," Wilson said.

"Did you have any previous experience with bloodhounds, Mr. Wilson?" asked Ray Pierson.

"No, not before April of 1925."

"During your training with the dogs, did you attempt to cross trails or use multiple people to work the dogs?"

"No, because we worked in public places, where there were already plenty of scents."

"Did you have good luck with the dogs?"

"Well," George Wilson said, running his hand through his dark hair. "I had better luck working with just one dog, instead of both."

"Were you successful on any cases with both dogs?" Pierson asked.

"Some," Wilson said.

"But were you unsuccessful in others?" Pierson said, pressing.

"Yes," Wilson admitted.

"After the dogs had been taken to the Knoblock farm and into the bedroom, they followed a trail out of the house, lost it several times, and then finally lost it all together," Wilson said. "The officers found some more tracks about a half-mile away from where the dogs lost the trail, and I took the dogs over there to pick it up again."

Having heard all of the testimony, the judge sat back in his chair and considered the testimony.

Six attorneys leaned forward, afraid to blink.

"The defense has failed to prove the Emporia bloodhounds and the Emporia handler competent and qualified. As the Kansas City bloodhounds established their trail based on the work of the Emporia bloodhounds, the Kansas City bloodhounds are also not qualified. As the bloodhounds are the only solid connection between the murder of Florence Knoblock and Blackie Stevens," Judge Richardson said, "it is the decision of the court that the jury will disregard all evidence pertaining to the tracks, the bloodhounds from Emporia and Kansas City, and any evidence pertaining to Blackie Stevens."

*****

"It will be all right, John," Owen Samuel said. "We still have your testimony."

A lot of good that did him at the first trial, Knoblock thought, and turned his head to stare out at the rain.

File Type: Interview
Subject: Mary Lou, Roger Knoblock's daughter
Date: August 8, 2008

Diana: What did you grow up hearing about your grandmother's murder?

Mary Lou: Very little. My father did not speak about it. All I was told was that my grandmother was murdered and that someone was found guilty and hanged for it.

Diana: Someone was hanged for it?

Mary Lou: That's what I was told.

Diana: Were you ever told who?

Mary Lou: No. As I said, this wasn't something my father talked about. [pause] I'm wondering if you could send me some newspaper articles?

Diana: I'd be happy to send you the first few big articles and the sheriff's testimony and your grandfather's testimony from your grandfather's trial. That should at least give you the basic information. We can talk about arranging for the rest of the articles later.

Mary Lou: My grandfather was on trial?

Chapter Thirty-One
Five Hours, Twenty-Three Minutes

Lyon County Courthouse
Emporia, Kansas
Saturday, May 15, 1926

On Saturday morning, more than one hundred and fifty men and women poured into the Lyon County Courthouse to hear the testimony of John Knoblock. Redmond thought he looked more nervous than he ever had before, until W. C. Harris began to ask him questions. Then he sounded worn down, like a man who had told the same story so many times, he could no longer put any emotion in it.

*****

Lyon County Courthouse
Emporia, Kansas
Monday, May 17, 1926

The closing arguments made, Judge Richardson gave the jury their instructions. First and foremost, they were reminded that they had each agreed to stay as long as necessary to reach a verdict if at all possible. Second, the jury had the option to convict John Knoblock of a lesser offense, including second degree murder down to assault and battery. At fifteen minutes past five that evening, the case went to the jury.

*****

Lyon County Courthouse
Emporia, Kansas
Tuesday, May 18, 1926
10:30 a.m.

John Knoblock sat in his chair, his little boy in his lap. He concentrated on breathing slowly. In. Out. In. Out. A trickle of sweat ran down from his forehead. The jury had only officially deliberated on the case for five hours and twenty-three minutes.

"Has the jury reached a verdict?" Judge Richardson asked.

"We have, your honor," the foreman, Edward Haas, said and passed a scrap of paper to the bailiff to hand to the judge.

John Knoblock passed Roger to Mary Knoblock. Despite his son, despite his entire family and Florence's family, his friends, and more than one hundred and fifty complete strangers in the courtroom, John Knoblock never felt as alone as he did awaiting his fate.

"We the jury find the defendant, John Knoblock, not guilty," Haas said.

A hush settled over the crowd.

John Knoblock laid his head on his folded arms on the table and cried.

File type: Interview and Impressions
Subject: Marian Hamman, Florence Knoblock's
niece
Date: October 9, 2008

"My only real memory of Florence Knoblock
was from when I was very little. We were
playing out in the yard, and she came out
and said in a stern, no-nonsense voice,
'Are you kids going to get in here? It's
time for supper!'"

I was fortunate enough to be interviewing
Marian Hamman, Florence Knoblock's niece.
Marian's mother was Frances McCormick, the
sister who lived in Hartford and gave birth
the day after Florence died.

I sat next to Marian in her cozy little
nursing home room, where she had been living
since she began to suffer from transient
ischemic attacks, often called TIAs or
ministrokes. Her roommate, someone who had
seen over one hundred years, dozed during
most of our conversation.

Marian was one of those people who exuded
kindness. She wore large plastic-framed
glasses on a very sweet face. I was tickled
to see that she had inherited the famous
Mozingo red hair, even if it was streaked
with gray.

"Florence was well liked," Marian said.
"She was older when she got married. She was
a schoolteacher, and she played the piano.
All of the Mozingo girls taught school at
some point. But at the time Florence was
killed, Ruth and Edna were working in Topeka
at the telephone office."

"Could you tell me about John Knoblock?"
I asked.

"Everyone said John had some odd
mannerisms," she said. "He was quiet, but
he was a good man. He was a carpenter, and
he and John Kellerman, Ella's husband, were
friends."

"Can you tell me what you know about the
day Florence was murdered?" I asked.

"It really stirred up everybody," Marian
said. "People were afraid to be left alone.
I don't remember much, and I wasn't told
much. I was only three at the time. My
mother was always angry that she wasn't
told until after the baby was born."

Marian shifted around in her recliner
until she was more comfortable. "My Aunt
Vesta, Florence's youngest sister, was very
young at that time. My grandma was going to
send Vesta to Florence's house that morning
on a pony but for some reason didn't. It
shook her up to think about what might have
happened if she had."

Marian spoke slowly and carefully, making
it very easy for me to record her words.
Despite the strokes, her grasp on these
old memories was firm, even if she repeated
herself because she couldn't remember what
she had already told me.

"Grandpa [John Mozingo] was a very
respected man. The reason why John Knoblock
got off, everyone thought, was because of
John Mozingo's support."

"What happened afterward?" I asked.

"Our family never was sure the Negro did
it, but no one in our family believed John

Knoblock did it," Marian said. "No one was against him. My dad never believed he did it. I think of everyone, only Edna and Ruth wondered, deep down, if John was guilty.

"Afterward, nobody talked about it. Margaret[25] and I found some papers in a trunk once, but we were caught looking through them, and the next time I looked, they were gone. My grandma carried some papers around in her purse, always, but they're gone, too."

"What happened to John and Roger afterwards?" I asked.

"Roger was four when his mother was murdered," Marian said. "Grandpa wanted to adopt Roger and raise him, but John said no. John had already lost everything. He said he couldn't lose Roger, too. John was a carpenter, and Roger lived with the Mozingos during the summer, and in town so he could go to school during the school year. John remarried to a woman with a horrible temper. She used to throw things. They divorced, and later, he remarried again. They lived in California, where Roger finished school. After the murder, there was a sale, and my grandparents bought Florence's cupboard and her kitchen things. They stored them away in the big barn."

"How did the community treat your family afterward?"

"I tried not to let people know who I was," Marian said, with a smile. "Not because I

---

25 Marian's sister, Margaret, was born the day after Florence Knoblock was murdered.

was ashamed, but because I thought they'd
talk more, let things slip, if they didn't
know who I was. When I was in high school,
I remember a teacher saying, 'If ever there
was anyone guilty of a murder, it was John
Knoblock.' When I was younger, I had a Sunday
school teacher who I loved, and I would have
believed anything she said until I heard
her say, sort of offhand, 'If you ever need
a good lawyer, get the ones that got that
Knoblock fellow off.'"

"Why do you think your family never talked
much about what happened to Florence?" I
asked.

"All of us kids, we were curious. Even
Roger was curious. And there was that one
time Margaret and I found the box in a
suitcase under the bed that disappeared
after we were caught with it. But I think—"
Marian paused, collected her thoughts—"If
people really care about their people, they
don't talk because it hurts too much."

Chapter Thirty-Two
Broken Promises

Graceland Cemetery
Burlington, Kansas
Sunday, May 30, 1926

Dora Goodrick bent down to place a bouquet of purple irises and early blooming white peonies at the foot of Florence Knoblock's headstone. Despite a year passing, the grave still looked new, the ground not quite yet settled to match the older graves surrounding it. Charles and Grace had walked out with her, offered their silent prayers, then returned to the Ford in order to give Dora a few moments alone.

"I don't know why I am standing here, speaking out loud," Dora said. "I'm sure, if you can hear me at all, you could just as easily hear my thoughts." She stepped forward and traced her index finger over Florence's name carved into the stone.

"You probably already know that John was acquitted during the trial in Emporia. I'd like to say they found him innocent," Dora said, "but I think people are going to believe what they want to believe. He'll be okay though, I think. And your boy, too. I'm so sorry you're not here to see how much he's grown."

Dora wiped the tears on her cheeks with the back of her hand. "John is looking for work. I don't know if he'll stay near his folks and yours or if he'll move on. You probably know more than I do about that."

Her vision blurred. She dug a handkerchief out of her handbag and blotted her eyes.

"I'm sure you know all about what I saw that day. I can't begin to tell you, little sister, how my heart breaks every time I consider how Charles and I were standing in our field, watching others near your house, not realizing what was happening to you. Just a few days earlier, I promised to help you with the problem you were having with that man, and I didn't. I just stood in my field and did nothing while he came right up to your doorstep. I'm so sorry, Florence, I let you down."

Dora wiped her nose. "You've probably seen that people haven't been real kind to your husband these past few months. I don't think they meant anything personal by it, but fear makes reasonable men do foolish things. Your family hurt more from what our neighbors did than from losing you, and believe me, they hurt a lot from that. I hope you'll find it in your heart to forgive me, Florence, for not coming forward. I can't allow my family to be punished the way yours was. I can't even let that awful man's family be punished when I can't be sure what he did or didn't do. There has been so much suffering already, and the only way any of us will be able to carry on is if we move on now. I'm so sorry, Florence, but it's all I can do."

Dora placed a kiss on her finger tips and gently touched the warm headstone before walking down the muddy path to where Charles and Grace waited for her.

File Type: Interview
Subject: Bill Shoup, grandson of Sam Shoup
Date: August 19, 2008

Note: The Shoup family has worked the same quarter section of land for over one hundred years. Casper and Sarah Shoup were already living on their land when their son, Samuel H. Shoup, was born in 1878.

Sam Shoup's young life was laden with tragedy. In 1887, just before Sam's ninth birthday, his father died of a gunshot wound, determined to be accidental. According to the *Burlington Republican-Patriot*, Mrs. Shoup returned to the house from the smokehouse and "found him dead, lying partly on his left side, with the right hand on his breast and the left by his side. The youngest of the children, a baby one and a half years old, was left in the room with him, and was playing about the bed . . ." The coroner's inquest deduced that he rolled over on his gun, which he kept under the pillow. Twenty years later, Sam's sister, Virginia, also died of an accidental gunshot wound. According to the *Burlington Republican*, her brother Sam "had been hunting the day before and had placed the rifle over the kitchen door at night and the jar of closing the door Saturday morning caused the rifle to fall. It struck the table and was discharged, the load entering Miss [Shoup]'s body just below the heart." Unlike her father, Virgie (as she was called) consciously suffered from her wound for three days before she died.

Tragedies aside, the Shoup family had done well in Coffey County, acquiring more land, starting other businesses, and was, in general, very involved in their community. Sam Shoup died in 1957. His wife, Rose, died in 1956.

Bill: I don't really know anything about the Knoblock murder. I'd heard of it, but that's about it.

Diana: Could you tell me a little about your grandparents?

Bill: Well, my granddad [Sam] was hard of hearing when he got older, and if he didn't quite hear what you said, he'd say, 'How?' which was really funny. And my grandma, when she got excited, she'd say, 'Whoopee!' We had to move their house when the John Redmond Reservoir went in. The original site for the house is now part of the Otter Creek Management Area. I'm really glad they didn't live to see the house moved. There was a big barn on the place, and we moved it to some property ten miles south. My dad, Glenn, he moved to Gridley for a while, but after my granddad retired, my dad and I did the farming. You should really talk to my sister. She could tell you more.

Diana: Is there anything else you can tell me? What did your grandparents look like?

Bill: They were pretty average height. I'd guess grandpa was five-nine, grandma about five-five. And when my granddad was younger, he was kicked severely by a horse and had a bad limp.

Chapter Thirty-Three
Florence

Knoblock farm, six miles west of Burlington, Kansas
Saturday, May 30, 1925
9:30 a.m.

Florence stood on the bottom step of the porch as her husband, John, loaded eggs, cream, and strawberries into the car.

"Let's go, Roger," John called, and Roger started to run for the car before thinking better of it. He ran back to Florence and gave her a smacking kiss on the cheek.

"'Bye, Mama," he said and barely stood still long enough for Florence to kiss him on the forehead before rushing back to the car.

Florence waved to her two men from the porch and watched them pull out into the road before going back into the house.

Her little chicks peeped and cheeped from the dining room table. Forty of them had hatched. She picked up a baby chick and stroked its fluffy head. It wouldn't be long before they were big, pecking, clucking chickens, but at the moment, they were darling babies who needed some mothering.

Secretly, Florence was happy to have the house to herself for a little while. Chores went faster without two men—sometimes two boys—underfoot. In those few snatches of quiet moments, she could collect her thoughts and renew herself.

The bread dough on the oil stove was rising and would soon be ready to bake. She whirled around the kitchen in her housedress, humming, tidying, straightening, and washing dishes. The rain last night had put her in a melancholy mood. She had sensed her unwanted admirer in the yard again a few nights before, and the fear had left her queasy. She had talked to Dora Goodrick just a few days before, asking her advice on how to dissuade him and his interest in her, but she had none to offer.

But last night, the storm had swept through, washing away the fear and worry as surely as it washed away the dust on the porch. Today was full of sunshine and promise.

Florence opened the inside doors to the porches, allowing the fresh air to carry the clean smell of wet grass and wildflowers from the pastureland into the house. They would have to hang the screens on the windows soon, before the mosquitoes and flies became a nuisance.

The clatter of hooves thudded outside, and Florence looked out the window. Dora's boy, Carl, rode across the Goodricks' yard, then followed the tree line along the Knoblock side of the section, slowing the horse to a trot.

Florence checked the time. She would need to get supper started soon, but first, she would treat herself to a cup of tea. She filled the kettle and set it on the stove. She pulled a cup and saucer as well as the canister of tea leaves out of the cupboard and set it on the work counter.

Her loaf was ready for the oven; she just needed to transfer it out of the crock and into a pan. Without looking, Florence reached down to the shelf where she stored her favorite bread pan.

Nothing.

She sighed.

Florence bent down to look on the shelves but couldn't find it. On her knees, she pulled pots and pans and baking sheets out of the cupboard, hoping her bread pan was tucked behind something.

Footsteps reverberated on the east porch steps.

She bumped her head on a low shelf.

"Florence?"

Florence sighed again. She didn't want her tranquility interrupted by company, though at least the company was coming up the east porch instead of the dining room. She had yet to sweep up John and Roger's hair from their earlier game of barbershop, and it lay strewn across the floor.

"Come on in," she said.

And she resumed her search for the bread pan as her visitor walked through the door.

File Type: Interview
Subject: Carol Hamman, great-niece of
Florence Knoblock
Date: January 22, 2010

Carol: We went to a funeral over the summer.
Another Mozingo cousin told us that Roger
told her that John Knoblock confessed to
being responsible for his wife's murder on
his deathbed. But I don't believe that for
a minute. Maybe he said he was responsible,
but what he meant was that he should have
been there to protect her. But I don't think
he did it.

Epilogue

Just minutes after the verdict was brought into the courtroom, John Knoblock and his relatives left for their homes in Coffey County. The *Emporia Gazette* reported that "Knoblock has not decided what he will do, but he says he will not farm again. He will seek a job in another city . . . and take his son with him."[26]

John Knoblock would remarry twice more after Florence died, a fact that is not correctly noted in the official genealogy submitted to the Coffey County Historical Society and Museum. John married Elizabeth "Betty" A. Altman in 1929. Altman graduated from Colby High School in Colby, Kansas. Her parents lived in Eureka, Kansas, but she taught school and had a claim in Lusk, Wyoming. According to the June 11, 1929 *Daily Republican*, "The romance began when the groom met the bride in Marion . . . [where she] was working at the Ida Lee shop and Mr. Knoblock was working as a carpenter." With a twinge of dark humor, the article also said, "The bride, altho [sic] a stranger in Burlington comes here with a very pleasing personality . . . Mr. Knoblock . . . is well known over the county."

John and Betty were still listed as a couple in the 1930 census, but their marriage fell apart soon after. Betty moved

---

26 "Defendant Cries As Jury Reports," *Emporia Gazette*, May 18, 1926.

back to Wyoming and met her next husband, Wayne Dainton, in 1933 and married him in 1935. They remained married until her death in 1989.

Despite his acquittal, John Knoblock's life was never again the same. Marjorie Barrett, the daughter of Velma and Orville Haehn, said "They had to get out of Burlington. When [John's mother] went to church, no one would hold a songbook with her."

According to Duane Fitch, a retired postmaster who served as a historian in Coffey County until his death in 2008, "John [Knoblock] . . . farmed and he also carpentered, as I know of some houses and barns he built. He stayed around here until . . . after 1935, as he built a barn that year. Roger stayed with his grandparents and attended grade school here. I remember him playing in the neighborhood, as [he was] one of the larger boys and I was a smaller one."

In 1935, John moved to LeMoore, California, where he worked as a carpenter. He married Hazel Robinson in 1945, and they moved to Fresno. They remained married until his death in 1957.

Roger also remained in California, married, had children, and continued to live there until his death in 2011.

*****

Fate deals different hands to different people, and this is certainly true in regard to the many people whose lives were touched by Florence Knoblock's death. John Mozingo and his wife, Mary, died just two years apart, in 1936 and 1938, respectively. Florence's siblings went on to live long, full lives, producing many nieces and nephews Florence would never see in person. I found it especially tragic that, had she lived, she might have lived into her eighties or nineties as several of her sisters and brother had done.

Sheriff Frank Hunter lost his bid for reelection and moved to Lansing, Kansas to become a security guard at the penitentiary.

A. A. Rickman, who served as a bailiff in the first trial, and George Griffith, a deputy under Frank Hunter, were shot while apprehending a robbery suspect in 1930. Rickman was killed; Griffith survived being shot in the head (and having 53 shots removed).

Ray Pierson, the young county attorney who prosecuted John Knoblock, was killed in a horrific car accident in 1953. His wife, Alice, and the driver of the vehicle that hit the Pierson's car were also killed. The photos of the wreck are stored in a folder at the Coffey County Historical Society. They make me appreciate every single advance ever made in automobile safety since then.

Joe Rolston, another prosecuting attorney, continued to practice law until he was 87 years old. He died a week after retiring in 1949. Owen Samuel, one of John Knoblock's attorneys, practiced law for forty years and served as a probate judge for Lyon County. He died in 1966. His partner, the former judge W. C. Harris, was elected as a state senator before dying in 1940.

The steadfast juror Charles Strickland died in 1932 at the age of 75. The mysterious Ed Tolbert's life intersected with Coffey County for only a short while. Originally from Abilene, he moved to Coffey County to help his mother work her land after his father died; he lived out his life in the Colorado Springs area, dying in 1969.

Dr. A. N. Gray, the first doctor to report to the scene of the murder, lived out his life in Burlington and remained a very active health care professional until the week of his death in 1956, at the age of 86.

Dora and Charles Goodrick maintained connections to the Coffey County area throughout their lives, as did their daughter, Grace. Dora lived to see her 101st birthday. All three Goodrick children married. Carl served his career in the military and retired to Oklahoma, passing away in 1978. Lester retired from the post office and lived out his golden years in Florida, dying in 1974. Grace married local boy Homer Hatch and had six children. She died in 1972.

The star reporters, John Redmond and Bill White, would be remembered differently by their respective towns. John Redmond is still considered a town father figure and is loved and respected by his community. After multiple floods devastated Coffey County, Redmond led the campaign to have a reservoir built in the county. The desperately needed reservoir he worked so hard to make a reality was ultimately named after him. Bill White never quite came out from under the shadow of his father, the great William Allen White, despite his own honest talent. His name graces Emporia's Civic Auditorium, a building whose construction he heavily opposed. Redmond died in 1953, White in 1973. Both men maintained a lifelong commitment to their newspapers.

It is unclear what happened to two of the key missing witnesses in the Knoblock case. I was not the only one who wondered what happened to the coroner, J. O. Stone, after the Knoblock murder. John Redmond reported that people asked about Coroner Stone throughout and after the first trial. "The question was a natural one as it would be expected the coronor [sic], being one of the first to reach the scene of the murder, would be been called upon to testify," Redmond wrote in the January 26, 1926 edition of the *Daily Republican*. "Coronor [sic] Stone has been gone for some weeks and no one seems to know where he is, but it is not generally expected that he will return as the officers are said to be looking for him, and his wife recently sued for divorce and alleges in her petition that Mr. Stone is a fugitive from justice."

Determining the identity of J. O. Stone was a bit of a mystery. While I identified him as Joseph O. Stone, throughout the course of the Knoblock murder investigation, the newspapers and court documents refer to him only as "J. O. Stone." Most likely, he was Joseph Oliver Stone, who appeared in Coffey County sometime before January 31, 1923, when he married Mrs. Elizabeth A. South. Mrs. South was a prominent and upstanding citizen, a woman very active in the community and with the Women's

Christian Temperance Union at the local, county, and state levels and who organized the construction of the Carrie Nation Home in Kansas City. Elizabeth A. (Bunton) married her first husband, S. C. South, in 1872; he died in 1913. While the paper's wedding announcement praised Mrs. South, the *Daily Republican* gently implied that Joseph O. Stone was, perhaps, not as dedicated to any particular cause or trade: "Mr. Stone has been engaged in different lines of activity but has not decided upon what he will do in Burlington, but will enter into some kind of activity."

Mrs. South-Stone, as she was called, added J. O. Stone to the titles of her property, where his name was listed as Joseph Oliver Stone. The next year, in August of 1924, the *Daily Republican* announced J. O. Stone's intention to run for coroner of Coffey County. "Mr. Stone's friends say he is well qualified to attend to the duties of this office," the paper recorded.

The weekend of May 30 and May 31, 1925, J. O. Stone would have served as coroner on two gruesome deaths: Florence Knoblock's murder and the suicide of Reece Marker, a forty-six-year-old man who came to terms with depression and financial despair by hanging himself. Stone was still in town in the middle of July, when the Coroner's Jury met one last time to officially declare the cause of death in Florence Knoblock's case.

J. O. Stone's name did not appear on the lists of individuals subpoenaed to testify at the preliminary hearing in November of 1925. There is no mention of him in the papers at all until December 7, when his wife, Mrs. South-Stone, was reported to have suffered a light stroke. "Mr. Stone, who is employed at the state hospital at Parsons, was notified of her illness and hurried home, arriving here Saturday [December 5] morning," the *Daily Republican* reported.

But after that, his whereabouts were murky. The state was unable to deliver the subpoena to him in time for the January trial and, as mentioned, his wife filed for divorce. The courthouse papers give only one clue as to where he might be. Harris and Samuel filed a motion on John Knoblock's behalf that the second trial be delayed because they believed they had located J. O. Stone and needed time to reach him. Stella Menard had testified that she assisted the coroner in his search of the bedroom, and only J. O. Stone could definitively refute that testimony. According to the motion filed April 15, 1926, "J. O. Stone is somewhere in the vicinity of Los Angeles, California where he resides with or in the neighborhood of some married daughters and some sisters, whose names and residences affiant has not been able to learn for the reason that the whereabouts of said J. O. Stone in Los Angeles, California, only came to affiant within the past week or ten days."

Unfortunately for Mrs. South-Stone, her husband did not reappear. She did divorce him, sold her property in the town she had called her home for thirty-six years, and moved into the Carrie Nation Home she helped establish. She died March 6, 1927, her obituary making no reference to her former spouse.

But why did he abandon his public office and his wife? Could he not handle the job? Was the stress of an ailing wife too much for him? Was he frightened or bribed into leaving town? As far as I could find, he's simply not mentioned again.

*****

Sherman "Blackie" Stevens was even more of a mystery. The first problem was that there was no consensus as to his actual name. The *Daily Republican* calls him Sherman Stevens, often referring to him as "Blackie" or "Deacon." According to the June 3, 1925 edition of the *Emporia Gazette*, "The colored man's name is not Stevens but Stephenson, it was learned today when [Judge] Rudrauff saw the man. Rudrauff was probate judge pro tem two years ago and married the colored man. The Negro admitted he had been married by the judge and said his wife left him [at] Christmas and was in Illinois."

With that information, I was able to find a marriage license, issued to S. H. Stephenson of Independence, Kansas, age 31, and Mary Graham of Burlington, Kansas, age 30.

Beyond the sheriff's testimony that Stevens continued to check in with him from the town of Garnett for several weeks after his release, it is unclear what happened to him. If he left by choice, it was a wise decision. In the mid-1920s, the central area of Kansas had a surge in KKK membership, and the *Daily Republican* regularly ran advertisements for KKK events during Knoblock's second trial. "Klan officers election at the usual time in the usual way and the usual place. Klansmen your presence is desired. —Exalted Cyclops." In the earliest stories on the Knoblock murder, Redmond reported that citizens joked about whether or not to lynch Stevens. It is a testament to the sheriff and his deputies that they investigated Stevens as carefully as they did.

They could have lynched him. But I think Coffey County looked at this heinous crime and recognized that even if they killed the colored man, if he wasn't the murderer, it meant that the murderer was still on the loose.

*****

Who killed Florence Knoblock? We will likely never know the truth. There is evidence that at least two, possibly three (depending on if Rosa Knapp saw a third individual other than Carl Goodrick or possibly Sam Shoup) were seen at the Knoblock house after John and Roger drove away that fateful morning. Dora Goodrick did testify that Florence Knoblock was troubled by a man who was showing her unwanted attention, and it is possible that that man may have been Sam Shoup. However, the family legend indicates that the man who may have been Shoup rode his horse to the Knoblock farm after John and Roger left that morning, and the evidence—footprints near the creek, a bloody stick, evidence of someone hiding in an old outbuilding—indicate that someone was on foot. Did the family legend misremember the truth, or did a third person make his way to and from the house while no one was watching? After all, Rosa Knapp testified to seeing a man, but not a horse.

On December 17, 1926, another Coffey County farm woman, Julia A. Reed, was murdered and left on her kitchen floor in a position very similar to that of Florence Knoblock's, her head nearly cut off with a shaving razor. Her husband, Jesse, readily admitted to the crime. When asked about a connection to Florence Knoblock's murder, Jesse said there was none, other than it having served as the inspiration for how to kill his own wife. Jesse was deemed insane and was sent to the State Asylum for the Dangerous Insane in Leavenworth County, Kansas, where his name appears among the inmates in the 1930 U.S. Census.

I had spent nearly two years finding everything I could that related to Florence Knoblock's murder. I had piles of newspaper articles from papers all over the United States, courthouse documents, U.S. Census records, maps, photographs, and interview notes. I recreated Florence's story as carefully as possible, though I will admit freely that the Goodrick family's involvement was assembled based on a series of interviews and brief mentions in the newspapers and is heavily based on my own opinion regarding the information available. Despite the thousands of column inches, documents, and hours of gossip dedicated to solving Florence Knoblock's murder and despite the discovery of some old family stories, which, if true, could have altered the course of the investigation had they been known in 1925, it is still unclear which men were mere witnesses and which man was the true murderer.

Sources

I drew on numerous sources to assemble the story of Florence Knoblock's murder, the investigation, and the subsequent trial. Several small-town newspapers dedicated tremendous amounts of space to the Knoblock murder, especially John Redmond's paper, the *Daily Republican* in Burlington; the *Emporia Gazette*; the *Emporia Weekly Gazette*; the *Olpe Optimist*; the *Madison News*; the *Hartford Times*; and the *Gridley Light*. Because the trial transcripts no longer exist, the extensive newspaper documentation was essential to my ability to reconstruct the testimony during the trial. The Coffey County Historical Society and Museum was an invaluable source of information for the county's history. Their genealogy room is stocked with microfilm reels of all of the newspapers that existed in Coffey County, and their organized collection of obituaries, marriage announcements, births, family trees, and general history were of tremendous help, especially in locating descendants of the primary figures involved. The museum also has excellent displays capturing what life in Coffey County was like at various periods of time, and the Bethel Methodist Church, which served the Pleasant Township and was the site of Florence Knoblock's funeral, is now a permanent exhibit on the museum grounds.

The staff at the Coffey County Courthouse was an excellent source of information, particularly in the district court office, the register of deeds, and the county clerk's office.

In Lyon County, the Lyon County Courthouse district court clerk's office allowed me to sit down with the surviving original paperwork from John Knoblock's second trial. Emporia Public Library houses many of the Lyon County newspapers as well as small-run publications on histories from Lyon County and neighboring counties.

The State Library of Kansas' online databases were extremely helpful, most especially by offering access to Heritage Quest, which offers searchable scans of the U.S. Census Records through 1930. I also heavily used the state library's Blue Skyways databases for community information. The State Library of Kansas' State Data Center was the place to ask any statistical information I could think of for the state of Kansas.

Other important web sources include those of the Kansas State Historical Society; NewspaperArchive.com; Niobrara County Library in Lusk, Wyoming; Pikes Peak Library District in Colorado Springs, Colorado; the family genealogy page run by Mark and Catherine Byard at http://www.jude25.net/roots/; and the Social Security Death Index at http://ssdi.rootsweb.com (which is no longer freely available).

In addition, I was able to interview—either in person or by phone, letter, or e-mail—many descendants of the people originally involved in Florence Knoblock's story and have mentioned them as their information appears in each chapter.

Descriptions of individuals in this book were assembled from newspaper articles running between 1925 and 1926, photographs, obituaries, U.S. Census records, and interviews.

Chapter One: Across the Fence

Descriptions and family information came from interviews with Dorene Smith and Helen in July of 2008 and a personal visit to the Pleasant Township.

Chapter Two: Murder

Most of this chapter came out of the pages of the *Daily Republican*, beginning with the first article written on the crime: "Skull Crushed And Throat Cut: Mrs. John Knoblock Is Found By Her Husband Saturday Afternoon," June 1, 1925. Additional information came from newspaper coverage at both the preliminary hearing and the first trial: "John Knoblock Preliminary Still In Progress Today—Many Witnesses Examined," November 10, 1925; "Examining The Witnesses In Knoblock Murder Case and Fighting Every Point," January 14, 1926; "Knoblock Trial Drags Along—Two Witnesses Declare Razor Was Not Under Boy's Clothes," January 15, 1926; and "State Not Quite Through: Defense Will Begin Monday— Knoblock Admissions Go In," January 16, 1926. Descriptions of the property were based on newspaper descriptions and my own visit to the property.

Chapter Three: After

In addition to the sources listed in Chapter One, Sherman "Deacon" "Blackie" Stevens is first mentioned in "'Deacon'

Stevens A Negro Suspect Is Held In Jail" in the *Daily Republican*, June 1, 1925. Descriptions of Ella and John Kellerman, Vesta Mozingo, and Sam Shoup came from photographs at the Coffey County Historical Society and Museum, Byard's genealogy website, and interviews and e-mail exchanges with Sharan Hamman, Marian Hamman, Dorene Smith, Bill Shoup, and Rose Shoup. Reverend Neden's name is spelled differently at various times; "Neden" appears in the coverage of the trial in "Bench Warrant Issued For Blood Hounds' Owner For Failing To Come Here," *Daily Republican*, January 20, 1926, and variations, including "Nedham," appear elsewhere. I found a Reverend Joseph Neden cited as the officiate in a few funerals and selected that spelling.

Chapter Four: Bloodhounds

Newspaper sources include "'Deacon' Stevens A Negro Suspect Is Held In Jail" in the *Daily Republican*, June 1, 1925; "Blood-Hounds Follow Trail Eleven Miles," *Daily Republican*, June 1, 1925; "May Have Murderer: Burlington Awaits Report On Fingerprints," *Emporia Gazette*, June 2, 1925; "Says Dogs Missed Skulker's Tracks After Murder," *Daily Republican*, July 21, 1925; "John Knoblock Preliminary Still In Progress Today— Many Witnesses Examined," *Daily Republican*, November 10, 1925; and "Blood Hound Man Appears In Court—Tells About Dogs," *Daily Republican*, January 21, 1926. Descriptions of George Wilson were developed from e-mail interviews with Sue Fulcher Pearson and Belinda Sims. Mark Haag of Emporia, Kansas, an avid hunter who has worked with bloodhounds, answered many questions about what bloodhounds can and cannot do.

Chapter Five: Burial

Newspaper sources include "Hundreds Attend Last Sad Rites Of Mrs. Knoblock," *Daily Republican*, June 3, 1925. Descriptions of the conversation between John Knoblock and

Dora Goodrick are based on Dora's testimony at the first trial, recorded in "Examining the Witnesses In Knoblock Murder Case And Fighting Every Point," *Daily Republican*, January 14, 1926. Descriptions of the Bethel Methodist Church are based on my own observations during my visit to the church, which is now located on the Coffey County Historical Society and Museum grounds.

Chapter Six: Rumors
    Newspaper sources include "Deacon Stevens Claims He Was In Independence At The Time Of The Murder," *Daily Republican*, June 2, 1925; "Murder Mystery Still Unsolved—Only One Arrest," *Daily Republican*, June 3, 1925; "Hundreds Attend Last Sad Rites Of Mrs. Knoblock," *Daily Republican*, June 3, 1925; "Call In Detectives: Knoblock Murder Probe Will Be Pushed: Colored Man Under Arrest May Establish Alibi—Makes Strong Denial," *Emporia Gazette*, June 3, 1925; "Mystery Is Growing: New Developments Tend To Clear Negro," *Emporia Gazette*, June 4, 1925; "Negro's Guilt Not So Certain—Officers Hunt," *Daily Republican*, June 4, 1925; "Secrecy In Probe: Woman's Body Is Exhumed For New Inquest," *Emporia Gazette*, June 5, 1925; "Some Weird Tales Being Circulated About Burlington," *Daily Republican*, June 5, 1925; "Call Out A Posse: Burlington Thought Murderer Was Captured, Night Ride Only To Find Pedestrian," *Emporia Gazette*, June 6, 1925; "Murder Mystery Remains Unsolved After One Week," *Daily Republican*, June 6, 1925; "Crowd Gathers In Response To Alarm—Vance Fox Held," *Daily Republican*, June 6, 1925; "Rumors Flying Saturday Night—Town Crowded," *Daily Republican*, June 8, 1925; "Escapes From Asylumn [sic]," *Madison News*, June 11, 1925; "New Clew [sic] To Murder: Illegal Operation May Have Been Performed," *Emporia Gazette*, June 13, 1925; "No Truth In Rumor: Officials Deny Theory Of Operation," *Emporia Gazette*, June 15, 1925; "Says No Truth In Mascunis Story—No Developments," *Daily Republican*, June 15, 1925;

Mrs. John Mozingo Made Very Ill By Thoughtless Talk," *Daily Republican*, June 17, 1925; "Intruders Are Liable To Get Shot," *Daily Republican*, June 27, 1925; and "Another Tourist Wandering Around Brought To Jail," *Daily Republican*, June 11, 1925.

Chapter Seven: Burns Detective Agency

John Knoblock's quotes in the interview with the unidentified *Emporia Gazette* reporter come from "Knoblock Tells His Story: No Truth In Rumors, Says Farmer," *Emporia Gazette*, June 16, 1925. Other newspaper sources include "Burns Operative Makes Statement Concerning Rumors," *Daily Republican*, June 17, 1925; and "Burns Operative Off The Job—Still No Arrest," *Daily Republican*, June 22, 1925. Mr. Maple, the Burns Detective, is mentioned only elusively in a few articles. I developed his character and conversations with John Redmond, Frank Hunter, and Ray Pierson based on the few mentions he received in those articles. He was not called to testify at the preliminary hearing or either trial. Discussion about other possible suspects comes from the testimony in the preliminary hearing and first trial, when various neighbors mention that Florence being harassed by someone, and from my interview with "Helen," who told me her family's story about Florence being bothered by a man whose advances she did not return.

Chapter Eight: Released

Newspaper articles include "Release Deacon Stevens Knoblock Murder Suspect—No Other Arrests Made," *Daily Republican*, July 15, 1925; and "Stevens Is Released: Negro Held In Case Is Freed," *Emporia Gazette*, July 15, 1925. The spiritual Sherman Stevens sang to himself was never mentioned in the papers; I chose to assume that a man nicknamed "Deacon" was spiritual. Lyrics for the 1920s spiritual "I'm Troubled In Mind" were found at negrospirituals.com, and the public domain sheet music can be found at http://www.musicofyesterday.com/

sheetmusic/I/Im_Troubled_In_Mind.php. Sheriff Frank Hunter's lamentations are based on several newspaper articles: "Two Stop Signs As An Experiment," *Daily Republican*, July 7, 1925; "Make Arrests In Effort To Stop Spitting," *Daily Republican*, July 11, 1925; "Everyone Stops For Stop Signs—Very Few Kicks," *Daily Republican*, July 21, 1925; "No Developments But Many Rumors In Knoblock Case," *Daily Republican*, July 17, 1925; and "Detective At Work: Burlington Did Not Know Of Knoblock Investigator; Sheriff Hunter Resents Belief That Officers Disregarded Clews [sic] And Loafed On Job," *Emporia Gazette*, July 20, 1925." Mention of John Knoblock retaining the services of his attorneys is first found in "Negro Held In Knoblock Case Is Freed," *Madison News*, July 16, 1925. John Mozingo's visit to the offices of Harris & Samuel in Emporia was recorded in "Knoblock Questioned," *Emporia Gazette*, August 7, 1925.

Chapter Nine: Arrested

The Kansas State Historical Society's website was a great resource for information on Attorney General Charles B. Griffith, who was known for his efforts to shut down the Ku Klux Klan in Kansas. KSHS also has a picture of Griffith at http://kshs. org/p/kansas-historical-quarterly-kansas-battles-the-invisible-empire/13247. His interest in the Knoblock case first appears in the *Daily Republican* article, "Hope $700 Reward Will Bring Forth Motive For Crime," June 29, 1925. Other newspaper articles include "Attorney General Griffith Is Working On Knoblock Case—Mystery Is Still Unsolved," *Daily Republican*, July 28, 1925; and "Little Done When Knoblock Fails To Report At Topeka," *Daily Republican*, August 7, 1925. John Knoblock's arrest was mentioned in many Kansas newspapers, though I primarily used the *Daily Republican* ("John Knoblock Arrested For Murder Of His Wife Florence Emma Knoblock," August 8, 1925) and *Emporia Gazette* ("Knoblock Is In Jail: Murder Victim's Husband Charged With Crime," August 8, 1925) as my sources. Information about Knoblock making bail was found in "John Knoblock Is Released On Bond—Postpone Hearing," *Daily Republican*, August 15, 1925.

Frank Hunter's day-to-day concerns as sheriff are mentioned throughout issues of the *Daily Republican*; I particularly wanted to mention "Investigates Two Rabies Epidemics Near Burlington" and "G. L. Knoblock Escapes From The State Pen," both in the August 21, 1925 edition of the *Daily Republican*, and "Thieves Pull A Series Of Jobs Thursday Night" in the August 22, 1925 edition of the *Daily Republican*.

Other pertinent news articles include "Knoblock Out On Bond," *Emporia Gazette*, August 15, 1925; "Alleged Wife Slayer On Bond," *Kansas City Star*, August 15, 1925; "Knoblock Hearing Set For Wednesday—May Be Postponed," *Daily Republican*, September 7, 1925; "Knoblock Is Free: Court Dismisses Murder Charges," *Emporia Gazette*, September 9, 1925; and "Case Against John Knoblock Is Dismissed By The State To Avoid Immediate Trial," *Daily Republican*, September 9, 1925.

Chapter Ten: Rearrested

To avoid redundancy, I did not include everyone who testified at the preliminary hearing or all of the testimony of the individuals I did include. Complete details can be found in the newspaper articles covering the arrest and preliminary hearing, including "John Knoblock Arrested Again This Morning On Charge Of Wife-Murder," *Daily Republican*, November 2, 1925; "Knoblock Rearrested," *Emporia Gazette*, November 2, 1925; "Knoblock Re-Arrested," *Olpe Optimist*, November 2, 1925; "Knoblock Gives $25,000 Bond And Is Released," *Daily Republican*, November 3, 1925; "May Have Motive," *Emporia Gazette*, November 3, 1925; "Will Call Many Witnesses For Knoblock Case," *Daily Republican*, November 6, 1925; "Are Preparing For Hard Fight At Preliminary," *Daily Republican*, November 7, 1925; "Crowd Jams Court Room

For The Knoblock Murder Preliminary—Deacon Stevens Can't Be Found," *Daily Republican*, November 9, 1925; "Hear Knoblock Today," *Emporia Gazette*, November 9, 1925; "John Knoblock Preliminary Still In Progress Today—Many Witnesses Examined," *Daily Republican*, November 10, 1925; "No Motive Shown In Knoblock Case," *Emporia Gazette*, November 10, 1925; and "Knoblock Bound Over On Charge Of Murder— Gives Bond For $25,000," *Daily Republican*, November 11, 1925. The identity of the *Emporia Gazette* reporter is never named, but because there were female reporters and editors at the *Gazette*, I opted to give the reporter a female identity.

Chapter Eleven: Fair Trial

Newspaper articles include "Result Of Hearing Seem Satisfactory To All Interested," *Daily Republican*, November 12, 1925; "John Knoblock Asks Court For Change Of Venue And Declares He Can't Get Fair Trial Here," *Daily Republican*, December 9, 1925; "Getting Affidavits Against Change In John Knoblock Case," *Daily Republican*, December 12, 1925; "Knoblock Hearing Here Next Monday—File Information," *Daily Republican*, December 15, 1925; "Many People Want To Hear Argument In Knoblock Case," *Daily Republican*, December 17, 1925; "Call Witnesses To Testify In Knoblock Case," *Daily Republican*, December 18, 1925; "Judge Richardson Hearing Affidavits And Argument In Knoblock Murder Case," *Daily Republican*, December 21, 1925; "Case Against Knoblock Will Be Tried In Burlington Starting Monday, January 11," *Daily Republican*, December 22, 1925; and "Preparing For Battle In Knoblock Murder Trial—Hundreds Sign Affidavits," *Daily Republican*, December 23, 1925.

Chapter Twelve: Dockets

Information about the court dockets came from "District Court Bar Docket Out—Not Many Cases," *Daily Republican*, January 2, 1926; and "Judge Richardson Sets Court Docket—

Murder Case First," *Daily Republican*, January 6, 1926. Proper courtroom behavior, including the notion that visitors should bathe, really did run in the January 7, 1926 edition of the *Daily Republican* under the headline, "Trial Of John Knoblock Will Be A Trial, Not A Spectacle—Judge Richardson Works On Plans." Information about the extraordinary number of citizens subpoenaed comes from "Defense Wants Blackie Stevens Here For Knoblock Trial—Is Hint At What Defense Will Be," *Daily Republican*, January 8, 1926; and "Everything Ready For Knoblock Trial—Defense Calls 47," *Daily Republican*, January 9, 1926. Information about Carl Goodrick's run-in with the investigator for the Kansas attorney general was revealed during Owen Samuel's opening arguments during the first trial, as recorded in "Samuel Outlines Testimony To Be Offered By The Defense To Prove Knoblock Innocent," *Daily Republican*, January 19, 1926.

Chapter Thirteen: Jurors
    The jury selection process was recorded in great detail, beginning with "Draw Extra Jurors For Knoblock Case And May Need More," *Daily Republican*, January 6, 1926, which listed the original potential jurors called to report. Questions asked of jurors, and their answers, were recorded in "Trial Of John Knoblock Begins In Coffey County District Court—First Thing Is To Secure A Jury," *Daily Republican*, January 11, 1926; "First Juror Chosen: Only One Man Qualified For Knoblock Trial," *Emporia Gazette*, January 11, 1926; "Making Good Progress Toward Securing Jury To Try John Knoblock, *Daily Republican*, January 12, 1926; "No Knoblock Jury," *Emporia Gazette*, January 12, 1926; "Witnesses Are Excused From Room During Trial—Jury Finally Secured," *Daily Republican*, January 13, 1926; and "Trial Under Way: Jury Of Farmers To Hear Knoblock Case," *Emporia Gazette*, January 13, 1926.
    The volume of information available from both of the Knoblock trials is overwhelming. Newspapers listed every

prospective juror and every subpoenaed citizen, summarized the testimony and the goings-on in the courtroom, and took the pulse of the city. Testimony did not always happen in a logical order; sometimes witnesses were ill, at school, or unable to travel, and their testimony was worked in whenever they could be there. Many witnesses also offered essentially the same testimony. To make chapters on the trial logical yet still faithful to the original testimony, I occasionally rearranged the testimony, included only portions of testimony, and generally did not include redundant testimony unless it was crucial to recording the trial. Descriptions of witnesses came from newspaper articles, U.S. Census records, obituaries, and interviews with descendants. I sometimes was forced to use my best judgment in determining which attorney was questioning a particular witness. Roger Knoblock was allowed to attend his father's trial, and both the *Daily Republican* and the *Emporia Gazette* are peppered with small write-ups on his behavior in the courtroom. The showgirl, a member of the Brunk's Comedians tent show, is referred to only as "Mrs. Lavelle" in both court documents and "Judge Richardson Intimates Application for Continuance," *Daily Republican*, April 7, 1926. "Mrs. Lavelle" does not appear in the list of show rosters printed in *Henry L. Brunk and Brunk's Comedians: Tent Repertoire Empire of the Southwest* by Jerry L. Martin (Bowling Green University Popular Press 1984). However, similar names, including "Leavell" and "Levell," do appear on the rosters of the long-running tent show.

Chapter Fourteen: Blankets and Razors
Newspaper articles include "Examining The Witnesses In Knoblock Murder Case And Fighting Every Point," *Daily Republican*, January 14, 1926; "Chain Of Circumstances The State Will Try To Prove," *Daily Republican*, January 14, 1926; "Trial Slowing Up: Few Witnesses Are Heard In Knoblock Case," *Emporia Gazette*, January 14, 1926; and "Knoblock Trial Drags Along—Two Witnesses Declare Razor Was Not Under Boy's

Clothes," *Daily Republican*, January 15, 1926. The description of Stella Menard is based on descriptions of her behavior on the stand by both Bill White and John Redmond.

Chapter Fifteen: Crime Scene

Descriptions of other newspaper reporters covering the trial were found in "Notes On The Trial," *Daily Republican*, January 13, 1926. A. C. Babcock is also mentioned by the *Emporia Gazette* on January 13, 1926 in "Trial Will Be Theme For Stories." The description of Bill White was developed from various descriptions of him in the book, *William Lindsay White, 1900–1973: In the Shadow of His Father*, by Jay E. Jernigan (University of Oklahoma Press 1997). Newspaper articles covering this portion of the trial include "Thursday Morning's Proceedings In The Knoblock Trial," *Daily Republican*, January 15, 1926; "Trial Slowing Up: Few Witnesses Are Heard In Knoblock Case" *Emporia Gazette*, January 14, 1926; "Notes On The Trial," *Daily Republican*, January 15, 1926; and "State Rests Tonight," *Emporia Gazette*, January 15, 1926.

Chapter Sixteen: Motive

Information about Ed Tolbert was found thanks to the U.S. Census records, Emily Anderson at the Pikes Peak Library District (who e-mailed me Tolbert's obituaries from the *Colorado Springs Gazette*), and information at the Coffey County Courthouse Register of Deeds office. Newspaper articles for this chapter include "State Not Quite Through: Defense Will Begin Monday—Knoblock Admissions Go In," *Daily Republican*, January 16, 1926; "Seek Murder Motive: Knoblock's Relations With Sister-In-Law Probed," *Emporia Gazette*, January 16, 1926; and "State Finishes Presenting Case Against Knoblock," *Daily Republican*, January 18, 1926.

Chapter Seventeen: Journalism

A description of the lunch provided by the Burlington Women's Relief Corps was recorded by Bill White in "Defense

Under Way," *Emporia Gazette*, January 18, 1926. John Redmond really did report on Bill White having to dispose of his lunch in "Notes On The Trial," *Daily Republican*, January 18, 1926. He wrote about the newspaper process in that same article.

Chapter Eighteen: Defense
   Bill White did write comical descriptions of various people in the courtroom in "Defense Under Way," *Emporia Gazette*, January 18, 1926, and I recorded them faithfully in this book. Other newspaper articles include "State Finishes Presenting Case Against Knoblock," *Daily Republican*, January 18, 1926; "Notes On The Trial," *Daily Republican*, January 18, 1926; "Mr. Samuel Will Give Defendant's Side Of The Case," *Daily Republican*, January 18, 1926; "Samuel Outlines Testimony To Be Offered By The Defense To Prove Knoblock Innocent," *Daily Republican*, January 19, 1926; "Witnesses Giving Knoblock Defense To Murder Charge," *Daily Republican*, January 19, 1926; "Stand By Knoblock: Relatives Substantiate Defense Version," *Emporia Gazette*, January 19, 1926; "Monday Afternoon's Proceeding In The Knoblock Murder Case," *Daily Republican*, January 20, 1926; "Tuesday Morning Testimony In Knoblock Case," *Daily Republican*, January 20, 1926; "Bench Warrant Issued For Blood Hounds' Owner For Failing To Come Here," *Daily Republican*, January 20, 1926; and "Charges Are Denied: Mozingo Girls Defend Their Conduct," *Emporia Gazette*, January 20, 1926.

Chapter Nineteen: Uncommonly Affectionate
   Testimony came from newspaper articles, including "Bench Warrant Issued For Blood Hounds' Owner For Failing To Come Here," *Daily Republican*, January 20, 1926; "Charges Are Denied: Mozingo Girls Defend Their Conduct," *Emporia Gazette*, January 20, 1926; "Knoblock On Stand: Murder Trial Defendant Tells Story To Jury," *Emporia Gazette*, January 21, 1926; "Defendant Will Testify In His Own Behalf Today—Is

Expected To Be Last," *Daily Republican*, January 21, 1926; and "Wednesday Morning's Proceeding In The Knoblock Murder Case," *Daily Republican*, January 21, 1926.

Chapter Twenty: The Judge
Information about W. C. Harris' campaign to have Judge I. T. Richardson disbarred can be found running almost continuously in the *Emporia Gazette* from October 1924 through January 1925, beginning with "No Delay By State: Petition In Richardson Case Amended Today," October 21, 1924. Owen Samuel was implicated in these same wrongdoings. All charges were dropped. The *Daily Republican* reported on inappropriate courtroom behavior in "Notes On The Trial," January 21, 1926. The Supreme Court's decision on *State v. Scott* would have been very current to the Knoblock trial and profoundly impacted the way Knoblock was tried (*State v. Scott*, No. 25772, December 6, 1924; on rehearing, May 9, 1925, 117 Kan. 303, 235 P. 380). Judge I. T. Richardson's lengthy instructions were published in their entirety in "Judge Richardson's Instructions To The Knoblock Jury," *Daily Republican*, January 23, 1926.

Chapter Twenty-One: Tracks
Newspaper articles include "Defendant Will Testify On His Own Behalf Today—Is Expected To Be Last," *Daily Republican*, January 21, 1926; "Knoblock On Stand: Murder Trial Defendant Tells Story To Jury," *Emporia Gazette*, January 21, 1926; and "Thursday Morning Proceeding In The Knoblock Murder Case," *Daily Republican*, January 22, 1926.

Chapter Twenty-Two: Recollection
This chapter was developed almost entirely from the *Daily Republican* article, "'Did You Kill Your Wife?' 'No Sir.' Said Knoblock—All The Evidence Is In," on January 22, 1926. Additional information came from "Knoblock On Stand: Murder Trial Defendant Tells Story To Jury," *Emporia Gazette*, January

21, 1926; and "Case To Jury Soon: Lawyers Sum Up Evidence In Knoblock Case," *Emporia Gazette*, January 22, 1926. The information from John Knoblock's testimony has been presented in first person in a linear format; in the actual trial, Knoblock answered a variety of questions that did not necessarily tell the story in a logical order.

Chapter Twenty-Three: Unhappy
The testimony presented in this chapter came from "'Did You Kill Your Wife?' 'No Sir.' Said Knoblock—All The Evidence Is In," *Daily Republican*, January 22, 1926.

Chapter Twenty-Four: Deliberation
Citizens of Coffey County packed into the courthouse to hear the closing arguments of both sides, which were recorded in "Lawyers Argue Knoblock Case Today," *Daily Republican*, January 22, 1926; "Case To Jury Soon: Lawyers Sum Up Evidence In Knoblock Case," *Emporia Gazette*, January 22, 1926; "No Verdict Yet After Five Hours," *Daily Republican*, January 23, 1926; "Still No Verdict After Many Hours—Want Testimony," *Daily Republican*, January 25, 1926; "Echoes Of The Trial," *Daily Republican*, January 25, 1926; "Knoblock Jury Disagrees Eleven To One: Knoblock Jurors Agree To Disagree After 18 Ballots," *Daily Republican,* January 26, 1926; "Echoes Of The Trial," *Daily Republican*, January 26, 1926; and "Knoblock Jury Hangs, Dismissed," *Emporia Gazette*, January 25, 1926.

Chapter Twenty-Five: Strategy
Newspaper articles include "Defense Lawyers To Ask Arrest Of Blackie Stevens," *Daily Republican*, January 26, 1926; "May Try Stephenson: Knoblock Case Has Taken A Queer Turn," *Emporia Gazette*, January 26, 1926; "John Knoblock Placed In Jail Two Hours Wednesday Afternoon Quickly Gives New $25,000 Bond," *Daily Republican*, January 28, 1926; "Knoblock's

Attorneys File Complaint Against Blackie For Mrs. Knoblock's Murder," *Daily Republican*, January 30, 1926; "To Argue Motion To Dismiss Case Against Blackie," *Daily Republican*, February 15, 1926; "Stevens Case Is Continued Until Next Wednesday," *Daily Republican*, February 17, 1926; "Hear Motion To Dismiss Stevens Case Wednesday," *Daily Republican*, February 22, 1926; "Expect Move For Change Of Venue," *Daily Republican*, February 23, 1926; "Postpone Hearing Of Deacon Stevens To Friday Morning," *Daily Republican*, February 24, 1926; "Hear Argument About Dismissal Of Stevens Case," *Daily Republican*, February 26, 1926; "Blackie Stevens Is Released From Charge Of Murder," *Daily Republican*, February 27, 1926; "Knoblock Wants Change Of Venue From Burlington," *Daily Republican*, March 3, 1926; "J. Knoblock Would Compare His Finger Prints With Murderer's—Asks Court Order To Get Prints," *Daily Republican*, March 15, 1926; "Postpone Change Of Venue Hearing Till Thursday, March 18," *Daily Republican*, March 16, 1926; "Judge Richardson Here For Hearing On Venue Petition," *Daily Republican*, March 18, 1926; and "Second Knoblock Murder Trial Will Be Held In Burlington Beginning Thursday, April 15," *Daily Republican*, March 10, 1926. In addition, copies of the motions can also be found at the District Court Clerk Offices in both the Coffey County Courthouse in Burlington, Kansas, and the Lyon County Courthouse in Emporia, Kansas.

Chapter Twenty-Six: Commemoration
Dora and Grace are listed as subpoenaed to appear on April 17 in "Knoblock Trial Opens Tomorrow—List of Jurors," *Daily Republican*, April 14, 1926.

Chapter Twenty-Seven: Change of Venue
Newspaper articles include "Knoblock Trial Opens Tomorrow—List Of Jurors," *Daily Republican*, April 14, 1926; "Trying For Jury In Knoblock Case—Some Are Excused," *Daily Republican*, April 15, 1926; "Slow Work Getting Jury

In Knoblock Murder Case—Only Two Pass So Far," *Daily Republican*, April 16, 1926; "Jury Box Filled And Then Emptied In 2 Short Hours," *Daily Republican*, April 17, 1926; "Pass Four Jurors In Knoblock Case In First Two Days," *Daily Republican*, April 17, 1926; "Jury At Standstill: Two Jurors Are Excused, One More Accepted," *Emporia Gazette*, April 19, 1926; "No Thought Of Change Of Venue In The Knoblock Murder Trial— Getting A Jury Is Slow Work," *Daily Republican*, April 19, 1926; "Knoblock Murder Trial Goes To Emporia: Knoblock Given Change Of Venue—Trial May Fifth," *Daily Republican*, April 20, 1926; and "Change Of Venue Ordered By Judge," *Emporia Gazette*, April 20, 1926.

Chapter Twenty-Eight: Emporia
Information about the city of Emporia, the Broadview Hotel, higher education, displeasure with the location of the courthouse, and the populations of small Lyon County towns came from the *History of Emporia And Lyon County* by Laura M. French (Emporia Gazette Print 1929). The history of Emporia State University's name can be found at "A Timeline of Emporia State's History" at http://www.emporia.edu/about/timeline.htm. Newspaper articles cited in this chapter include "Defense Already Calls Witnesses In Knoblock Case," *Daily Republican*, April 21, 1926; "Draw Jurors Monday," *Emporia Gazette*, April 24, 1926; "Knoblock Papers Sent To Emporia Ready For Trial," *Daily Republican*, April 26, 1926; "Subpoenas Issued For 104 Witnesses In Knoblock Trial," *Daily Republican*, May 1, 1926; "Knoblock Jury Easier To Get In Lyon County," *Daily Republican*, May 3, 1926; "Editor To Emporia To Report Trial Of The Knoblock Case," *Daily Republican*, May 4, 1926; "Knoblock Trial Opens In Lyon County District Court— Begin Task Of Getting A Jury," *Daily Republican*, May 5, 1926; "Accept Two Jurors: Knoblock Trial Makes Satisfactory Progress," *Emporia Gazette*, May 5, 1926; "Interesting Passage In Court Over An Objection By Mr. Samuel Enlivens Knoblock

Murder Trial," *Daily Republican*, May 6, 1926; "Accept 12 For Jury: May Begin Hearing Evidence Friday," *Emporia Gazette*, May 6, 1926; "Hurry Up Call For More Jurors In John Knoblock Murder Trial—Special Tale Of Sixty Drawn," *Daily Republican*, May 7, 1926; "Expect Jury Soon: May Hear Knoblock Evidence Monday Morning," *Emporia Gazette*, May 7, 1926; "Still Laboring On Knoblock Jury—31 Additional Jurors Called— Witnesses To Come Monday," *Daily Republican*, May 8, 1926; "Expect A Jury Soon: Only Five Challenges Left At 3 O'clock," *Emporia Gazette*, May 8, 1926; "Should Begin Taking Evidence In Knoblock Case This Afternoon—Another Tale Of Jurors Called," *Daily Republican*, May 10, 1926; and "Ready For Evidence: Knoblock Jury Completed This Afternoon," *Emporia Gazette*, May 10, 1926. Additional information about the jurors was found through 1920 U.S. Census records and obituaries.

Chapter Twenty-Nine: Encore
    This book's account of the second trial is highly abbreviated, focusing less on the testimony (which was almost identical to that in the first trial) and more on the people of Emporia and the experience of hearing the trial in the Emporia community. However, details are available in the following articles: "Harris Outlines Theory Of State For Prosecution," *Daily Republican*, May 11, 1926; "Samuel Gives Defense's Idea Of The Murder," *Daily Republican*, May 11, 1926; "Sheriff Hunter Takes The Stand—Tells His Story," *Daily Republican*, May 11, 1926; "State Builds Its Case," *Emporia Gazette*, May 11, 1926; "Making Very Rapid Progress In Presenting Case Of State In Second Trial Of Knoblock," *Daily Republican*, May 12, 1926; "State To Rest Soon: Prosecution May Complete Evidence Today," *Emporia Gazette*, May 12, 1926; "Defense Is Presenting Its Side—Testimony May All Be In Saturday—Knoblock To Stand In Own Behalf," *Daily Republican*, May 13, 1926; "Defense Has Inning: Friends And Relatives Stand By Knoblock," *Emporia Gazette*, May 13, 1926; and "The Knoblock Trial," *Emporia Gazette*, May 13, 1926.

Chapter Thirty: Will the Bloodhounds Save Him?

Dozens of newspapers around the United States, including those listed in this chapter, printed a picture of John Knoblock and his son, Roger, which was distributed by the Newspaper Enterprise Association. Other newspaper articles used in this chapter (and articles not used but that will offer the reader more information regarding the trial) include "Legal Battle Over Bloodhounds Opens In Knoblock Murder Case—Try To Tell Of Tracks At Farm," *Daily Republican*, May 14, 1926; "Griffin Arrested For Perjury In Testimony About Tracks—Defense Says It Is An Outrage," *Daily Republican*, May 14, 1926; "Witness Is Arrested: Charge Earl Griffen [sic] Lied In Knoblock Case," *Emporia Gazette*, May 14, 1926; and "Court Cuts Out Testimony About Bloodhounds," *Daily Republican*, May 15, 1926.

Chapter Thirty-One: Five Hours, Twenty-Three Minutes

Newspaper articles include "John Knoblock Appears Today In Own Behalf," *Daily Republican*, May 15, 1926; "Knoblock Is On The Witness Stand," *Emporia Gazette*, May 15, 1926; "John Knoblock Gives His Side Of The Mystery," *Daily Republican*, May 17, 1926; "To Spend Today Arguing About Knoblock Case," *Daily Republican*, May 17, 1926; "Court Instructs Knoblock Jury Of Law In The Case," *Daily Republican*, May 17, 1926; "Case To Jury Soon," *Emporia Gazette*, May 17, 1926; "Judge Richardson Outlines The Law In Knoblock Trial," *Daily Republican*, May 18, 1926; "John Knoblock Is Found Not Guilty By Jury," *Daily Republican*, May 18, 1926; and "Knoblock Is Acquitted Of Murder Charge: Defendant Cries As Jury Reports," *Emporia Gazette*, May 18, 1926.

Chapter Thirty-Two: Broken Promises

This is a stylized chapter based on my interview with Helen in July 2008.

Chapter Thirty-Three: Florence

This chapter is based on information inferred from the many articles and pieces of testimony described in the *Daily Republican* and *Emporia Gazette* and interviews with people who knew her or knew of her as well as my own imagination.

Epilogue

Additional information about Betty Altman was found in her obituary, which ran in the September 6, 1989 edition of the *Lusk Herald*, made available through the Niobrara County Library's website. Obituaries for most subjects were found in the *Daily Republican* (which later became the *Coffey County Republican*) and the *Emporia Gazette*. An addition obituary for Carl Goodrick was found in the *Claremore Press* in Claremore, Oklahoma. Other sources are as mentioned in the chapter, including "Defendant Cries As Jury Reports," *Emporia Gazette*, May 18, 1926. Special thanks to Erin Burdick at the Coffey County Historical Society and Museum for alerting me to the murder of Julia Reed by sending me a copy of the story "Tries to Cut Wife's Head Off With Razor: Mrs. Jesse A. Reed Is Killed—Throat is Cut and Hacked—Husband Is Held in Jail," *Daily Republican*, December 18, 1926.

CPSIA information can be obtained at www.ICGtesting.com
Printed in the USA
LVOW10s0553151113

361422LV00002B/59/P